AF600575

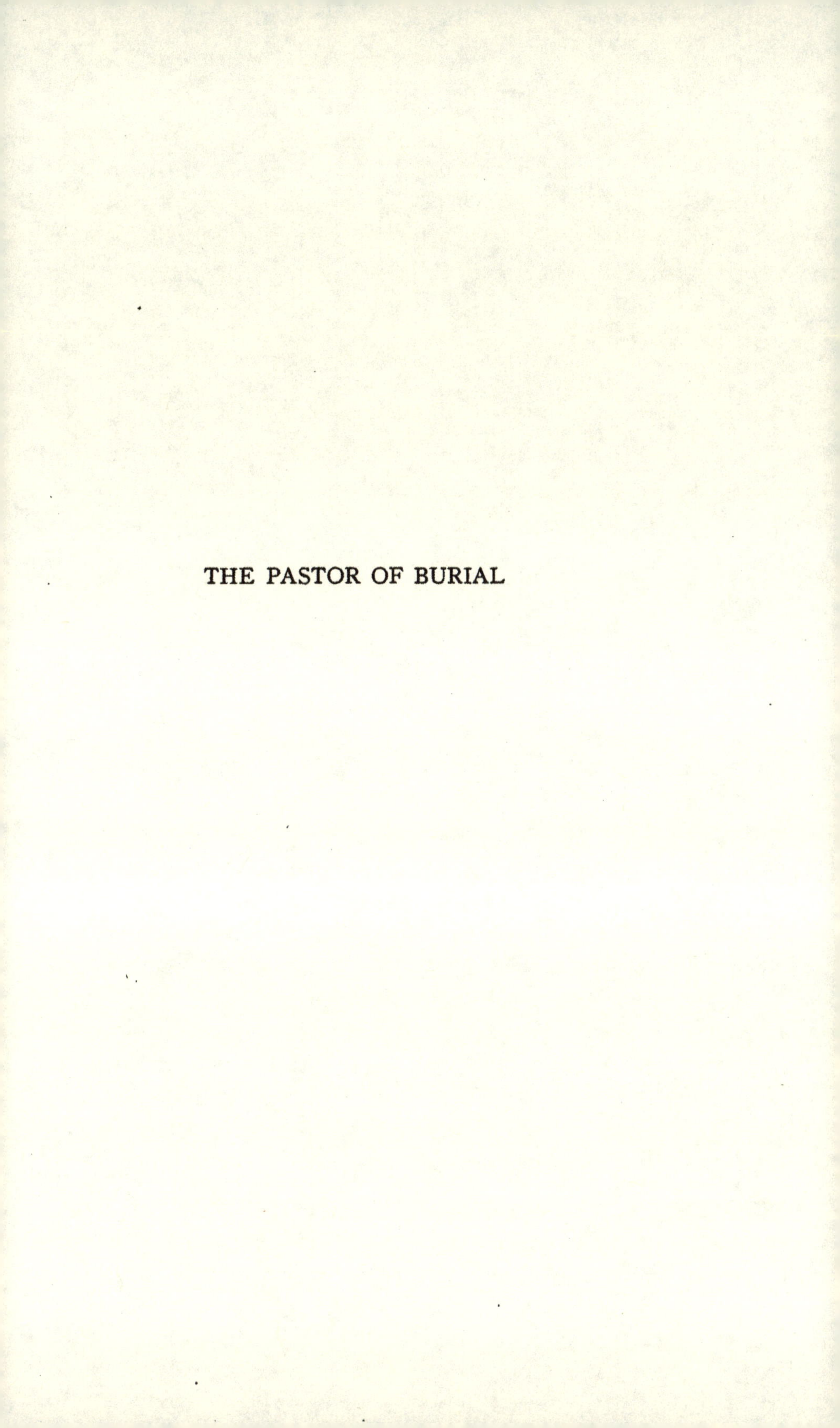

THE PASTOR OF BURIAL

THE CATHOLIC UNIVERSITY OF AMERICA
CANON LAW STUDIES
No. 234

THE PASTOR OF BURIAL

A Historical Synopsis and a Commentary

BY THE
REVEREND JOSEPH F. HALE, M.A., J.C.L.
PRIEST OF THE DIOCESE OF WINONA

A DISSERTATION
SUBMITTED TO THE FACULTY OF THE SCHOOL OF CANON LAW OF THE CATHOLIC UNIVERSITY OF AMERICA IN PARTIAL FULFILLMENT OF THE REQUIREMENTS FOR THE DEGREE OF DOCTOR OF CANON LAW

THE CATHOLIC UNIVERSITY OF AMERICA PRESS
WASHINGTON, D. C.
1949

Nihil Obstat:
EDUARDUS G. ROELKER, D.D., J.C.D.,
Censor Librorum
Washingtonii, die 7 iunii, 1946

Imprimatur:
✠ LEO BINZ,
Episcopus Titularis Pinarensis
Administrator Apostolicus
Winonae, die 28 iunii, 1946

MURRAY & HEISTER—WASHINGTON, D. C.
PRINTED IN THE UNITED STATES OF AMERICA

TABLE OF CONTENTS

PART II—CANONICAL COMMENTARY

CHAPTER III

CHAPTER IV

CHAPTER V

FOREWORD

From the very beginnings of Christianity the Church has always exercised a particular care in regard to the faithful departed. The rites associated with their burial, which have become so sacred to her and to her children, demand the presence and the ministrations of the priest. He escorts the body from the home to the church, offers the holy sacrifice of the Mass for the repose of the soul of the departed Christian, officiates at the absolution, and, finally, gives the last blessing at the interment.

In the course of the centuries there has developed a considerable body of canonical legislation relative both to the determination of the priest who officiates at the funeral and burial and also to his obligations and rights, both material and spiritual. The spiritual rights involved are the following: the right to receive the body at the home, the right to escort the body to the church, the right to conduct the exequies in the church, and the right to accompany the body to the place of burial.

The purpose of this dissertation is twofold. It will trace in summary form the development of the canonical legislation from its origin down to the promulgation of the Code of Canon Law, determining which priest officiated during the funeral and burial of the faithful departed. It will then present a canonical commentary on the legislation of the present day.

The dissertation is divided into two parts. The first part, the historical synopsis, will consider especially the origin and development of the fundamental right of the pastor to conduct the funeral and the burial of his parishioners; but also, since the parishioner possessed the right to be buried in a church which he had selected or in which there was a tomb of his family, the spiritual rights of the pastor in this regard in the event that a church other than his own parish church was selected by the deceased for burial, or the deceased was to be buried in the family tomb.

The second part of the dissertation is a canonical commentary on the laws of the Code relative to the same subject matter. In addition, there will be determined the minister authorized to officiate at the funerals and burials of certain classes of persons. The legislation of the Code of Canon Law which refers to this subject is contained in canons 1215–1233.

The writer takes this occasion to express his sincere gratitude to His Excellency, The Most Reverend Leo Binz, D.D., Coadjutor Bishop and Apostolic Administrator of the Diocese of Winona, for the opportunity of graduate study in Canon Law. The writer also wishes to express his sincere thanks to the members of the Faculty of the School of Canon Law for their kind assistance and guidance in the preparation of this dissertation, and to his family and friends for their interest and encouragement.

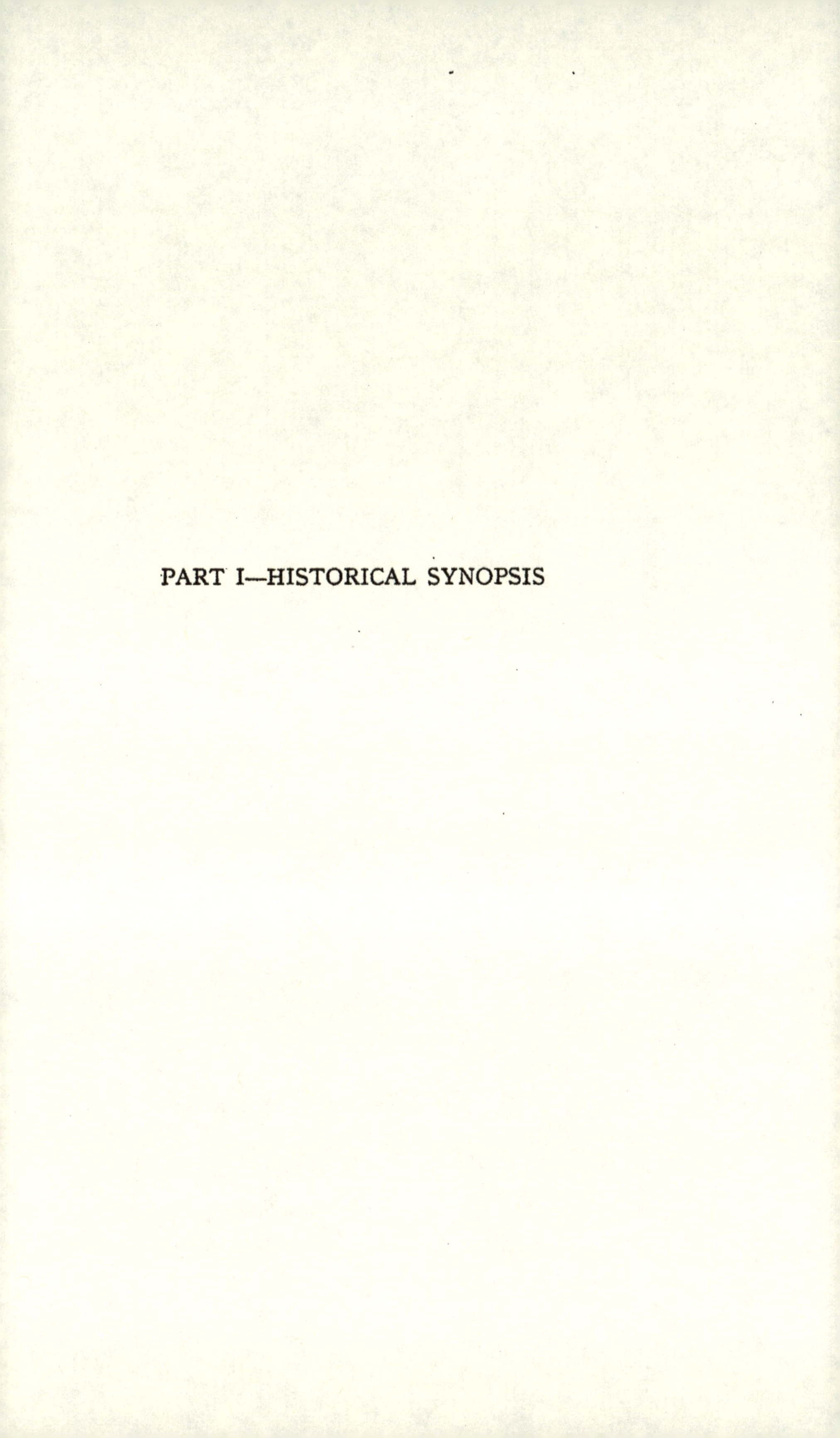

PART I—HISTORICAL SYNOPSIS

CHAPTER I

THE DOCTRINE OF THE *Corpus Iuris Canonici* AND OF THE GLOSSATORS AND COMMENTATORS

ARTICLE I. THE RIGHT TO BESTOW BURIAL

A. The Right of the Parochial Church

The rise of the parishes towards the end of the persecutions, owing to the growth of Christianity, led to a greater definition ultimately of parish rights in general and of the right of ecclesiastical burial in particular. The *Liber Pontificalis* recorded of Pope Dionysius (259–268): "Hic presbyteris ecclesias divisit et coemeteria et parochias constituit." [1]

Based undoubtedly upon this historical fact was the letter attributed to this pontiff. This famous pseudo-Isidorian decretal, which was found in so many collections of canons in the middle ages, was a reputed instruction of Pope Dionysius to Severus, Bishop of Cordova in Spain, who had consulted him concerning his arrangements for the care of the faithful in the church at Rome. Dionysius replied that he had given individual priests to individual churches; that he had divided the parishes and cemeteries for them, and had determined the proper rights of each, so that no one of them would invade the limits of another parish or infringe on the rights of the pastor; that each priest was to act only within his parish lines, and thus he would guard the church and the flock committed to his care, prepared to give an account concerning his charge before the tribunal of the Divine Judge, and to receive not judgment but glory for his deeds.[2]

[1] Duchesne, *Le Liber Pontificalis, texte, introduction, et commentaire* (2 vols., Paris, 1886–1892), I, 122—"La première partie de ce decret, celle qui regarde le gouvernement des églises et des cimitières de Rome, correspond bien aux necessités du temps qui suivit immediatement la persecution de Valérien. Notre auteur aura peut-être tiré cela de quelque document ou de quelque tradition."

[2] Jaffé, *Regesta Pontificum Romanorum ab condita Ecclesia ad annum post*

Whatever may be judged concerning the authenticity of this letter of Dionysius, it indicated the manner in which the local government within the Church developed. Bishops ruled their dioceses; parishes developed under the care of a pastor who was subject to the bishop; the pastors had various rights which were exercised within distinct boundaries.[3] The right to give ecclesiastical burial was among these rights. The fact that this letter was found in the collections of Burchard of Worms (+1025) and Ivo of Chartres (1040–1116) attested to its common acceptance as a foundation for the division of dioceses into parishes, for the rights of pastors, and especially for their right of giving ecclesiastical burial. Gratian considered it of great importance.[4]

Although Pope Leo III (795–816) may not have explicitly taught that the right of burial was the right of the parochial church, yet it would be impossible to understand his language unless that were presumed. He taught that every one had the right to choose his place of burial, and, in the event that he chose to be buried in a church other than his proper parish church, a third part of all that was left in his last will to the church chosen by him as his last resting place had by the law to be paid to his parochial church, or that in which he had been accustomed daily to be refreshed with heavenly food. The pastor had a right to this payment because he was the worker worthy of his hire; if this payment was not made, free choice of burial was not to be conceded. Most severely did he reject any abuse of this right that proved detrimental to the rights of the pastor and of the parish church.[5] This was just one example in the Decretals of Gregory

Christum natum MCXCVIII (2. ed. by Kaltenbrunner [ad annum 590], Ewald [590–882], and Loewenfeld [882–1198], and so referred to often as JK, JE, and JL, 2 vols. in 1, Lipsiae, 1885–1888), n. 139. This work hereafter will be cited as Jaffé. For information relative to the date, composition, juridic force and authority of the Pseudo-Isidorian Decretals, cf. A. Van Hove, *Commentarium Lovaniense in Codicem Iuris Canonici,* Vol. I, tom. I, *Prolegomena ad Codicem Iuris Canonici* (Mechliniae et Romae: Dessain, 1928), pp. 160–167. Hereafter this work will be cited as Van Hove.

[3] Rufinus, *Summa Decretorum* (ed. H. Singer, Paderborn, 1902), ad. c. un., C. XIII, q. 1, p. 332.

[4] C. un., C. XIII, q. 1.

[5] C. 1, X, *de sepulturis,* III, 28; Jaffé n. 2536. In the text of Friedberg

IX (1227–1241) regarding the necessity of recognizing the rights of the pastor by the payment of the canonical portion.

The *dictum* of Gratian appended to the canon of the Council of Tribur (895) showed the mind of the Church in the twelfth century.[6] He asserted that a person who changed his domicile from one province to another lost his domicile in the first province and became subject to a new jurisdiction. He declared further that, since this person paid his tithes to a distinct and different church, it was in this church of his new domicile that he was to be buried. Rufinus (+ca. 1190) explained that Gratian here referred to the personal tithes which were paid out of the income derived from other things than from the cultivation of the soil, and which had to be paid to that church where one lived and heard divine services, that is, to one's parish church.[7]

In the twelfth century also, Pope Alexander III (1159–1181) recognized this right of the pastor in a letter in which he spoke of the complaint on the part of certain canons against a prior who had buried one of the canons' parishioners. Alexander commanded the bishop to whom the letter was addressed to see to it that the prior restored the body of the parishioner to the canons.[8]

---

the number is erroneously given as 5795–816: the numbers 795–816 indicate the time within which the decretal was issued, or the dates of Leo III's reign.

[6] *Dictum,* p. c. 6, C. XIII, q. 2. Hefele-Leclercq, *Histoire des Conciles* (10 vols., in 19, Paris: Letouzey et Ané, 1907–1938), Vol. IV, Part II, p. 700.

[7] *Summa Decretorum,* ad c. un., C. XIII, q. 2, pp. 332–334.

[8] C. 5, X, *de sepulturis,* III, 28: Jaffé, n. 13971. In the text of Friedberg the reading is: "Ex parte canonicorum Obrigensium nobis est intimatum, quod prior de Insula quendam parochianum suum post appellationem ad nos factam in sua ecclesia sepelivit." He also gives the variant readings: *Ebrigen.: Obligen.: Eburgenses* (*Ebrugenses.*). Gonzalez-Tellez (*Commentaria Perpetua in Singulos Textus Quinque Librorum Decretalium Gregorii IX* [Venetiis, 1699], ad lib. III, tit. 28, c. 5) favors *Edinburgenses.* In his footnote n. 1 to this canon he says: "In sexta collectione legitur Abrugen. et Glossa marginalis emendat Obargens. seu Obligens. sed legendum credo Edinburgen. quae Ecclesia est in Laudonia Scotiae provincia;" in footnote n. 2: "Prior de Insula. Monasterium est canonicorum regularium in Scotia, sub nomine Insulae; et etiam dicta Ecclesia Cathedralis, dicta Insularum, est canonicorum regularium, ut refert Pennotus, lib. 2, histor. canonic. regul. cap. 36, n. 5. Unde cognosci non potest, de quo Priore agatur in praesenti."

Pope Innocent III (1198–1216), when he conceded the privilege of burying the faithful to certain churches of Hospitallers, judged it necessary that the canonical portion should be paid to the parish church, and that parishioners of other churches should not even be accepted for burial unless the latter had chosen to be buried in churches of the Hospitallers. He demanded further that the Hospitallers should restore to the parish all that they had received at the time they had buried two children who were below the legitimate age for personally determining the place of their burial. His reasoning was obvious. No other church than the parish church had the right to bury its parishioners. Even if other churches were endowed with the privilege of burying those who chose to be buried in them or in their cemeteries, there had to be a recognition of the parish church by the payment of the canonical portion on the part of the church of burial. The use of this privilege, as will be indicated, depended upon the free election of the deceased. If parishioners of a certain parish were not old enough to make this choice of burial, the burial of them by clerics in charge of another parish was completely contrary to the law and a serious attack on parish rights. Hence, in the latter case it was not only the canonical share, but the offerings received at the time of burial in their entirety that had to be given to the parochial church. In the judgment of Innocent, an act of injustice had been committed; hence complete restitution had to be made. He considered that the right of the pastor to conduct the burial of his subjects had been infringed upon.[9] In his recognition of the necessity of the payment to the pastor of the canonical portion, in every case, by those privileged to officiate at burial, and of the complete sum received when the conditions for the use of the privilege were not fulfilled, Innocent III upheld the right of the parochial church to give burial to its subjects.

The IV General Council of the Lateran (1215), presided over by this great pope, upbraided severely the clergy, both secular and religious, who to the detriment of the parish churches added to the

[9] C. 10, X, *de sepulturis*, III, 28; Potthast, *Regesta Pontificum Romanorum inde ab anno post Christum natum MCXCVIII ad annum MCCCIV* (2 vols., Berolini, 1874–1875), n. 2806. Hereafter this work will be cited as Potthast.

contract, when they let out homes and lands to rent, a pact that the renters would pay their tithes to them and choose burial in their churches. The council, knowing well that such acts proceeded only from avarice, determined that whatever was received as the result of such pacts should be restored to the parochial church.[10]

Pope Boniface VIII (1294–1303) in several instances stood for the right of the pastor of the parish church to officiate at the burial of its dead. In clarifying a point in regard to the church entitled to the payment of the canonical portion when one, who was no longer a parishioner of the church of his ancestors, had chosen to be buried in a church other than that of his ancestors, he asserted that the payment was not owed to the church of his ancestors, which was no longer the parochial church of the decedent, but to precisely that church in which the deceased had been accustomed to hear Mass, attend divine services and receive the sacraments. This church, which incidentally was excluded as the place of burial of the decedent, was obviously, nevertheless, the parish church of the deceased. It was not then the church of one's ancestors whose rights had been infringed upon, but only the parochial church.[11]

At the same time he further elucidated this point by determining that whoever, having a domicile in a city, sometimes went to his country villa for recreation or the cultivation of his farm, and then happened to die there without having chosen his place of burial, was not to be buried in the church of the country villa, but in his parochial church or in that rather in which there had existed for a long time a burial place of his ancestors.[12] An obvious difficulty arises if the attention is concentrated on the word " rather." This receives its explanation from the next article of this thesis,

[10] Mansi, *Sacrorum Conciliorum Nova et Amplissima Collectio* (53 vols. in 60, Paris-Arnhem-Leipzig, 1901–1927), XXII, 1043. Hereafter this work will be cited as Mansi.

[11] C. 2, *de sepulturis,* III, 12, in VI°.

[12] C. 3, *de sepulturis,* III, 12, in VI°: Is qui, habens domicilium in civitate vel castro, quandoque ad villam ruralem se transfert recreationis causa, vel ut ruralia exerceat in eadem; si non electa sepultura decedat ibidem, non in ecclesia dictae villae, sed in sua parochiali, vel in ea potius in qua majorum ipsius ab antiquo sepultura exstitit, sepeliri debebit, dummodo absque periculo ad ipsam valeat deportari.

which deals with the common law concerning the place of burial. For the time being it may be noted that the faithful could choose their place of burial; if they did not choose it, they were to be buried in their parish churches. However, it has been noted that Pope Boniface held that the canonical portion was to be paid to the parish church in the event that both churches, that is, the church of one's ancestors and the parish church, were excluded for another in the choice of a place of burial.

Pope Clement V (1305–1314), in his Constitution "*Dudum,*" recognized the right of the pastor to conduct the funeral of his subjects at the same time that he granted the privilege to the Friars Minor to conduct the funeral of those who elected to be buried in the church of this mendicant order.[13]

The parish was a place in which there resided a group of people, allotted to a certain church and contained within definite boundaries. Its limits designated by the bishop, it was particularly that church in which the people heard Mass and assisted at divine services, and in which the priest who ruled it administered the sacraments to the faithful. The parish could be administered by members of the secular or the regular clergy.

B. The Privileged Right of Other Churches

Besides the parochial churches, other churches could by way of privilege enjoy the right of bestowing ecclesiastical burial, that is, of receiving the bodies of the deceased. There were of course numerous privileges of this kind concerning which mention is not contained in the Decretals. For instance, Pope Innocent III (1198–1216) granted this right, as shown above, to certain churches of Hospitallers in the diocese of Clermont in France.[14] Pope Clement IV (1265–1268) granted it to the Friars Minor.[15] Pope Boniface VIII (1294–1303) granted it to the same order and also to the Order of Preachers in his Constitution "*Super cathedram.*" Later he extended it to the Hermits of St. Augus-

[13] C. 2, *de sepulturis,* III, 7, in Clem.

[14] C. 10, X, *de sepulturis,* III, 28; Potthast n. 2806.

[15] *Bullarum Diplomatum et Privilegiorum Sanctorum Romanorum Pontificum, Taurinensis Editio* (25 vols., Augustae Taurinorum, 1857-1872), III, 741. Hereafter this work will be cited as *Bull. Rom.*

tine.[16] Benedict XI (1303–1304)[17] and Clement V (1305–1314) confirmed this grant. Pope Clement granted to the friars of the Friars Minor and of the Order of Preachers the right of burying the faithful in their churches and cemeteries. He added, however, that when they buried those who had elected to be buried by them, they were to pay the canonical portion to the pastor, thus recognizing the fundamental right of the pastors to bury their own parishioners.[18] Other grants of this privilege were made during subsequent years. Pope John XXII (1316–1334) gave it to the Carmelites;[19] Pope Julius II (1503–1513) to the Minims of St. Francis of Paula;[20] Pope Leo X (1513–1521) to the Camaldulensian monks.[21]

Among the writers of the middle ages the "*ius sepeliendi*" signified the right of a church to bury the deceased in its cemetery. Arguing from the letter of Pope Dionysius to Severus, Bishop of Cordova, Bernard of Pavia (+1213) said that this right, in so far as it was not a parochial right, arose from the concession of the pope.[22] As has been seen, the supreme pontiffs in fact granted it to many orders. Hostiensis (+1271) remarked that not every church had the right of receiving the bodies of all the faithful for burial, even if they had it for the burial of certain persons or for the burial of the friars, but only those churches which had parishioners subject to them or to which the privilege had been given.[23]

Panormitanus (1386–1453) declared that since the concession of this right was to the detriment of parochial churches, the pope, who was able to transfer the rights of one person to another, should usually be petitioned to make such a concession. Yet he

---

[16] C. 1, *de sepulturis,* III, 6, in Extravag. com.

[17] C. 1, *de privilegiis,* V, 7, in Extravag. com.

[18] C. 2, *de sepulturis,* III, 7, in Clem.

[19] C. un., *de iudiciis,* II, 1, in Extravag. com.

[20] *Bull. Rom.,* V, 421.

[21] *Bull. Rom.,* V, 549.

[22] Bernardus Papiensis, *Summa Decretalium* (ed. Laspeyres, Ratisbonae, 1860), Lib. III, tit. 24, p. 101.

[23] Hostiensis (Henricus de Segusia), *Commentaria in Quinque Decretalium Libros* (5 vols. in 3, Venetiis, 1581), ad c. 1, III, 28, s. v. *Et eligere.* Hereafter this work will be cited as *Commentaria.*

concluded that the bishop could grant it also, but only for a just cause and with the consent of his chapter. To him the reason for requiring the fulfillment of such conditions was that this privilege or concession had to be reckoned among the difficult and prejudicial cases, which the bishop, as he said, could not handle except in this manner.[24] He said that proof was hardly necessary to establish the fact that the pope could grant this privilege. However he recurred in justification of it to the letters of Pope Dionysius and of Pope Clement III (1187–1191).[25] The teaching that the pope and the bishop could grant this right of burial remained constant through the entire period up to and including the time of the Council of Trent (1545–1563).

From the fact that they were exempt, the superiors of monasteries had the right to bury their own subjects in their churches and monasteries. This right was strongly upheld in the thirteenth century by Innocent III (1198–1216), and especially by Gregory IX (1227–1241). The last named pope in his Constitution "*Nimis iniqua*" upbraided many prelates who, because of their excessive greed, had put many burdens upon the religious who had left all for God. He complained that they compelled the friars to bury their deceased brethren in the parish churches and to have their obsequies celebrated there.[26] At the time of Innocent IV (1243–1254) the terms of this constitution were renewed.[27] However, after the latter's death the dispute between the secular and the regular clergy involved rather a discussion of the right of the friars to bury all who chose to be buried in their churches.

ARTICLE II. THE PLACE OF BURIAL

The discussion concerning the right to bury the deceased naturally gives rise to the question about the place of burial. It has been seen that through the middle ages the parochial church had the right granted by the common law, but that also many religious

---

[24] Abbas Panormitanus (Nicolaus de Tudeschis), *Commentaria in Quinque Libros Decretalium* (5 vols. in 7, Venetiis, 1588), ad. c. 9, III, 28, n. 8 and 9. Hereafter this work will be cited as *Commentaria.*

[25] C. 9, X, *de sepulturis,* III, 28; Jaffé, n. 16941.

[26] C. 16, X, *de excessibus praelatorum,* V, 31; Potthast, n. 8786a.

[27] Potthast, n. 11878.

orders had that right by way of privilege. Attention will now be fixed on the common law of the same period in so far as it concerned the rights of the faithful in regard to burial, and in relation to those rights, on the prominence enjoyed by the parochial church.

Against the right of burying the dead as enjoyed by the parish church through concession of the common law, and by the churches of some of the religious orders through privilege, it will be ascertained that the faithful were given the right of choosing a place of burial. It will be learned also that, if this selection had not been made during the life of the deceased, then the burial was to occur in the church where the burial place of one's ancestors was located; and that, finally, if there was lacking this kind of burial place, one was to be buried in his parochial church.

A. The Church Specifically Selected

The free choice of the place of burial on the part of the faithful arose from the fact that such a choice was always regarded as a part of one's last will and testament, which was always to be fulfilled in all of its parts. In the *Decretum Gratiani* and in the Decretals of Gregory IX, the treatment of burial followed the section on wills, inasmuch as the deceased in his last will frequently determined where and in what manner he would be buried.

This high regard for the last will concerning the final disposition of one's body was evidenced in a letter of Pope St. Gregory the Great (590–604) of the year 598.[28] He asserted that the last will of the deceased was to be fulfilled in every detail.

The Council of Tribur (895) supposed this right of selection of one's burial place when it listed a number of places which, if selection of them for burial occurred, would be more fittingly chosen in the order given.[29]

Gratian, besides including in his *Decretum* the excerpt from the letter of Gregory the Great and the canon borrowed from the Council of Tribur, cited also a purported letter of Pope Mel-

---

[28] C. 4, C. XIII, q. 2—*Monumenta Germaniae Historica, Epistolarum,* Tomus I, Pars II, *Gregorii I Papae Registrum Epistolarum* (Hartmann, Berolini, 1887–1899), 240–242.

[29] C. 6, C. XIII, q. 2—Hefele-Leclercq, *Histoire des Conciles,* tom. IV, pars II, p. 700.

chiades (311–313).[30] This pope was supposed to have been asked whether any one could rashly reject as his burial place that of his ancestors and choose a new one for himself. He is reputed to have answered that if any one were to do so he should be excommunicated. The question of course dealt with the rashness of the party and his inconsiderateness with respect to the family tomb.

The *dictum* of Gratian made it very clear that it was one thing to spurn the burial place of one's parents through rashness, for example out of pride, out of hatred, or because one had been lured by rash promises and gifts, and quite another to choose a new burial place for a reasonable cause. He asserted also that no matter what others said about the fact that any one who was free to make a last will was not for that reason free also to choose a place of burial, such a choice of burial was in fact nothing else than an expression of one's last will. Although he admitted that from some examples offered by the lives of the Patriarchs and of the saints one could draw an argument for the burial always and necessarily with one's ancestors, yet he contended that from even a greater number of examples of the ancient Patriarchs and of the saints the freedom to choose one's place of burial was fully warranted and firmly established. His conclusion was that one was free to be buried with one's ancestors, but that one was likewise free, in view of the diversity occasioned by temporal and local circumstances, to choose a tomb other than that of one's forebears.[31] He granted that it was fundamentally not permissible to change whatever was defined by law, but that what was not defined could rightfully follow the judicious direction of our free wills. He added that where one was to be buried was not defined by law, and therefore the specification of the place of burial depended on one's free choice.

Gathered in the Decretals of Gregory IX (1227–1241) was the letter of Pope Leo III (795–816), which upheld so strongly the freedom of election of the place of burial. He had declared: "*Nulli tamen negamus propriam eligere sepulturam, et etiam*

---

[30] C. 7, C. XIII, q. 2. Friedberg notes that this chapter is wholly uncertain in its authorship and authenticity.

[31] *Dictum,* p. c. 7, C. XIII, q. 2.

alienam: Dominus enim et Magister alienam elegit ut propriam." [32] Thus he had set opposite the ancient custom of being buried with one's ancestors the example of our Blessed Lord.

There was much dispute among the writers in the thirteenth century concerning the letter of Innocent II (1130–1143) to the Archbishop of Cagliari.[33] This pope had taken exception to the election of a place of burial in a less christianized locality, referring in this manner to a locality where Masses or divine services were more rarely celebrated. He had rather favored burial among one's ancestors in this particular case, and had emphazised the point that if any one chooses a burial place, he ought to choose a place where he would frequently receive the benefit of divine services. To put an end to the dispute, Pope Boniface VIII (1294–1303) definitely stated that he did not wish to assail the choice of any one who had rejected as his place of burial the ancestral tomb and had chosen to be buried even in a place where religion flourished less than there.[34]

The Decretists and Decretalists from the twelfth to the fifteenth century referred to the right of the faithful to choose their place of burial. Rufinus (+ca. 1190) referred to the canon of Pope Leo III as the ordinary law.[35] Bernard of Pavia (+1213) discussed at some length the exercise of this right on the part of various classes of persons.[36] Hostiensis (+1271) remarked that any adult who had the use of reason could in his last will freely choose the place of his burial to be wherever he wished, unless he did so with evil intent;[37] and he definitely manifested that he

---

[32] C. 1, X, *de sepulturis,* III, 28; Jaffé, n. 2536. Cf. Panormitanus, ad c. 1, III, 28, n. 1, ". . . [Statuit] aliam regulam affirmativam, quod quisque de novo potest sibi eligere sepulturam et praetermittere sepulchrum majorum, instar Christi; nam si voluisset, sepultus fuisset in sepulchro majorum suorum, tamen elegit sepeliri in sepulchro Joseph. . . . Stat enim permissive et non dispositive. Nam Christus non disposuit, ut ibi sepeliretur, sed permittendo videtur elegisse."

[33] C. 3, X, *de sepulturis,* III, 28; Jaffé, n. 8275. This letter is attributed to Innocent III (1198–1216) in the Decretals of Gregory IX.

[34] C. 2, *de sepulturis,* III, 12, in VI°.

[35] *Summa Decretorum,* ad c. un., C. XIII, q. 1, p. 334.

[36] *Summa Decretalium,* p. 102.

[37] *Commentaria,* ad c. 1, III, 28, s. v. *Et eligere.*

wanted no one to think that he condemned the choice one made of the place of one's burial. It was all too clear, he said, from the very fact that one had reached the age of puberty, that one could choose the place of his burial, but he also insisted that the choice be made in accordance with the freedom as granted by the law.[38] He maintained that the last will could be changed at the discretion of the testator. He declared that, since the testator did not make laws for himself, he could not so bind himself that later he could not change his last will if he happened to change his mind. He stated flatly that, since a person was free to make a last will, he could change it whenever he wished. He fully conceded this same option to the choice of a burial place in a last will.[39] Bernard of Parma (+1266), who was the author of the *Glossa Ordinaria* to the Decretals of Gregory IX, wrote in the same vein.[40] Panormitanus (+1453) stood for the absolute freedom of choice in this matter, so long as it was exercized in accord with the other provisions of the common law.[41]

To ensure further the freedom of the choice of burial, Pope Boniface VIII (1294–1303) issued his Constitution "*Animarum periculis,*" in which he forbade the secular and the regular clergy to induce the laity to vow, swear or otherwise promise the selection of their church as the place of burial, or the retention and non-alteration of the choice as previously made. He declared that an election made under such inducement was absolutely null; that the laity who were so induced were nevertheless to be buried in the churches in which they should have been buried according to law, if they had died without having chosen another place of burial. He commanded the clergy, both secular and religious, that if they had acted in this way they were not only to restore to their proper churches the bodies which were sought by those churches, but also within ten days to return all the offerings which in any way had been tendered to and received by them on the occasion of the funeral. He added that, if they did not

---

[38] *Commentaria,* ad c. 1, III, 28, s. v. *Nulli autem.*

[39] Hostiensis, *Summa Aurea* (Venetiis, 1570), Lib. III, *de sepulturis,* s. v. *an licitum.*

[40] *Glossa Ordinaria,* ad c. 1, X, *de sepulturis,* III, 28, s. v. *Eligere.*

[41] *Commentaria,* ad c. 1, III, 28, n. 1.

make such restitution, the churches themselves and their cemeteries were forthwith under interdict and thereupon would remain under interdict until a full restitution of the offerings and the bodies had been made by them.[42]

Pope Clement V (1305–1314) in the General Council of Vienne (1311–1312) renewed this same prohibition in his Constitution "*Cupientes,*" barred with suspension the transgressors of this prohibition from the office of preaching, excommunicated them in the event that they violated this suspension, and reserved the absolution from the penalties to the Holy See.[43]

> Sane, temerarios violatores constitutionis illius, quae religiosis et clericis saecularibus prohibet, ne aliquos ad vovendum, iurandum, vel fide interposita, seu alias promittendum inducant, ut sepulturam apud eorum ecclesias eligant, vel iam electam ulterius non immutent, similem sententiam (poena in dicta constitutione contenta in sua perdurante robore,) incurrere volumus ipso facto, ab alio quam a sede apostolica, praeterquam in mortis articulo, nullatenus absolvendos, nullis privilegiis, aut statutis, cuiuscumque tenoris exsistant, super his valituris.

Pope Sixtus IV (1471–1484) specified anew the punishment of excommunication *latae sententiae* for this same crime which assailed the right of free choice of one's burial place.[44]

Ordinarily then the faithful could choose a place of burial as long as the place which was chosen by them had the right of receiving them for burial. It has been previously noted that the parish churches in virtue of the common law, and the churches of

---

[42] C. 1, *de sepulturis,* III, 12, in VIº.

[43] C. 3, *de poenis,* V. 8, in Clem.

[44] C. 2, *de treuga et pace,* I, 9 in Extravag. com.: "Quodque etiam nec fratres, nec curati inducant aliquo modo laicos ad eligendum sepulturam apud eos, et bene caveant propter poenas, quae imponunt canones, quum sit libera . . . iniungentes archiepiscopis, episcopis, plebanis, rectoribus, curatis, nec non prioribus, guardianis et singulis fratribus Ordinum Mendicantium sub poena excommunicationis latae sententiae, quam contra facientes et quemlibet eorum contra facientem incurrere volumus eo ipso, a qua absolvi nequeant, nisi de expresso consensu partis laesae, et debita satisfactione praevia, inviolabiliter observent, et quantum in eis est ab aliis observari faciant."

some of the regular clergy by reason of privilege granted, had this right. However, there were exceptions to this right of choosing a place of burial. Since the choice of burial was rooted in the capacity to make a last will, those who were incapable of human acts were naturally excluded. The law of the Decretals gave particular attention to two exceptions, involving namely those who had not attained the age of puberty and those who were members of religious orders.

Classed as below the age of puberty were all boys who were not yet fourteen years of age and all girls who were not yet twelve years of age. Pope Boniface VIII (1294–1303) declared that, although the father could bury, wherever he wished, his minor sons who were unable to make a choice before they reached the age of puberty, if such was the custom of the land, he could not do this where a custom of this kind did not exist, for then the children were to be buried with their ancestors or in the parish church. Those below the age of puberty were evidently excluded from making a choice, for the place was chosen for them either by the father, if custom permitted, or, in the absence of any choice made by him, the place was designated for them according to the rule of the law enacted by the pope. It was custom that allowed the choice to be made by the father. The prohibition which barred the children from exercising any option in this matter was simply founded in their incapacity for making a last will.[45]

Pope Lucius III (1181–1185) had been reluctant to determine the right of minors in regard to the choice of burial. Accordingly he had left it to custom to determine these rights.[46] However, according to the words of Boniface VIII any person above the age of puberty could certainly choose for himself the place of his burial. Boniface VIII declared that the father could make this choice for his son who was below the age of puberty only when there existed a custom which favored that parental right. The father, then, was excluded from exercising this choice for those of his children who had reached the age of puberty. It must be

---

[45] C. 4, *de sepulturis,* III, 12, in VI°; *Gl. ord.* ad c. 7, X, *de sepulturis,* III, 28, s. v. *minores.*

[46] C. 7, X, *de sepulturis,* III, 28; Jaffé, n. 15734.

admitted with Ioannes Andreae (1272–1348) that the right to make a will regarding matters of spiritual import was conceded by Boniface VIII to minors who had reached the age of puberty.[47]

Hostiensis (+1271) believed most firmly that a religious could choose the place of his burial, since, as he maintained, the religious was freed from the yoke of religious obedience at his death.[48] He contended that the law which called for the burial of a monk in his own monastery applied only then when the monk had not chosen some other place.[49] However, Boniface VIII allowed monks to make such a choice only if they were far from their own monastery, and moreover could not readily be brought back to it upon their death. He declared that apart from this exception religious were incapable of choosing the place of their burial, "*cum velle et nolle non habeant,*" and accordingly were to receive burial at their proper monasteries.[50] No religious, then, unless he was in a place far from his monastery, could choose the place of his burial. What was to be done if he had died in such a place without having chosen his burial place? Some said that he was to be buried in a monastery of his order if such a monastery existed in the place where he died. But the common opinion maintained that he was to be buried in the parochial church of the place where he died.[51]

Panormitanus (1386–1453) believed that abbots, as religious, could nevertheless choose the place of their burial, since they had "*velle et nolle*" in regard to the monks who were subject to them, and the abbots themselves were not subject to any other person. He appealed to the case of St. Benedict (c. 480–c. 550), who chose a place of burial for himself. However, he conceded that perhaps he was stretching a point, and finally admitted that he did not find this point treated specifically by any author.[52]

Professed religious, then, were not allowed to choose a place of burial for the same fundamental reason that excluded those who

---

[47] *Gl. ord.*, ad c. 4, *de sepulturis,* III, 12, in VI°, s. v. *filiusfamilias.*

[48] *Commentaria,* ad c. 7, III, 28, v. *ad eum statum.*

[49] *Loc. cit.*

[50] C. 5, *de sepulturis,* III, 12, in VI°.

[51] *Gl. ord.* ad c. 5, *de sepulturis,* III, 12, in VI°, s. v. *casus.*

[52] *Commentaria,* ad c. 7, III, 28, n. 5.

had not reached the age of puberty, namely, they were not able to make a will. If they died close to their monasteries, so that they could easily be brought to them, then they were to be interred at their monasteries. The monastery church was for them the church where they had been accustomed to receive the sacraments and to assist at the divine services. If they died outside the monastery and could not easily be brought home, then they were to be buried as lay persons in the place of their choice, or, if a choice had not been expressed, then in the parish church within whose parochial limits they died. Novices, since they enjoyed "*velle et nolle,*" could choose the place of their burial.[53]

To St. Augustine of Hippo (+430) Gratian attributed the saying: "*Unaquaeque mulier sequatur virum sive in vita sive in morte.*"[54] From this it could seem that the wife should always be buried in the burial place of her deceased husband. Yet this was not the opinion of Gratian. He believed that she too had a free choice regarding the place of her burial. Ioannes Teutonicus (+1246) remarked that the saying of St. Augustine implied no more than counsel, and that accordingly the wife had a free choice in determining where she wished to be buried.[55]

Pope Lucius III (1181–1185) stood for her equal freedom with her husband's in the choice of a burial place. He said that each of them had equal capacity, inasmuch as the choice of a place of burial pertained rather to that state or condition in life in which the wife was freed from the dominion of her husband.[56] Yet, Pope Boniface VIII returned to the counsel of St. Augustine for the case wherein the wife had not specifically chosen her burial place. He declared that a wife who upon successive marriages had not chosen a place of burial was to be buried with her last husband, whose domicile and honor she retained. The dignity of the wife was derived from the person of her husband.[57]

---

[53] Cf. *Gl. ord.* ad c. 24, X, *de privilegiis,* V, 33, s. v. *concessum,* for a discussion of the rights of the *oblati et conversi;* also Panormitanus, ad c. 9, III, 28, n. 3.

[54] C. 3, C. XIII, q. 2.

[55] *Gl. ord.* ad c. 3, C. XIII, q. 2, s. v. *in morte.*

[56] C. 7, X, *de sepulturis,* III, 28; Jaffé, n. 15734.

[57] C. 3, *de sepulturis,* III, 12, in VIo.

In the event that a wife died before her husband without having chosen a place of burial, Panormitanus believed that the dictates of custom determined the place of her burial. He deemed it just and equitable that, if the husband had prepared a place of burial for himself, then the wife should be buried there also. However, he likewise conceded that there were cases in which she could be buried in her own family's tomb, e.g., when the husband did not have his own burial place and really intended to be buried with his ancestors, but in consequence of his absence when the wife died had never had a chance to express his will.[58] Panormitanus then raised another question: if the wife had chosen her own burial place and had died before her husband, where was the husband to be buried? The author was torn between two solutions. Perhaps, he said, the husband should be buried with her because of the union that existed between them during life. Yet he considered that opinion as a better solution which held that he was to be buried with his ancestors, for it was the wife that had to follow the husband, not vice versa.[59]

B. The Family Tomb

It was an ancient custom among peoples to be buried with their ancestors. In the Old Testament one reads frequently that the deceased Patriarchs were buried with their ancestors.[60] The same custom prevailed in the early ages of the Church. In the canon ascribed to Pope Melchiades (311–313) it was declared that no one should rashly reject as the place of his interment the ancestral burying place.[61] Pope Leo III (795–816) decreed that each person should be buried in the tomb of his ancestors. At the same time he admitted that every one had the right to choose his place of burial.[62]

Pope Boniface VIII (1294–1303) decided that if someone died at a summer villa without having chosen a place of burial he was

---

[58] *Commentaria,* ad c. 7, III, 28, in 7.

[59] *Loc. cit.*

[60] E.g., Genesis, XXV; 9; XLIX; 29–31.

[61] C. 7, C. XIII, q. 2. Friedberg notes that this quotation from Pope Melchiades is wholly uncertain in its authorship and authenticity.

[62] C. 1, X, *de sepulturis,* III, 28; Jaffé, n. 2536.

to be buried in his parochial church, or rather in that church in which there existed a tomb of his ancestors, as long as the body could be brought thither for burial.[63] Thus he accented the locality of the burial place of the family as next in order when a specific burial place had not been chosen.

The tomb of one's ancestors, called the "*sepulchrum maiorum*" or "*gentilitium,*" was the tomb in which one's forebears were buried. It ordinarily happened that one of the ancestors determined on a certain place of burial for himself and his family, thus gaining the right to be buried in this tomb. This right was handed on to his descendants. It was only fitting that in the absence of a specifically selected place one should be buried in the family sepulchre. Panormitanus remarked that all men were bound by natural ties of affection to the members of their families, and that all are presumed to prefer to be buried with those near and dear to them, rather than with strangers.[64]

Naturally, various cases were contemplated and discussed by the Glossators and Decretalists after the time of Boniface VIII (+1303). Ioannes Andreae (1272–1348) declared that a son could be buried in either tomb when the great-grandfather and the grandfather were buried in one church, and the father was buried in another as specifically chosen by him. He also held that, if three ancestors of a son were buried in three different places, the son should be buried with the father.[65] Panormitanus agreed with Ioannes Andreae except for the case in which the father had been buried in a certain church in opposition to his specifically expressed will for a different church as the place of his burial. In this case, the son was to be buried in the church in which the family tomb was located.[66]

As has been mentioned above, if the wife did not choose the place of her burial, she was to be buried not with her own family but in the tomb of her husband. Her case, then, was an exceptional one with reference to the rule that one should be buried with one's ancestors.

---

[63] C. 3, *de sepulturis,* III, 12, in VI°.

[64] *Commentaria,* ad c. 1, III, 28, n. 5.

[65] *Gl. ord.* ad c. 3, *de sepulturis,* III, 12, in VI°, s. v. *ab antiquo.*

[66] *Commentaria,* ad c. 1, III, 28, n. 5.

C. The Parochial Church

If one had not chosen a place for his burial and did not have a family tomb, he was to be buried in the cemetery of his parochial church. The right of the parish church to bury its parishioners has been mentioned previously in this study. There were cited on that occasion a number of canons which upheld the right of the pastor to officiate at the burial. It seems sufficient here to mark the position which the parish church had in its relation to the church of personal selection and the church of the family tomb.

Pope Leo III (795–816) determined that each person should be buried with his ancestors, but to no one did he deny the right to choose the place of his burial. However, he demanded at the same time that in both instances a third part of all that had been left to either of these churches on the occasion of the funeral should be paid to the parish church. Thus he recognized the following order for the places of burial: first, the place of one's choice; secondly, the tomb of one's ancestors; thirdly, the parish church.[67]

Pope Boniface VIII (1294–1303), in his decision concerning the person who had gone to his country place and had there died without having chosen his place of burial, determined the same order thus:

> Is qui, habens domicilium in civitate vel castro, quandoque ad villam ruralem se transfert recreationis causa, vel ut ruralia exerceat in eadem; si non electa sepultura decedat ibidem, non in ecclesia dictae villae, sed in sua parochiali, vel in ea potius in qua maiorum ipsius ab antiquo sepultura exstitit, sepeliri debebit, dummodo absque periculo ad ipsam valeat deportari.[68]

Hence the law of the Decretals was explicit. If choice of the place of burial had not been made and if there was no ancestral tomb, the body was to be buried in the parish church of the deceased as long as it could be brought there without danger. Panormitanus sagely remarked that since the right of burying its parishioners was a parochial right, the pastor had an established

---

[67] C. 1, X, *de sepulturis,* III, 28; Jaffé, n. 2536.

[68] C. 3, *de sepulturis,* III, 12, in VI°.

prior claim and title for burying in his church all who died within the confines of his parish. He declared further that therefore the burden of proof rested on the one who asserted that the deceased person was to be buried in a church other than the parish church. He concluded that the right of the pastor yielded solely to firmly established proof that one had actually chosen a place of burial or had a family tomb.[69]

The pastor accordingly possessed the right of burying all those who at the time of their death had a domicile in his parish. If a person had a domicile in two parishes, then he could be buried in either parish, since both pastors possessed an equal right.[70]

If one had a domicile in a parish and died while he was living as a traveller in another parish, then the pastor of his domicile possessed the right to officiate at the funeral as long as the body could be transported thither without danger. If one who had a domicile in a parish went to another parish to dwell there for a time apart from any intention of remaining, and then died there, a doubt arose regarding the proper and lawful place of burial. Since he had customarily received the sacraments in the parish where he was living, it seemed that he should be buried there. On the other hand, his reception of the sacraments at that church was simply occasioned by his temporary sojourn there, and by that fact alone that church did not become his parish church. Panormitanus favored the pastor of the domicile as the one whose right it was to officiate at the burial.[71]

There was a dispute also concerning the place of burial of the one who died in a locality while he was merely passing through it, and whose body could not be transported to his home parish. Hostiensis (+1271) believed that the body should be buried in the cathedral church;[72] St. Raymond of Pennafort (1175–1275) maintained that it should be buried in the local parochial church.[73] Vagrants, since they had no proper parish, were to be buried in the parish in which they died.

---

[69] *Commentaria,* ad c. 5, III, 28, n. 1.

[70] C. 2, *de sepulturis,* III, 12, in VI°.

[71] *Commentaria,* ad c. 10, III, 28, n. 10.

[72] *Commentaria,* ad c. 1, III, 28, s. v. *Et eligere.*

[73] *Summa* (Verona, 1744), Lib. I, Tit. 16, p. 134.

Nuns enjoyed the same privilege as the monks did in this matter so far as their own burial was concerned. Novices also were generally looked upon as enjoying the privileges of their orders. At the same time, when they became novices, they had changed their domiciles and were receiving the sacraments daily in a church distinct from their old parish churches. The Council of Trent (1545–1563) declared that those who were real servants in the monasteries and dwelt within the walls and homes of the monks and lived under their obedience, so that they really belonged to the family of the monastery, could receive the last sacraments from the monks, and burial in the cemetery of the regular clergy without the intervention of the pastor.[74]

The peculiar status of the wife in the matter of burial, which has already been mentioned, exempted her also from the claims of parochial burial rights.

With these noteworthy exceptions to the parochial burial rights, the common law prevailed for all others.

ARTICLE III

THE CONDUCT OF THE FUNERAL

The burial right did not attach to every church. Churches which were parochial possessed this right under the concession of the common law. The pastor had the strict right to conduct the funeral. By custom this consisted of three acts, the conduct of the body to the church, the performance of the obsequies, and the escorting of the body to the place where it was to be interred or entombed. Since the pastor had the right to conduct the funeral of his parishioners, he had the right to perform these three acts.

The problem became somewhat complicated when one of his parishioners had chosen to be buried in a monastery or in a church of the regular clergy to which had been conceded the right of burial. What part was the pastor entitled to play in that instance? Could the clergy of the church of burial conduct the whole funeral without having to recognize at least some right on the part of the pastor?

---

[74] Conc. Trident., sess. XXIV, *de ref.*, c. 11.

Ioannes Andreae (1272–1348) mentioned the opinion of Ioannes Monachus (Lemoyne), who held that, if there existed a custom to that effect, then the corpse had to be brought first to the parochial church. He further maintained that, even if no such custom existed, the body was nevertheless to be brought to the parochial church so that the Mass could be celebrated over the body there, inasmuch as the deceased should receive his last farewell from his pastor.[75]

Oldradus de Laude (+1335), on the contrary, is said by Ioannes Andreae to have asserted that, notwithstanding the prohibition of the pastor, the friars could enter the parish to conduct the body in procession to their church. His chief reason was that the regular clergy had been granted the right freely to bestow burial. Once this right was granted, everything subservient to it or necessary for attaining it was granted also. The principle that the means to the end are conceded along with the concession of the end itself was basic in his argumentation. The right to bury, he said, could not be considered free if the act of burying was impeded even for a time. The word " free " meant simply that no one's consent was required. Hence he concluded that the regular clergy could go in procession to the home of the deceased for the removal of the body to their churches without any obligation to wait until the pastor delivered the body to them at his church or at their own.[76]

The discussion concerning this point was occasioned, no doubt, by the publication in quick succession of three Constitutions, "*Super cathedram*" by Boniface VIII (1294–1303),[77] "*Inter cunctas*" by Benedict XI (1303–1304),[78] and "*Dudum*" by Clement V (1304–1314),[79] during the first decade of the fourteenth century. The Constitution "*Inter cunctas*" of Benedict XI, which had revoked the Constitution of Boniface VIII, and then in turn was revoked by the Constitution of Clement V, stated flatly:

[75] *Gl. ord.* ad. c. 2, *de sepulturis,* III, 7, in Clem. s. v. *integre.*

[76] *Gl. ord.* ad c. 2, *de sepulturis,* III, 7, in Clem. s. v. *libera.*

[77] C. 2, *de sepulturis,* III, 6, in Extravag. com.

[78] C. 1, *de privilegiis,* V. 7, in Extravag. com.

[79] C. 2, *de sepulturis,* III, 7, in Clem.

> . . . iubemus, ut corpora defunctorum, qui apud eorundem Fratrum loca elegerint, dum viverent, sepulturam, processionaliter cum cruce, thuribulo, et aqua benedicta, cantando seu legendo officium mortuorum, vel psalmos, et alienas ingredientes parochias, possint assumere et ad suas deferre ecclesias tumulanda.

This was an outright grant to the Friars Minor and the Order of Preachers to enter any parishes in procession with a cross to remove the body for burial. Although this privilege was revoked by Clement V, nevertheless the discussion went on.[80]

Later in the same century Franciscus de Zabarella (1335–1417), and still later Panormitanus (1386–1453), upheld the right of the regular clergy freely to go in procession to the house in order to remove the body for burial. Franciscus de Zabarella used the arguments of Oldradus de Laude.[81] Again great emphasis was placed on the word " free " in connection with the bestowing of the burial. Clement V, it was maintained, granted the right of " free burial " to the regulars at the same time that he revoked the Constitution of Benedict XI. Zabarella approved the admission of Oldradus, namely, that if there existed a custom that the body be brought first to the parochial church and was there to be delivered over to the regular clergy of the church which had been chosen for burial, then the custom had to be observed. Otherwise, he maintained, the Mendicants could go in procession with the cross to the home of the deceased and bear the body to their own churches for Mass and interment. The word " free " denoted for him a certain absolute prerogative and an absolute dominion over the act with which this word was linked, that is, the burying of persons who had selected a monastic or other nonparochial church for the place of their burial. Hence he concluded that it was wholly licit for the regular clergy to have complete charge of the entire funeral.[82]

Panormitanus used the same arguments to maintain the same

---

[80] Cf. Schroeder, *Disciplinary Decrees of the General Councils* (St. Louis: B. Herder Book Co., 1937), pp. 382–386, for a more detailed history of this controversy.

[81] *Gl. ord.* ad c. 2, *de sepulturis,* III, 7, in Clem., v. *libera.*

[82] *Loc. cit.*

position. He added that there was no law which positively authorized this mode of procedure, but that his expressed opinion seemed to him to be in accord with the mind of the law.[83]

The opinions mentioned above were not confirmed by the action of Pope Sixtus IV (1471–1484) in his Constitution "*Regimini universalis Ecclesiae*" of the year 1474.[84] This bull was commonly called the "*Mare Magnum*" of the regular clergy. It was addressed to the Friars Minor, and its provisions were extended a few months later to the Order of Preachers. He declared that the Friars had the right to bury those who wished to be buried by them. He further explained that this right of "free burial" signified that the Friars themselves could in procession with a cross enter the parishes in which the bodies of the deceased were resting in order to remove the remains, and to carry them to their own churches for burial, but only provided that an established usage or custom favored this practise, or else that the pastor had refused to conduct the body to their church, though he had been requested by the regular clergy to do so. Pope Leo X (1513–1521) in the V General Council of the Lateran (1512–1517) followed very closely in sentiment, and even in expression, the bull of Sixtus IV in his Constitution "*Dum intra,*" which he issued on December 19, 1516.[85]

Consequently, contrary to the doctrine of Oldradus and Panormitanus, the regular clergy did not have by common law the right to remove the remains of those who had chosen to be buried in their churches. The right of bestowing free burial did not include the right to enter the parishes in procession for this purpose; the regulars needed first to consult the pastor. However, they could come in procession to remove the remains in two instances, namely, if the pastor refused to conduct the body to the church, and if there was a custom which favored their right to remove the

---

[83] *Commentaria,* ad c. 6, III, 28, n. 4.

[84] *Bull. Rom.,* V, 219.

[85] Leo X (in Conc. Lateranen. V), const. "*Dum intra*", 19 dec. 1516, § 9.—*Codicis Iuris Canonici Fontes cura Emi. Petri Gasparri editi* (9 vols., Romae: Typis Polyglottis Vaticanis, 1923–1939 [Vols. VII, VIII, et IX ed. cura et studio Emi. Iustiniani Card. Serédi]), 72. Hereafter this work is cited as *Fontes.*

body from the home of the deceased to their own churches for the obsequies.

Since the clergy whose churches were selected as a place of burial were not allowed to come into the parish to remove the remains of the deceased, the duty obviously devolved upon the pastor to conduct the body from the home to the church of the regulars. He had not only the right but also the duty, to conduct the corpse to the place of its burial. Evidently it could not be the duty of the rector of the church which had been chosen for burial. Yet every Catholic had a right to a Christian burial and all that it entailed. Hence it was the pastor upon whom rested the duty to bring the corpse to the church of burial.

It appears from all that has been said concerning the free right of burial as granted to some of the orders, that the pastor's duty ended when he delivered over the body to the regular clergy at their church. It was they who then celebrated the Mass and conducted the body to the place of its interment or entombment. Nothing in the law militated against either of these acts. Whatever restriction there was concerned the right of the regular clergy to enter the parishes of others to conduct the body from the home to their own church. Pope Clement IV (1265–1268) forbade the secular clergy to conduct any benediction, processions or offices of the dead, as well as the exequies, in the churches of the Friars Minor without their express permission.[86]

There arose many further questions concerning the acts of the pastor and of others, but these were to find their solutions in the responses of the Roman Congregations. These responses will be treated later, for the solutions of the difficulties considered in these responses fall within the period subsequent to the General Council of Trent (1545–1563).

[86] *Virtute conspicuus*, 21 iul. 1265—*Bull. Rom.*, III, 841.

CHAPTER II

FROM THE COUNCIL OF TRENT TO THE PRESENT DAY

ARTICLE I. THE PARISH CHURCH

A. The Contingent Proper Place of Burial

At the time of the Council of Trent (1545–1563) it was apparent from the common law that the parish church, or, as it was expressed so frequently, " the church where one was accustomed to be refreshed with heavenly food and to attend divine services," was the proper church of burial for the faithful, unless according to law the deceased had chosen another place of burial or possessed a family tomb. This ordinary law by that time was well established. Yet, during the post-Tridentine period there emanated from the Roman Congregations many decisions which either supported it directly or simply presupposed it. There were issued also two papal constitutions which are particularly worthy of attention.

As early as the year 1580 the Sacred Congregation of Bishops and Regulars in writing to the Bishop of Sinigaglia determined that Franciscan tertiaries who wore only the cord of the Franciscan habit and lived in their homes as other lay people were to be treated in regard to burial as lay persons who had not chosen where they wished to be buried. In other words, they were to be buried in their parish church.[1]

At Foligno, the confusion which resulted in consequence of the fact that the cathedral church claimed to have the right to bury all travellers and servants in the city was ordered brought to an end by the same Sacred Congregation in 1592. It was declared that those persons who were not precisely travellers, but lived in the city for some time, had to be brought for burial to the parish

---

[1] S. C. Ep. et Reg., *Senogallien.*, 22 nov. 1580—*Fontes*, n. 1374. Cf. for a like decision, S. C. Ep. et Reg., *Parmen.*, 11 aug. 1702, ad 4—*Fontes*, n. 1819.

church within whose limits they had been living at the time of their death.[2] The Sacred Congregation desired that the bishop provide that his regulation be observed, and that thus there would exist a full compliance with the sacred canons.

In a most explicit manner the Sacred Congregation in 1606 repeated the earlier law with reference to the case of certain Franciscan tertiaries at Novara.

> S. C. . . . censuit, statuit et decrevit, quod sorores tertii ordinis S. Francisci habitantes in propriis domibus possint ubi voluerint sibi sepulturam eligere, et si decedunt non electa sepultura, sint sepeliendae in sepulchris maiorum, vel illis non existentibus, in ipsarum Ecclesiis parochialibus; neque sint sepeliendae in Ecclesia fratrum Minorum de observantia, nisi in eis sepulturam eligant vel habeant maiorum sepulchra.[3]

Pope Innocent X (1644–1655), in confirming the decisions of the Sacred Congregations concerning the compromise reached by the pastors and the religious orders of Majorca, stood most firmly for the right of the parochial church. Though he approved on the whole the agreement by which the regular clergy would be able, without asking the pastors beforehand, to enter the parishes in order to bring the bodies of those who had chosen burial in the churches of the regular clergy to these churches for burial, inasmuch as there had been an immemorial custom to this effect in many of the cities and towns, he did not grant this privilege to any churches of the regular clergy in which there was not such a custom. The four other points confirmed by him maintained in full vigor the rights of the parochial church. First, the "*quarta funeraria*" was to be paid to the pastor of the deceased when a parishioner was buried in a church of the regular clergy. Secondly, children below the age of puberty, as long as there was not a family tomb, were to be buried in their proper parochial church. Thirdly, the mother of such children could not choose their place of burial unless there existed a legitimate custom. Lastly, lay members of confraternities sponsored by the religious

---

[2] S. C. Ep. et Reg., *Fulginaten.*, 9 iun. 1592—*Fontes*, n. 1458.

[3] S. C. Ep. et Reg., *Novarien.*, 15 mart. 1606—*Fontes*, n. 1638.

orders, if they had not chosen a specific place of burial, were to be buried in their proper parish church.[4]

The Sacred Congregation of the Council on three occasions in the seventeenth and eighteenth centuries maintained the necessity of a parochial funeral for the lay servants of monasteries who did not precisely dwell within the walls of the cloister and who had not chosen a place of burial.[5] At Salerno, in the late seventeenth century, a conservatory of women oblates had been established without prejudice to the rights of the pastor of the parish in which the institute was located. The pastor had even acted as the chaplain for the first nine years of its existence. When a distinct chaplain was appointed, he began to assume all the parochial rights, including that of burying all the women who had died in the institute. The pastor had recourse to the Sacred Congregation, which declared that, the rights of the pastor remaining intact, the women of the institute who had not chosen a specific place of burial were at death to be buried in the parochial church, and that the pastor was to receive all the offerings made on the occasion of their burial.[6]

Pope Benedict XIV (1740–1758) in his Constitution "*Etsi pastoralis,*" issued on May 26, 1742, for the Italo-Greeks, enunciated once more the principles in regard to the position of the parochial church.[7] After he had determined that infants pertained to the jurisdiction of the pastor in whose rite they had been baptized, he declared that if they died before they attained the use of reason they were to be buried by the pastor in whose rite they had been baptized and in their proper parishes, unless baptism had been conferred on them either because of some grave necessity, namely, when they were near death and the proper pastor, or a priest of the proper rite, was not available, or in view of an Apostolic dispensation, namely, when the faculty was granted that

---

[4] Innocent X, const. "*Ex iniuncto*", 22 febr. 1645, § 6—*Fontes,* n. 230.

[5] S. C. C., *Lauden.,* 14 apr. 1685, ad 3—*Fontes,* n. 2885; *Spoletana,* 19 apr. 1692, ad 3—*Fontes,* n. 2928; *Ulixbonen. Occident.,* 22 nov. 1721, 19 sept. 1722, ad 2, 3—*Fontes,* n. 3234, 3247.

[6] S. C. C., *Salernitana,* 8 et 28 iul., 19 aug. 1702, ad 4—*Fontes,* n. 2997.

[7] Benedictus XIV, const. "*Etsi pastoralis*", 21 maii 1742, § II, n. XI—*Fontes,* n. 328.

they might be baptized in the Latin rite, but that thereafter they should still pertain to their own rite. In these cases it was not considered that they had passed from their own to another rite. The same rule also applied after they had attained the use of reason, unless they had expressed their wish to be buried in the church of another rite. If anyone who had been baptized in the Latin rite chose to receive burial in a Greek church, the rules of law were to be observed. The corpse was to be escorted by the proper pastor of the deceased to the church of burial, and the proper pastor was likewise to receive the "*quarta funeralis.*"

There were other decisions of the Sacred Congregations relative to this point, but they will be considered more opportunely when the right of the pastor of burial is the precise subject for discussion.

That the parochial church was the proper place of burial for the parishioners when they had not selected a specific place for their burial and they did not have a family tomb, was taught by all the authors during this time. From Pirhing (+1679) to Many (+1922) no controversy regarding this law is traceable in any of the canonical works.[8] Ferraris (+ca. 1763) designated the doctrine as common and universal.[9]

The historical application of the general principle can best be understood through a logical treatment of the material. Since burial was determined by the status of the parishioner, it is accordingly necessary to consider first the parishioner in his relationship to the parish to determine the pastor who was to officiate at his

---

[8] Pirhing, *Jus Canonicum Nova Methodo Explicatum* (5 vols. in 4; Dilingae, 1674–1678) lib. III, tit. XXVIII, nn. 5–8 (hereafter this work will be cited Pirhing); Reiffenstuel, *Jus Canonicum Universum* (5 vols. in 7; Parisiis, 1864–1870) lib. III, tit. XXVIII, n. 12 (hereafter this work will be cited Reiffenstuel); Schmalzgrueber, *Jus Ecclesiasticum Universum* (5 vols. in 12; Romae, 1843–1845), lib. III, tit. XXVIII, n. 9 (hereafter this work will be cited Schmalzgrueber); Barbosa, *De Officio et Potestate Parochi* (Romae, 1774), C. XXVI, n. 1; Devoti, *Institutionum Canonicarum Libri IV* (Romae, 1830), lib. II, tit. IX, n. V: Many, *De Locis Sacris* (Parisiis, 1904), n. 170.

[9] *Prompta Bibliotheca Canonica Iuridica Moralis Theologica necnon Ascetica Polemica Rubricistica Historica* (9 vols., Romae, 1885–1899), v. *Sepultura*, n. 20. Hereafter this work will be cited *Prompta Bibliotheca.*

burial. The parishioner may have had a domicile in one parish and also may have died there; he may have had a domicile in several parishes and may have died in one of them; he may have died accidentally outside his proper parish or parishes; or he may have died without having acquired a domicile or quasi-domicile in any parish.

B. The Pastor of Burial of the Deceased Who Had One Proper Parish and Died There

If the deceased had one proper parish and died in it, the pastor who officiated at the funeral was, by reason of his office, the proper pastor of this parish. Whatever has been cited above from the Constitutions of the popes, from the decisions of the Sacred Roman Congregations and from the authors of the period, concerning the fact that the church to which the body was to be brought for burial was by common law the proper parish of the deceased, the same is of application here also. However, there were issued many other decisions of the Sacred Congregations that were particularly apropos.

In the seventeenth century, the Sacred Congregation of Rites declared that the pastor of the parish was the pastor of burial in reference to the burial of the canons of a collegiate parochial church,[10] and also in reference to the burial of prisoners incarcerated in a prison situated within the confines of a certain parish.[11] It held also that the proper pastor was the pastor of burial of his parishioners rather than any dignitary even of a cathedral chapter,[12] any canon or any other priest. Furthermore, none of these was to be called to officiate at obsequies if the pastors were reluctant, unwilling or opposed to having them do so.[13]

The Sacred Congregation of the Council in the same century published several pertinent decisions. It declared that the bodies of lay persons who, without having chosen a place of burial, had died in the convents of the regular clergy were to be buried

---

[10] S. R. C., *Montis Regalis*, 17 mart. 1663, ad 4—*Fontes*, n. 5537; *Caietana*, 13 sept. 1670, ad 1—*Fontes*, n. 5578.

[11] S. R. C., *Romana*, 15 ian. 1667—*Fontes*, n. 5563.

[12] S. R. C., *Senen.*, 9 iun. 1668—*Fontes*, n. 5570.

[13] S. R. C., *Rossanen.*, 21 ian. 1673—*Fontes*, n. 5590.

by the pastors.[14] As was mentioned above, it ordered that the lay servants of monasteries who had not lived precisely within the walls of the cloister were to be buried by their proper pastor,[15] as were also the women members of an institute which had been founded without prejudice to the rights of the pastor.[16]

In 1753 the Sacred Congregation of the Council settled the very interesting case of the priest, Valentine Forconi, by declaring as the pastor with burial rights the pastor of his parochial church. Valentine had been a native of the parish church of St. Catervus. He had been appointed to service in his home parish upon his reception of minor orders, and had also exercised major orders there after he had become a priest. He took sick while the pastor was away from the parish, but the curate administered the last rites to him. Before he died, a new pastor had been installed. This priest did not know the rights of the parish, and when he had heard from a friend of the deceased that he ought to be buried in the cathedral, he readily assented and even accompanied the body to that church.

But not long after, having become better informed, the new pastor of St. Catervus' parish sought redress from the Sacred Congregation for the recovery of the body and for the restitution of the emoluments which had accrued to the cathedral church. His plea was presented in telling fashion. In his brief the pastor stressed the fact that it was rights of honor alone that could rightfully be claimed by the cathedral church; that when there existed distinct parishes the cathedral church could not arrogate to itself the right of the pastors, who after all enjoyed a legally founded claim in the matter of burying all parishioners who had not clearly selected some other place for their burial, or who could not, in the absence of a family sepulcher, hope for burial there; that the ecclesiastical status of the deceased priest did not engender any right for the cathedral church, since he had never been retained in its service as a canon or as a beneficiary, but had merely rendered voluntary service, if any.

---

[14] S. C. C., *Sarzanen.*, 28 apr. 1674—*Fontes*, n. 2835.

[15] S. C. C., *Lauden.*, 14 apr. 1685, ad 3—*Fontes*, n. 2885; *Spoletana*, 19 apr. 1692, ad 3—*Fontes*, n. 2928.

[16] S. C. C. *Salernitana*, 8 et 28 iul., 19 aug. 1702—*Fontes*, n. 2997.

To the double question which was then proposed: (1) whether the body of the deceased priest pertained to the parish of St. Catervus, and (2) whether it was to be returned, as also all the emoluments which had accrued to the cathedral church, the Sacred Congregation answered with a universal affirmative.[17]

In the middle of the nineteenth century the Sacred Congregation of Bishops and Regulars confirmed the decision of a bishop who had declared that a certain confraternity had to recognize the pastor's right to conduct the funerals of its members. This association had been acting in such a way that when one of their group died he was to be entitled to a funeral "*more pauperum.*" They had also been enrolling members "*in articulo mortis.*" In both acts they had defrauded the pastor.[18] On another occasion the same Sacred Congregation declared that in funeral matters dispersed religious were subject like other parishioners to the pastor of the parish in which they dwelt.[19]

In 1872 the Sacred Congregation of the Council was approached for a solution of the following case. A child had died at seven years of age. The little girl had spent much time under the care of the grandparents, and it was at their home that she died. Her parents had their home in a different parish. The child's funeral was conducted by the grandparents' pastor, who had also administered the sacraments to the dying child. When the pastor of the child's parents sought vindication for his right in the matter of the child's funeral, an attempt was made to prove that the grandparents had fully adopted the child. When proof for this failed, the Sacred Congregation vindicated the parents' pastor in his rightful claim, for the girl's domicile was that of her parents, and accordingly their pastor was acknowledged as having had the right to conduct the child's funeral and to bestow the burial.[20]

The Sacred Congregation of the Council in 1916 stated that members of a confraternity who had not explicitly chosen burial in the church of the confraternity were to be buried by the pastor

[17] S. C. C., *Tolentina,* 11 aug. 1753, ad 1 et 2—*Fontes,* n. 3633.

[18] S. C. Ep. et Reg., *Aesina,* 31 maii 1850, ad 2—*Fontes,* n. 1955.

[19] S. C. Ep. et Reg., *Pisauren. seu Minorum Conventualium,* 26 febr. 1864—*Fontes,* n. 1988.

[20] S. C. C., *Ilcinen.,* 24 febr. 1872, 25 ian. 1873—*Fontes,* nn. 4221, 4223.

of the parish church. A collective, interpretative or implicit choice of burial in the church of the confraternity, which had been for many of them at one time their parish church, was not judged sufficient to deprive their proper pastor of his rights.[21]

From the practice of the Roman Curia it is evident that throughout the past centuries it has stood for the right of the pastor to conduct the funeral of his parishioner if the latter died within the parish limits. The intention of the Sacred Congregations was to uphold the traditional law. They did so during this period by determining whether the deceased persons had domiciles in the parish. With that decision made the Sacred Congregations unfailingly accorded to the proper pastor the right of granting burial at his parochial church, as long as the parishioner had not selected some other church as the place of his burial, or as long as there was not a family sepulcher to receive his body in death.

C. The Pastor of Burial of the Deceased Who Had Two Proper Parishes and Died in One of Them

If the deceased had been a parishioner of two or more parishes, and had resided in one of them at the time of his death, he was to be buried by the pastor of the parish in which he had died. This principle was maintained by many of the authors after Ferraris (+ca. 1763).[22] Schmalzgrueber (1663–1735), on the contrary, had held that the right to bestow the burial pertained to the pastor of that parish in which the deceased during his lifetime had been accustomed to receive the sacraments and to attend divine services. If the sacraments had been customarily received at both parishes, then simply the pastor of prior intervention in the case determined which of the pastors had the right. He added that if this pastor failed to intervene or if a dispute arose among the

---

21 S. C. C., *Narnien.*, 15 dec. 1916, ad III—*Fontes*, n. 4372.

22 "Qui autem habet domum hiemalem, v. g. in civitate, et aestivam in rure, et sic aequali tempore, modo in una, modo in altera habitat seu moratur, sepeliendus est in parochia in qua decedit. Et ratio est quia parificatur cum eo, qui in duobus locis aeque principale domicilium habet, et sic efficitur utriusque parochiae parochianus, adeoque sepeliendus est in parochia, in qua decedit, cum ipsa sit pro tunc vera ipsius parochia."—*Prompta Bibliotheca*, v. *Sepultura*, n. 25.

pastors, then the bishop was to decide the matter.[23] Many (+1922) believed that the interpretation of the decretal of Boniface VIII,[24] which presupposed a perfect equality between the two pastors, favored this opinion, but he nevertheless acknowledged the doctrine of Ferraris as reflecting the common opinion.[25]

Schmalzgrueber held also that when the home of the deceased stood on the division line of the two parishes the pastor was to be determined in accord with the position of the door in relation to the house; and when the house had two doors, then by the position of that door which was the principal one or the one at which the house was more frequently entered. The principal door, as Schmalzgrueber thought, was generally the one which opened to the front of the house.[26]

A case involving the common opinion of the authors was decided by the Sacred Congregation of the Council in 1881.[27] Within the boundaries of the parish of *Ripalta Nuova,* near the city of Crema, a noble family had a villa, in which for about eight months of the year the family was accustomed to live, the rest of the year being spent in the city within the limits of the parish of St. James. The wife, Mary, in her last illness had been attended by the pastor of the rural parish. He gave her the last sacraments and buried her. The pastor of the parish of St. James claimed the right to all the emoluments of the funeral on the pretext that the woman was his parishioner alone. The Sacred Congregation denied his petition and responded in favor of the pastor of the rural parish, where the woman had died.

Regarding the right of bestowing burial the authors concluded that the pastor of a parish in which one had a quasi-domicile enjoyed the same right as the pastor of the parish of domicile. Thus, Pirhing (1606–1679),[28] Reiffenstuel (1642–1703),[29] Schmalz-

[23] Lib. III, tit. XXVIII, n. 40. Cf. Pirhing, lib. III, tit. XXVIII, n. 5.
[24] C. 2, *de sepulturis,* III, 12, in VI°.
[25] *De Locis Sacris,* n. 172.
[26] Lib. III, tit. XXVIII, n. 40.
[27] S. C. C., 12 mart. 1881—*Fontes,* n. 4251.
[28] Lib. III, tit. XXVIII, n. 7.
[29] Lib. III, tit. XXVIII, n. 28.

grueber (1663–1735),[30] Ferraris (+ca. 1763)[31] and Many (+1922)[32] maintained that those who had a quasi-domicile in one parish and a domicile in another were to be buried in the parish of their quasi-domicile if they had died there, even though they could easily have been transported to the church of their domicile. Hence the same conclusions were drawn for the pastor of quasi-domicile in reference to the burial of the parishioner as were indicated above in the case of the parishioner who had a domicile in two parishes. If the deceased parishioner had had two or even several quasi-domiciles, which latter status was thought by very many authors as at least a possible situation, then there was to be applied the same rule as that which determined the place of burial for a parishioner who had a plurality of domiciles.

D. The Pastor of Burial When the Parishioner Died Outside the Parish of Domicile or Quasi-domicile

The rule of Pope Boniface VIII in the earlier period had contained an exception to the general principle that the parishioner, as long as he had not chosen his burial place or did not have a family tomb, was to be buried in his parish church, and consequently by the pastor of the parish by reason of his office:

> Is qui, habens domicilium in civitate vel castro, quandoque ad villam ruralem se transfert recreationis causa, vel ut ruralia exerceat in eadem, si non electa sepultura decedat ibidem, non in ecclesia dictae villae, sed in sua parochiali, vel in ea potius in qua maiorum ipsius ab antiquo sepultura, exstitit, sepeliri debebit, dummodo absque periculo ad ipsam valeat deportari.[33]

During the later period the same proviso, i.e., "*dummodo absque periculo ad ipsam* [*ecclesiam*] *valeat deportari,*" governed the determination of the pastor of burial for those who died outside their parish.

The phrase "*absque periculo,*" which had been left undefined in

[30] Lib. III, tit. XXVIII, n. 39.

[31] *Prompta Bibliotheca,* v. *Sepultura,* n. 23.

[32] *De Locis Sacris,* n. 172.

[33] C. 3, *de sepulturis,* III, 12, in VI°.

the earlier law, was not determined with any more exactness by the law of the later period. The authors indeed tried to arrive at a more precise definition, but their attempt ended in producing the two opinions recorded by Ferraris.[34] Some said that the danger was present when a journey of one day was necessary to transport the body to the place of burial;[35] others left the determination regarding the presence of the danger to the judgment of a prudent man. Many, who wrote his treatise on sacred places in the year 1904, agreed with the second group, but thought that the will of the family of the deceased should be especially considered, since it devolved on them to transport the body. He considered this opinion to be the more common and the more probable one then current.[36]

The cases decided by the Sacred Congregation of the Council do not reveal any closer or clearer explanation of the meaning of the term. The distance of a mile from the city in which the proper parish of the deceased parishioner was located was not judged sufficient in one case to allow the rural pastor to bury a person who had been visiting him a few days.[37]

According to the clear principle of Boniface VIII, the authors constantly believed during this later period that the pastor of a deceased person who died outside of his proper parish was also the pastor of burial as long as the corpse could be transported to the parish without danger.[38] Their teaching was substantiated

---

[34] *Prompta Bibliotheca,* v. *Sepultura,* n. 41.

[35] Many, *De Locis Sacris,* n. 42—". . . *Una dieta aequivalet 20 milliariis Italicis, . . . communiter receptam . . .*"—According to the measuring system in use in this country, the day's journey would be the equivalent of twenty-one miles.

[36] *De Locis Sacris,* n. 171.

[37] S. C. C., *Ariminen.,* 18 dec. 1824, 29 ian. 1825, ad 1—*Fontes,* n. 3990.

[38] Pirhing, lib. III, tit. XXVIII, n. 8; Reiffenstuel, lib. III, tit. XXVIII, n. 26; Schmalzgrueber, lib. III, tit. XXVIII, n. 38—". . . Ratio est quia per hoc, quod quis transeat a loco domicilii ad alium locum, ibique ad tempus habitet, non amittit prius domicilium, nec fit incola, aut parochianus loci, ad quem migravit ob ejusmodi causam; addidi *de jure;* quia ex consuetudine, vel etiam ex conventione parochorum ab ordinariis approbata aliquando defunctus sepelitur ibi, ubi mortuus est, etiamsi loci illius parochianus non fuerit . . ."; Ferraris, *Prompta Bibliotheca,* v. *Sepultura,* n. 20.

by a response of the Sacred Congregation of the Council in 1825 in a case that arose at Rimini.[39] A priest who lived in a parish in the city left it to assist the pastor of a rural parish about a mile away in hearing confessions for a few days. While there he suffered a stroke and died. The rural pastor held the funeral, buried the priest, and would have retained all the emoluments received on the occasion of his burial had not the pastor of the parish of the visiting priest's domicile intervened. The Sacred Congregation declared that the pastor of the domicile alone had the right to conduct the complete funeral and burial of the deceased.[40]

In 1907 the Sacred Congregation of the Council decided that all the pastors in the city of Lucca could conduct the entire funeral of their respective parishioners who had died as patients in the city's general hospital. Even though the hospital was simply located in one of the parishes and likewise claimed parochial exemption, the pastor of domicile, and not the chaplain of the hospital church, was designated as the proper pastor of burial.[41] The bodies of the deceased parishioners could have been transported easily to their respective parishes. The claim to exemption on the part of the hospital was at most a very tenuous one. Since its original foundation in the thirteenth century, this hospital had witnessed many vicissitudes in its existence. It had so lost its identity in a merger with other *pia opera* and *hospitia* to form one institution that it could hardly be regarded as its original self.

Among the authors Many was the only one who mentioned the possibility of the existence of two or more parishes to which the deceased might be brought without danger. Although there was neither an explicit law nor any decision of the Roman Curia to enable one to answer definitely, he argued from the decretal of Boniface VIII,[42] which gave to two parishes equal right in the matter of receiving the "*quarta funeralis,*" and allowed that the

---

39 S. C. C., *Ariminen.,* 18 dec. 1824, 29 ian. 1825, ad 1—*Fontes,* n. 3990.

40 *Loc. cit.;* "An, et ad quem Parochum spectet ius tumulandi et funeris in casu? . . . Resp. ad 1. "Affirmative, ad Parochum domicilii . . ."

41 S. C. C., *Lucana,* 22 iun. 1907—*Fontes,* n. 4338.

42 C. 2, *de sepulturis,* III, 12, in VI°: "Cum ab eo, qui habet duo domicilia, se collocans aequaliter in utroque, in loco tertio eligitur sepultura, domiciliorum ecclesiae habebunt inter se dividere canonicam portionem."

body could be transported to either of them. Thus, for him, the pastor of burial was the pastor of any parish wherein the deceased had had a domicile or a quasi-domicile.[43]

It was generally taught therefore that, as long as the deceased who had died away from his parish could be brought to his parish church without danger, the pastor of his burial was he who was also his proper pastor. When he could not be so brought, the authors generally distinguished between those who, when death overtook them, had sojourned for some time in the place of their death, and those who had merely been passing through the city.

Reiffenstuel held that those who had lived in a parish other than that of their domicile, though with the intention of not staying for a long time, were nevertheless to be buried in the parish church where they had died, if they had not specifically chosen a different place of burial, or did not have a family tomb, or if their bodies could not be carried easily to their proper parish. He maintained this opinion, inasmuch as the pastor of the place where the traveller had died possessed a much more equitable claim to the bestowing of the burial than any others, since the pastor of the place where the traveller had stayed had likewise habitually administered the sacraments to him, and, finally, since the local pastor had a prior interest and vested title, as rooted in and supported by law, regarding the spiritual matters whose emergence in the parish called for pastoral attention.[44]

Ferraris, for his chief argument in support of this same opinion, had recourse to a decision which had been rendered in a case that arose in Foligno.[45] In this case the Sacred Congregation of Bishops and Regulars declared that those who were not simply passing through a city, but lived there for some time, were to be buried in the parish in which they had been staying at the time of their demise.[46]

The Sacred Congregation of the Council in 1832 declared that a certain canon, who was at the same time a titular archbishop, and who before his death had spent forty days in a parish for regain-

---

[43] *De Locis Sacris*, n. 172.

[44] Lib. III, tit. XXVIII, n. 26. Cf. Pirhing, lib. III, tit. XXVIII, n. 8.

[45] S. C. Ep. et Reg., *Fulginaten.*, 9 iun. 1592—*Fontes*, n. 1458.

[46] *Prompta Bibliotheca*, v. *Sepultura*, n. 22.

ing his health, should not have been buried in the cathedral of the city, but at the parish church where he had lived prior to his death. The entire argument which favored the pastor was based on the facts that the archbishop had spent some time within the limits of the parish in which he died, that he had not chosen a specific place of burial, and that his body could not without difficulty be brought back to his proper parish.[47] The Congregation ordered all the emoluments to be restored to the pastor. Even the body was to be exhumed and transferred privately to the parish church for burial.

Bonal (+1904)[48] and Many (+1922) were of the same opinion as Reiffenstuel. Many stated that almost all the authors believed that the traveller was to be buried by the pastor of the parish in which he had died, if before his death the traveller had sojourned in the parish for a fairly noticeable duration of time.[49]

The case in which the traveller died while merely passing through a city apart from all intention of tarrying there, and therefore could not without difficulty be brought back to his proper parish, gave rise to a dispute which existed among the authors even at Pirhing's time.[50] Schmalzgrueber recorded the opinion that such a traveller should be buried either in the cathedral church, or in the parochial church within whose parish limits he had died, especially if he had habitually received the sacraments within the same parochial territory. This author himself seemed to favor the parish church, yet he agreed with Pirhing and Reiffenstuel[51] that the custom of each place had to be followed in this matter.[52] Ferraris, who held for the burial in the cathedral of the city followed again the decision of the Sacred Congregation of Bishops and Regulars, which in 1592 had determined that those who died while they were merely passing through the city of Foligno were to be buried in the cathedral.[53]

---

[47] S. C. C., *Portuen. et Centumcellarum,* 23 iun. 1832—*Fontes,* n. 4039.

[48] *Institutiones Canonicae* (2 vols., Parisiis, 1898), II, 92.

[49] *De Locis Sacris,* n. 172.

[50] Lib. III, tit. XXVIII, n. 7.

[51] Lib. III, tit. XXVIII, n. 26.

[52] Lib. III, tit. XXVIII, n. 41.

[53] *Prompta Bibliotheca,* v. *Sepultura,* n. 22.

The dispute still continued through the nineteenth[54] and even into the twentieth century. Many, who entertained the opinion which favored the parish church, declared that the custom of each place was to be followed. He said, too, that custom as a matter of fact generally favored the parish church in France and Belgium.[55] Obviously, the authors were all agreed that if the town in which the traveller died was not a cathedral town, then the pastor of his burial was the pastor of the parish in which the traveller had died.

In regard to those who had neither a parish of domicile nor one of quasi-domicile, Schmalzgrueber remarked that the same controversy existed. Custom at his time indicated the pastor of burial for the wanderer, but Schmalzgrueber favored the pastor of the parish in which the wanderer had died.[56] By Many's time wanderers (*vagi*) were buried by the pastor within whose parish they had died.[57]

ARTICLE II. THE CHURCH SPECIFICALLY SELECTED

In the earlier period, apart from the members of religious orders, all the faithful, men and women alike, had a right to choose a place of burial for themselves in another church or cemetery outside the parish. Those who were still below the age of puberty were the only members of the laity excluded from this provision of law.

After the General Council of Trent, this universally applicable principle was maintained by some decisions of the Sacred Congregations. The Sacred Congregation of Bishops and Regulars upheld the proved choice of burial as made by a certain woman,[58] and furthermore declared that the choice of a place of burial was not essentially nullified by the foundation of a public cemetery, since the choice of the church of the funeral still remained to the

---

[54] Santi, *Praelectiones Iuris Canonici* (4 vols. in 2, Ratisbonae, Neo Eboraci et Cincinnati, 1886), II, 244.

[55] *De Locis Sacris*, n. 172.

[56] Lib. III, tit. XXVIII, n. 41.

[57] *De Locis Sacris*, n. 172.

[58] S. C. Ep. et Reg., *Maceraten.*, 7 oct. 1575—*Fontes*, n. 1317.

faithful, even though the burial could not be bestowed there.[59] The Sacred Congregation of the Council stated that pastors who impaired the choice of having burial bestowed in a certain church of the regular clergy were to be punished with the penalties established by law,[60] and that members of a parish in one diocese could choose to receive burial in a church of the regular clergy in another diocese.[61]

Pope Urban VIII (1623–1644) protected the right of freely selecting the place of burial through his command to the ordinaries to decree that pastors were not to ask for and receive more when burials were bestowed in the churches of the regular clergy than they asked for and received when the funeral services were held in their own churches.[62]

In the matter of selecting a place of burial the freedom of the wife,[63] as well as that of minors above the age of puberty,[64] as favored by the law of the earlier period, was again upheld by the Sacred Congregation of the Council.

There was no change in the law regarding the incapacity of persons who were under the age of puberty to choose a place of burial for themselves.[65] The father was still capable of making the choice for them, if custom approved such parental intervention.[66] The mother, too, could select a place of burial for them, if customary usage allowed her to do so.[67] The authors of the post-Tridentine period conceded the same right to the nearest relations, if there

---

[59] S. C. Ep. et Reg., *Aesina,* 31 maii 1850, ad 1—*Fontes,* n. 1955.

[60] S. C. C., *Lauden.,* 2 maii 1711, ad 3—*Fontes,* n. 3101.

[61] S. C. C., *Auximana seu Lauretana,* 8 iul. 1752, 24 mart. 1753, ad II—*Fontes,* nn. 3621, 3626.

[62] Urban VIII, const. "*Cum sicut dilectus*", 2 mart. 1638, § 1—*Fontes,* n. 218.

[63] S. C. C., *Vilnen.,* 15 dec. 1792, ad 1—*Fontes,* n. 3883.

[64] S. C. C., *Ariminen.,* 14 maii, 9 iul. 1825—*Fontes,* nn. 3994, 3997.

[65] Cf. Pirhing, lib. III, tit. XXVIII, n. 14; Reiffenstuel, lib. III, tit. XXVIII, n. 41; Many, *De Locis Sacris,* n. 164.

[66] S. C. Ep. et Reg., *Caputaquen.,* 17 nov. 1593—*Fontes,* n. 1498; S. R. C., *Civitatis Castellanae,* 12 dec. 1620—*Fontes,* n. 5283; S. C. C., *Forosempronien.,* 20 mart. 1643—*Fontes,* n. 2641.

[67] Innocentius X, const. "*Ex iniuncto*", 22 febr. 1645, § 6—*Fontes,* n. 230.

were no parents or grandparents, and to the guardian or tutor.[68] Even in the absence of justifying custom, the parents could choose the burial place of such of their children as were under the age of puberty, both before and after the death of the children, if the place which they chose was the family tomb.[69] If the place which they wanted to select was not the family tomb, then it was disputed whether the parents could similarly exercise a choice.[70] Even if the parents had not specifically chosen the family tomb for such of their children as were under the age of puberty, these were to be buried in the church where the family tomb was located, rather than in the parochial church.[71]

The pastor of burial for the cases in which the selection of place had been made naturally varied with each diverse choice. The pastor of the parish of the deceased had the right to conduct the body from the house to the door of the specifically selected church, but the pastor or rector of the selected church had the right to officiate at the rest of the ceremonies, i.e., at the office of the dead, in the Mass, and for the interment, if the church was exempt from the jurisdiction of the pastor.[72]

---

[68] Pirhing, lib. III, tit. XXVIII, n. 20; Leurenius, *Forum Ecclesiasticum in quo ius canonicum universum librorum ac titulorum ordine explanatur* (5 vols. in 4, Venetiis, 1729), lib. III, tit. XXVIII, q. DCCXCV: Many, *De Locis Sacris*, n. 164.

[69] S. C. C., *Novarien.*, 1 et 15 mart. 1704, ad 1—*Fontes*, n. 3015; *Reatina*, 10 et 31 mart. 1770, ad 1—*Fontes*, n. 3771.

[70] Many, *De Locis Sacris*, n. 162.

[71] S. C. Ep. et Reg., *Sulmonen.*, 8 iun. 1731, ad 2—*Fontes*, n. 1849.

[72] Cf. *infra*, pp. 204–211, 213–214.

PART II—CANONICAL COMMENTARY

CHAPTER III

THE FUNERAL CHURCH

ARTICLE I. THE OBLIGATION TO BRING THE BODY TO THE CHURCH FOR THE FUNERAL

In the historical section it was seen that the Church has been most solicitous in regard to the faithful in all questions related to Christian burial. The Code of Canon Law describes, if it does not define, Christian burial in saying that it consists in the transfer of the corpse to the church, the obsequies held over it therein, and its interment in a place legitimately set aside for the burial of the faithful departed.[1]

It has been the mind of the Church that the three distinct acts should always be performed on the occasion of burial. She has instructed pastors of souls that they ought most zealously to revere and employ the sacred ceremonies and rites which Holy Mother Church, relying on very ancient tradition and the precepts of the Supreme Pontiffs, is accustomed to use in the obsequies of her children, as embodying true mysteries of religion, as symbols of Christian virtue and as offering most salutary suffrages for the faithful departed.[2]

The obligation of using the rites as determined in the liturgical books has been recognized for centuries in the Church. The Code of Canon Law has made that obligation more clear in canon 1215, as follows:

---

[1] Canon 1204. Cf. Kerin, *The Privation of Christian Burial,* The Catholic University of American Canon Law Studies, n. 136 (Washington, D. C.: The Catholic University of America Press, 1941), pp. 97–125, for a discussion in regard to the definition of Christian burial.

[2] *Rituale Romanum Pauli V Pontificis Maximi iussu editum aliorumque Pontificum cura recognitum atque auctoritate Sanctissimi D. N. Pii Papae XI ad normam Codicis Iuris Canonici accomodatum* (Editio iuxta typicam Vaticanam, Novi Eboraci: Benziger Bros., 1944), tit. VI, c. 1, de exsequiis, n. 1.

Nisi gravis causa obstet, cadavera fidelium, antequam tumulentur, transferenda sunt e loco in quo reperiuntur, in ecclesiam, ubi funus, idest totus ordo exsequiarum quae in probatis liturgicis libris describuntur, persolvatur.

The obligation imposed by this law is strict and grave. The very words, "*nisi causa gravis obstet*," indicate this. It is also the common opinion of the authors in this matter.[3] The grave cause which excuses from the obligation of bringing the body to the church is to be judged on the basis of that cause which excuses similar cases. Certainly the danger of the spread of any epidemic disease, such as cholera and influenza, and the impossibility of following the ritual in time of war during a particular battle would be serious enough.[4] Among other excusing causes can be reckoned hygienic regulations in regard to those who have died of various contagious diseases,[5] and lack of time.[6] The civil laws that prohibit the transfer of the body to the church, such as exist in Spain,[7] and those that render it very difficult, as they are

[3] De Meester, *Iuris Canonici et Iuris Canonico-Civilis Compendium* (Nova Editio, 3 vols. in 4, Brugis, 1921–1928), III, n. 1184 (hereafter this work is cited *Compendium*); Coronata, *De Locis et Temporibus Sacris* (Augustae Taurinorum: Marietti, 1922), n. 155; Beste, *Introductio in Codicem* (editio altera, Collegeville, Minn.: St. John's Abbey Press, 1944), Commentary on canon 1215; Fanfani, *De Iure Parochorum ad Normam Codicis Iuris Canonici* (Taurini-Romae: Marietti, 1924), n. 329 (hereafter this work is cited as *De Iure Parochorum*); Cappello, *Summa Iuris Canonici* (3 vols., Romae: Universita Gregoriana [Vol. I, 3 ed., 1938; Vol. II, 3 ed., 1939; Vol. III, 1936]), II, n. 718 (hereafter this work is cited *Summa*); Cocchi, *Commentarium in Codicem Iuris Canonici ad Usum Scholarum* (8 vols. in 5, Taurinorum Augustae, 1922–1930 [Vol. V, *De Rebus*, 3 ed., Taurinorum Augustae: Marietti, 1932]), V, n. 55 (hereafter this work is cited as *Commentarium*); Ayrinhac, *Administrative Legislation in the New Code of Canon Law* (London: Longmans, Green and Co., 1930), n. 60; Rossi, *La Sepultura Ecclesiastica e l' "Ius Funerum" nel Diritto Canonico* (Bergamo: Arnoldi, 1920), n. 34 (hereafter this work is cited as *Sepultura Ecclesiastica*).

[4] Coronata, *De Locis et Temporibus Sacris*, n. 156; De Meester, *Compendium*, n. 1184.

[5] Rossi, *Sepultura Ecclesiastica*, n. 35; Cocchi, *Commentarium*, III, n. 55.

[6] Cocchi, *Commentarium*, V, n. 55.

[7] S. C. C., *Compostellana*, 1 aug. 1902—*Acta Sanctae Sedis* (41 vols., Romae, 1865–1908), XXXV (1902–1903), 283.

found in Brazil, would apparently constitute a sufficiently grave cause. When the Archbishop of San Sebastian in Brazil had made known to the Sacred Congregation of Rites that the rites as prescribed in the Roman Ritual were not observed for the reason that the remains were not brought to the church because civil laws required them to be interred within twenty-four hours after death, and also because the cemeteries, controlled by the government, were rather distant from the parishes, the Sacred Congregation, after having consulted the Pontifical Commission for the Authentic Interpretation of the Code, responded that as far as possible the Roman Ritual and canon 1215 were to be observed, and that the family of the deceased should be informed that a funeral with the funeral Mass could be held, according to the rubrics and the decrees interpreting them, even though the remains were present only in a moral sense.[8]

On the other hand, the Pontifical Commission for the Authentic Interpretation of the Code, on being asked whether the danger of nasal offense on the part of the faithful and the clergy constituted a grave cause, so as to excuse the omission of the act of bringing the bodies of the faithful from the place where they were to the church where the funeral was to be held, replied in the negative and added that the contrary custom was to be condemned.[9]

The obligation binds all individual members of the faithful inasmuch as all are forbidden to be buried otherwise than according to the ceremonies of Christian burial.[10]

The removal of the body to the church for the obsequies and the final interment, which of old formed a most praiseworthy custom, has entered into the public law of the Church. Wernz (1842–1914) reminded us that although Christians can renounce ec-

---

[8] S. R. C., *S. Sebastiani Fluminis Ianuarii in Brasilia,* 28 febr. 1920—*Acta Apostolicae Sedis, Commentarium Officiale* (Romae, 1909–) XII (1920), 128 (hereafter cited as *AAS*); reported in Bouscaren, *The Canon Law Digest* (2 vols., Milwaukee: Bruce, 1934–1943), I, 569.

[9] Pontificia Commissio ad Codicis Canones Authentice Interpretandos, "Dubia-n. 15," 16 Oct. 1919—*AAS,* XI (1919), 479; reported in Bouscaren, *The Canon Law Digest,* I, 569.

[10] Coronata, *De Locis et Temporibus Sacris,* n. 157; Cocchi, *Commentarium,* V, n. 55.

clesiastical burial that is to be conducted with great pomp and circumstance, they cannot exclude at their pleasure all the elements of ecclesiastical burial, since one's private will cannot change the public law which absolutely prescribes ecclesiastical burial for the faithful, unless the faithful have rendered themselves unworthy of it by their own obstinacy. Hence, he stated, if there is found even in a last will a clause by which ecclesiastical burial is renounced or forbidden, for a man otherwise worthy, the ecclesiastical judge and his relatives are obliged to consider that clause as not added to the will, and in practice to pay no attention to it; even less do erring relatives have any kind of a right to impede the ecclesiastical burial of one of the faithful departed who at the same time is not unworthy of ecclesiastical burial.[11] The same thought is expressed in a *dictum* of the Secretary of the Sacred Congregation of the Council in 1924.[12]

The grave obligation binds also the relatives and heirs of the deceased and the more gravely, the more closely related they are. Natural duties of piety or of justice and friendship would seem to demand this.[13]

Priests who have the care of the deceased are bound to escort the body to the church and to conduct the exequies over it.[14] This grave obligation extends to the three acts, namely, the transfer of the body to the church, the performance of the sacred rites therein, and the interment. As described in the Roman Ritual, there are five main parts of the whole arrangement of the obsequies.[15] The first deals with the transfer of the body, from the place in which

---

[11] Wernz, *Ius Decretalium* (6 vols., Romae et Prati, 1898–1905), III, n. 780, nota 35; Cf. also Cappello, *Summa,* II, n. 718.

[12] S. C. C., *Sancti Severi,* 12 ian. 1924—"Lex Canonica districte iubet omnes baptizatos sepultura ecclesiastica donandos esse, nisi eadem a iure expresse priventur, ita quidem ut fideles Christiani, quamvis renuntiare possunt ecclesiasticae sepulturae cum pompa faciendae, tamen omnem sepulturam ecclesiasticam pro suo arbitrio nullatenus excludere valeant. Agitur sane de iure publico, quod ex privatorum voluntate nequaquam mutari potest." —*AAS,* XVI (1924), 180.

[13] Coronata, *De Locis et Temporibus Sacris,* n. 157; Beste, *Introductio in Codicem,* Commentary on canon 1215.

[14] C. 1230, § 1.

[15] Rituale Rom., tit. VI, c. 3, *Exsequiarum ordo.*

it rests, to the church. At the specified time those who are to participate gather at the church where the funeral is to take place and proceed to the home of the deceased or the place where the corpse lies. Before the procession returns to the church, the pastor sprinkles the corpse with holy water, says the antiphon, "*Si iniquitates,*" the psalm one hundred twenty-nine, and repeats the antiphon. While the body is being carried to the church, the pastor sings the antiphon, "*Exsultabunt Domino,*" and the chanters, as the procession moves toward the church, take up the psalm, "*Miserere mei, Deus.*" [16] At the entrance to the church, the antiphon is repeated and while the corpse is being moved to its position in the church, the "*Subvenite*" is sung.[17] Then, in order, the office of the dead is said, Mass is celebrated, and the prayers of the absolution are recited.[18] Finally, the body is brought in procession again to its last resting place, where the prayers beginning "*Ego sum*" are said.[19]

The obligation is not as gravely binding in respect to all parts of the ceremonies of burial in the Ritual as it is in relation to the three essential elements. The carrying of the body to the church, the recitation of the absolution prayers, and the conduct of the body to the place of burial, are of stricter obligation than the recitation of the office of the dead or the celebration of Mass.[20]

The Ritual contains an instruction in regard to the office of the dead. If for a reasonable cause the entire office cannot be said, namely, because of a lack of time or the immediate necessity of other funerals, at least the first nocturn with lauds or even without lauds should be said, especially wherever there is a custom to this effect.[21] If time, or any other urgent necessity should be so pressing, that even the one nocturn without lauds cannot be said,

---

[16] Rituale Rom., tit. VI, c. 3, *Exsequiarum ordo,* n. 2.

[17] Rituale Rom., tit. VI, c. 3, *Exsequiarum ordo,* n. 3.

[18] Rituale Rom., tit. VI, c. 3, *Exsequiarum ordo,* nn. 4, 5, 6, 7.

[19] Rituale Rom., tit. VI, c. 3, *Exsequiarum ordo,* nn. 11, 13, 14.

[20] DeMeester, *Compendium,* III, n. 1184; Vermeersch-Creusen, *Epitome Iuris Canonici* (3 vols., [Vols. I et II, 6 ed., 1937–1940, Vol. III, 5 ed., 1936], Mechliniae-Romae: H. Dessain), II, n. 526 (hereafter this work is cited as *Epitome*).

[21] Rituale Rom., tit. VI, c. 3, *Exsequiarum ordo,* n. 16.

the other prayers and suffrages should never be omitted.[22] Rossi remarks that it is obvious that when there is a custom or a proportionate cause, even the partial recitation of the office can be dispensed with.[23]

In regard to the omission of the Mass, the Ritual states that in a case of necessity or on a day of great solemnity, the requiem Mass also can or ought to be omitted as long as the other prayers of the absolution and the subsequent conveyance of the body to the place of interment are correctly performed.[24] Authors commonly teach that a graver reason is required for the omission of the Mass than for the office of the dead.[25]

Coronata[26] and DeMeester[27] are of the opinion that in the parishes and hospitals of great cities where there are so many burials daily, and especially of those who are very poor, the obsequies can be carried out immediately, the office and the Mass having been omitted. Cappello[28] remarks that it is most fitting that the pastor celebrate the Mass for the repose of the soul of his deceased poor without receiving any stipend, provided that he too is not in straitened circumstances. The reason adduced to substantiate their opinion, namely, that there would be too severe a burden placed on the priests who had to conduct the funerals of the penniless without compensation, to their minds, renders it probable.

It is the evident mind of the Ritual that the Mass should be celebrated in so far as it is possible. It seems to the writer that

---

[22] Rituale Rom., tit. VI, c. 3, *Exsequiarum ordo,* n. 17. Cf. De Herdt, *Praxis Sacrae Liturgiae juxta Ritum Romanum* (8. ed., 4 vols., Lovanii: Universitas Catholica, 1889), III, n. 237 (hereafter this work is cited as *Praxis Liturgiae Sacrae*).

[23] *Sepultura Ecclesiastica,* n. 42.

[24] Tit. VI, c. 3, *Exsequiarum ordo,* n. 18.

[25] DeMeester, *Compendium,* III, n. 1184; DeHerdt, *Praxis Liturgiae Sacrae,* III, n. 237.

[26] *De Locis et Temporibus Sacris,* n. 158.

[27] *Compendium,* III, n. 1184.

[28] *Summa,* II, n. 719, " Ex lege liturgica, fas est Missam exsequialem pro defuncto paupere absque applicatione pro anima eius. Summopere tamen decet parochum Missam applicare pro paroecianis suis pauperibus, nulla quoque recepta eleemosyna, dummodo gravis egestas eum non excuset."

even in the cases mentioned above the pastor will find it possible to celebrate the Mass not infrequently at the funerals of his deceased paupers, if the counsel of Vermeersch is followed. This author states that if the pastor is generous in offering the Mass for his deceased poor on the occasion of their funerals, he can celebrate for them the low Mass of requiem instead of the sung Mass.[29]

As has been described above, the transfer of the body to the church is performed in a liturgical procession. In the United States it is not the custom ordinarily to conduct the body to the church in this way, but under the leadership of the undertaker, the pall-bearers, relatives and mourners form the funeral cortege with the aid of the hearse and accompanying automobiles.[31] The pallbearers, followed by the others, bring the body from the hearse to the door of the church, where they are met by the priest who is prepared to conduct the obsequies. He reads the usual prayers of the ritual at the door and ultimately at the repetition of the antiphon "*Exsultabunt Domino*" leads the procession formed by the pall-bearers, with the coffin, and the mourners to the place near the altar rail where the coffin rests during the performance of the exequies. Certainly, in some parishes of the country where there is a population predominantly Catholic in character, the ordinary liturgical function is still in use. Further, in some places, the priest even goes to the home to read the prayers outlined for this part of the funeral service, but he does not go or return in a liturgical procession.

The ordinary custom, prevalent here, appears to be reasonable, since it is morally impossible to have the funeral procession, led by the clergy in sacred vestments with the cross at their head. Were the procession to be held, there would be too great a danger of irreverence and ridicule in practically all sections of the country,

---

[29] *Epitome,* II, n. 526: "Frequentia funerum, uti in nosocomiis habetur, aut numerus eorum qui impensis solvendis impares sint, graves causae sunt omittendi officium, immo et missam. Quo facilius tamen etiam pauperibus missa concedi possit, licet pro ipsis missam de requie sine cantu loco Missae exsequialis cum cantu celebrare."

[31] Ayrinhac, *Administrative Legislation in the New Code of Canon Law,* n. 69.

for Catholics constitute only about one sixth of the population. Then, too, the distances between the house and the church in this country, especially in parishes that are extensive in territory, are too great to think of proceeding liturgically between the two places, even if the coffin is carried by automobile. The same causes may be cited by some as a cause sufficiently grave to excuse the omission of the act of conducting the body from the church to the cemetery.

The obligation to transfer the body to the church from the place where it lies, to perform the obsequies, and to inter the body with Christian rites, binds only once. It happens occasionally that bodies are exhumed and transferred to another tomb. The body originally may have been placed in a tomb, where it was intended that it should rest either perpetually or temporarily. If the order of the obsequies was not observed in its entirety at the first interment, it should now be carried out according to all the provisions of the canons. On the other hand, if the provisions of canon 1215 and those related to it were fulfilled at the time of the first burial, there is no necessity to repeat them.

Both of these conclusions are found in a case considered by the Sacred Congregation of the Council in 1924.[32] A certain Vincent, domiciled in the parish of St. John the Baptist in a certain city, was killed during the war and buried abroad in 1918. He was buried with the usual rites. His widow, in 1923, had the body exhumed and brought home for burial. In accordance with her wishes, a funeral was held in the cathedral church of the city, not in the church of St. John the Baptist. A protest arising from the pastor of the parish of St. John the Baptist, the question whether the right to conduct the funeral rites of the deceased belonged to him was asked of the Sacred Congregation of the Council. The reply was in the negative.

The reason for the response, found in the "*Votum Consultoris*" of the case, is of such great interest and so apropos that it merits the earnest consideration of all who have met the same problem in practice. In this section of the case, it is said that the obsequies

[32] S. C. C., *Sancti Severi,* 12 ian. 1924—*AAS,* XVI (1924), 188; reported in Bouscaren, *The Canon Law Digest,* I, p. 571.

as described in the Ritual are, in accord with the law of the Church, to be conducted only once; that, therefore, when one considers the case of the transferral to another place of burial of a corpse already buried, it is not necessary that the funeral be again carried out, if the exequies have been performed at the time of the first burial; that, when the funeral was held at that time, then in the case of the transferral of the body, the requiem Mass and other sacred rites, that may be performed on the later occasion, may, without violation of the common law, be celebrated by any priest asked to do so by the family of the deceased or by his friends or any persons interested in the case. Thus it is concluded for the particular case: "If the rites were omitted at the first burial, the rightful funeral services are to be carried out, and this in accord with the Code (can. 1216 ff.); if they were not omitted, it is not necessary either strictly so or in consequence of the prescription of the law of the Code, that the funeral services (the transferral of the body to the church, the requiem Mass, the interment with sacred rites) be repeated; of course, they can be held and quite appropriately. Since in this case the common law of the Code, which prescribes nothing other than the proper order of the obsequies, is not applicable, the right to carry out the functions does not belong *per se* (that is, as long as there is not a particular law to warrant it) either to the proper pastor, or to the pastor of the cathedral church, or, when there is no cathedral church, to the rector of the church where the cemetery is located." [33]

Those who are held to the obligation must bring the body to the funeral church, the "*ecclesia funeris.*" This church is deter-

[33] "Si hoc alterum (ritus sepulturae non persoluti fuerint), iusta funebria sunt peragenda, et quidem ad normam Codicis (Can. 1216 ss.); si primum (ritus sepulturae persoluti fuerint), necesse non est, stricte loquendo seu ex iuris praescripto, ut functiones funebres (translatio cadaveris ad ecclesiam, Missa de Requie, depositio cum ritu sacro) peragantur: opportune tamen fieri possunt. Cum in hoc casu non applicetur ius commune sive Codicis (Can. 1215 ss.) quod nonnisi ordinem exsequiarum proprie dictum praescribit, ius illas functiones peragendi non pertinet per se (i.e. salvo iure particulari) ad parochum proprium, neque ad parochum ecclesiae cathedralis, neque hac deficiente, ad rectorem ecclesiae in qua situm est coemeterium."—*AAS,* XVI (1924), 190, n. 4, in *Votum Consultoris.*

mined by the common law, both ordinary and special, or by choice. The ordinary law is expounded in canons 1216–1218; the special law is found in canons 1219–1222; and the choice of this church and the subsequent effects of this choice are regulated by canons 1223–1229. Simultaneously with the treatment of the determination of the funeral church according to the ordinary law, according to the special law, and according to the law regulating choice, there will eventually be brought forward for consideration the various canons that are more definitive in regard to the proper pastor of burial. The two subjects, namely the determination of the funeral church and the determination of the pastor of burial, are very closely connected. In fact, the right to conduct the funeral follows the duty of transferring the body to a determined church. It is obvious, therefore, that there must be a clear definition of the "*ecclesia funeris*" before it is possible to determine the pastor of burial.

ARTICLE II. THE FUNERAL CHURCH IS THE CHURCH IN WHICH THE EXEQUIES ARE HELD

The term "funeral church" is used frequently in the canons of Title XII, Chapter II, of the third book of the Code of Canon Law. This Title is concerned with "Ecclesiastical Burial." The first two canons deal with the disapproval of cremation and the definition of "Ecclesiastical Burial."[84] After these appear the following chapter titles: first, "*De coemeteriis*"; secondly, "*De cadaveris translatione ad ecclesiam, funere et depositione*"; thirdly, "*De iis quibus sepultura ecclesiastica concedenda est aut neganda.*" Throughout the entire title there recur constantly the terms "*sepultura ecclesiastica,*" "*sepultura,*" and "*funus.*" Before one proceeds to a definition of the term "funeral church," it seems fitting as well as necessary to investigate the manner in which the Code employs this term, and to recognize the fact that in the Code the other three terms here mentioned do not have the same meaning.

---

[84] C. 1204; Kerin, *The Privation of Christian Burial,* pp. 97–125.

A. The Distinction in the Terms "*Sepultura Ecclesiastica,*" "*Sepultura*" and "*Funus*"

The term "*sepultura ecclesiastica*" or ecclesiastical burial is a general term used as the caption of Title XII of this part of Book III of the Code. It consists in the transfer of the body to the church, in the exequies therein celebrated over the body, and in the interment of the body in a place rightly set aside for the burial of the faithful departed.[35] It is clear that it includes three acts, and that it is a term of much wider significance than the single word "*sepultura.*" The term "*ecclesiastica sepultura*" is used not only as the caption of this title, but also in the various canons in reference to the funeral services as well as to the interment in the place of burial.[36] Cappello,[37] Coronata,[38] and Vermeersch-Creusen[39] agree with Maroto (1875–1937)[40] that the term has this connotation.[41]

The term "*sepultura,*" when unqualified by "*ecclesiastica,*" designates a place of burial in those canons of the Code in which the place or cemetery of burial are mentioned.[42] This is evident

[35] C. 1204: "Sepultura ecclesiastica consistit in cadaveris translatione, ad ecclesiam, exsequiis super illud in eadem celebratis, illius depositione in loco legitime deputato fidelium defunctis condendis."

[36] Cc. 1212; 1214; 1239; 1240; 1241; Maroto, "De Axiomate 'Ubi tumulus ibi funus',": ". . . adhibetur namque in inscriptione totius tituli, in c. 1204 et in aliis canonibus ubi praeter locum sepulturae seu inhumationis recte subaudiri queunt etiam officia funebria praemissa."—*Apollinaris* (Romae, 1928–), I, 127; Kerin, *The Privation of Christian Burial,* 116.

[37] *Summa,* II, n. 762.

[38] *Institutiones Iuris Canonici* (5 vols., Taurini: Marietti, 1928–1936 [Vol. II, *De Rebus,* 1931]), II, nn. 794, 796, 813 (hereafter this work is cited *Institutiones*).

[39] *Epitome,* II, n. 512.

[40] *Loc. cit.*

[41] Those authors who retain the opinion that Christian burial consists essentially in the burial of the corpse in blessed ground do not agree that the term "Ecclesiastical burial" always refers to the funeral services. Cf. Wernz-Vidal, *Ius Canonicum* (7 vols. in 8, Romae: Apud Aedes Universitatis Gregorianae, 1927–1938 [Vol. II, *De Personis,* 3 ed., 1943; Vol. IV, *De Rebus,* Pars I, 1934]), IV, n. 577.

[42] Cc. 1218, §§ 2, 3; 1223, 1224; 1226–1229; 1231, § 2; 1232, § 1; Maroto, "De Axiomate 'Ubi tumulus ibi funus'.": ". . . *Sepultura,* e contra, unum verbum prolatum, videtur in Codice potius designare locum inhumationis vel

also in the canons where the one word "*sepultura*" is used.[43] The canons which use the words "*tumulare*" and "*inhumare*" as synonyms for "*sepelire*," and vice versa, add further proof that the meaning of "*sepultura*" is to be limited to the act of interring or to the specification of a place as a place of burial.[44]

The Code not only uses the unqualified term "*sepultura*" in a very restricted sense but also distinguishes it from the word "*funus*." This is clear especially when the two words are found in the same canon. For example, canon 1218, § 2 rules that the local Ordinary is to determine the circumstances which may render inconvenient the transfer of the corpse to the church of the funeral (*funeris*) or to the place of burial (*sepulturae*). Canon 1218, § 3 decides that the family, or the heirs, or those who have a legally recognized interest may always transfer the body to the funeral (*funeris*) church or to the place of burial (*sepulturae*), even though it may be financially or otherwise burdensome, as long as they pay the expenses. Canon 1223 grants the permission to everyone, unless he is prohibited expressly by the law, to select the church of his funeral (*funeris*) and the cemetery of his burial (*sepulturae*). Canon 1224 records those to whom the right to select the church of the funeral (*funeris*) or the cemetery of burial (*sepulturae*) is denied. There are of course many other examples.[45] This distinction between the funeral and burial is evident, too, in the canons that consider the funeral in itself,[46] and the burial respectively.[47] Further, the use of the particle "*aut*," when the terms are contrasted in the same canon, emphasizes the distinction between them.[48]

---

ipsam cadaveris inhumationem."—*Apollinaris*, I (1928), 130; Creusen, "Ubi tumulus ibi funus?": ". . . Quand le mot 'sepultura' est seul employé, il designe l'action de *sepelire, tumulare, inhumare*."—*Nouvelle Revue Théologique* (Tournai, 1869–), LIV (1927), 784.

[43] Cc. 1172, § 1, n. 4; 1209, § 3; 1228; 1229; 1230, § 7; 1233, § 1; 1235, § 1.

[44] Cc. 1203, § 2; 1203, § 1; 1205; 1213; 1215; 1229; 1231, § 1; 1232, § 2; 1235, § 2; 1237, §§ 1, 2; 1238.

[45] Cc. 1226; 1227; 1232; 1233.

[46] Cc. 1216; 1219; 1220; 1221.

[47] Cc. 1228; 1229; 1231, § 2.

[48] Maroto, "De Axiomate 'Ubi tumulus ibi funus'.": "Nunc Codex e

The Code has not only placed the two terms "*funus*" and "*sepultura*" in contrast to each other, but it has placed a very great emphasis on the funeral in the entire second chapter of Title XII. Of the three acts, the transfer of the corpse to the church, the celebration of the exequies, and the interment of the body, the celebration of the exequies or the funeral is given first and pre-eminent attention.[49] The funeral church itself as well as the funeral and the right to conduct the funeral are treated at great length in the canons. The minister of the funeral as well as the minister of the procession to the grave are to be selected from among the clergy of the funeral church. The funeral church generally determines the cemetery of burial. To the funeral church are due the emoluments received on the occasion of the funeral. In fact, it may be said that practically all the canons of the second chapter of Title XII are intimately connected with the funeral and the funeral church. The place of burial is not so much emphasized, and the church of burial not even mentioned.

The stress on the funeral church throughout this second chapter shows that the Code has rearranged this whole matter. It was commonly taught before the promulgation of the Code that the place of interment was the first thing to be considered. Its existence or choice determined the church of the funeral, the clergy,

---

contra iugiter unum et alterum distinguit, quoniam ecclesiam funeris et locum sepulturae separat, disiunctim exprimit et recenset, etiam tunc cum unum et alterum simul profert . . . ac praecipue ex particula *aut,* quae pluries in his canonibus occurrit, agnoscenda est vis disiunctiva inter ius funerandi et ius tumulandi, quae proinde habenda sunt non solum distincta sed per se separata:"—*Apollinaris,* I (1928), 137; Vermeersch, "'Ubi tumulus ibi funus': Axioma (?)": ". . . Dicemus igitur, hodierno iure tumulationem et funus ita esse separata, ut sine alio indicio non possis unum ex altero inferre."—*Periodica de Re Canonica et Morali,* XVI (1927), 65 (hereafter this periodical is cited *Periodica*).

[49] Maroto, "De Axiomate 'Ubi tumulus ibi funus'.": "Ex iis actibus primus, qui inspicitur et accuratius ordinatur, tamquam primarium sepulturae ecclesiasticae elementum, est funus simulque ecclesia funeris; deque funere, de ecclesia funerante ac eius electione, de ministro funeris ceterisque ad funus spectantibus caput ipsum praecipue ac pro longiore parte agit, cetera autem ad ipsum funus ecclesiamque funerantem veluti refert tamquam quid a funere ac ecclesia funerante dependens."—*Apollinaris,* I (1928), 278–279.

and the payment of the alms offered at this time.[50] "*Sepultura*" included the place of burial and the funeral and the rights to these, that is, both the "*ius tumulandi*" and the "*ius funerandi,*" but the second right depended on the first. Thus in the old law, the church in which there was a family sepulcher had the right to conduct the funeral as well as the burial of the persons to be buried there. The place chosen for the burial determined the church for the celebration of the funeral as long as the latter had the right to conduct a funeral.[51]

In the present Code, dependence of the funeral on the place of burial is not even tacitly expressed.[52] The church in which there is a family sepulcher has no right to conduct the funeral not only because of the contrary designation of the parish church, but also for the reason that it is generally prohibited by the Code to bury the dead in churches. The Code provides, indeed, that one may be buried in a family tomb,[53] but the church of the funeral is determined otherwise than by the location of that tomb.[54] The place chosen for the burial no longer determines the place of the funeral but on the contrary the general rule is that the body is to be entombed in the cemetery of the funeral church, with the provision made, of course, for the burial in the family tomb or in a grave chosen by the deceased.[55]

The change thus made by the Code in shifting the emphasis from the place of burial to the funeral church in determining rights was evidently needed in view of the fact that through the nineteenth century there was an extraordinary growth of public, that is, of civic or community cemeteries in Europe. Were the "*ius funerandi*" to be determined by the "*ius tumulandi,*" the right to

[50] Many, *De Locis Sacris*, n. 190.

[51] Many, *De Locis Sacris*, n. 226; Coronata, *De Locis et Temporibus Sacris*, nn. 186, 202; Cf., however, Van Espen, *Jus Ecclesiasticum Universum* (4 vols., Lovanii, 1753), II, Pars II, Sectio IV, Tit. VII, *De Sepulturis*, c. 5, nn. 4, 5, 6; Maroto, "De Axiomate 'Ubi tumulus ibi funus'."—*Apollinaris*, I (1928), 125.

[52] Maroto, "De Axiomate 'Ubi tumulus ibi funus'."—*Apollinaris*, I (1928), 263.

[53] C. 1229.

[54] Cc. 1216–1226.

[55] C. 1231, §§ 1, 2.

conduct the funeral would belong to no one, or would be at least in many cases left undetermined. As private cemeteries and those peculiar to a specific church decreased in number, the dependence of the funeral on the place of burial became more and more impractical. The prohibition of all burials in churches by the civil law also made the right of pastors to conduct the funeral more and more uncertain, especially as the years went on and families changed their domiciles or acquired new family plots either in a common Catholic cemetery or in those owned by the municipality.[56]

Vermeersch (1858–1936), in determining burial rights, declares that it is only logical that there should be less attention paid to the place of burial after the suppression of so many ecclesiastical cemeteries.[57] He added further that in the modern law the burial and the funeral are so distinct that without some other evidence one cannot determine that one is governed by the other, and that if present customs are considered, the burial must be regarded as the connatural complement of the funeral, rather than the opposite.[58]

Maroto, Vermeersch and others maintain that the changing conditions in the world were recognized by the Code. To meet them, the older law was totally rearranged in the present legislation. This was true not only in regard to the definition of Christian burial,[59] but also, in the determination of burial rights, in the new emphasis placed on the funeral church. Hence, in regard to the laws of Christian burial, they believe in accord with canon 6, 3°, that those canons which agree only in part with the former law must be interpreted according to the older law in the part in which they agree with it, but that, in the part in which they differ from the older law, the canons must be interpreted according to

---

[56] Maroto, "De Axiomate 'Ubi tumulus ibi funus'."—*Apollinaris,* I (1928), 274–278; Many, *De Locis Sacris,* n. 206.

[57] "'Ubi tumulus ibi funus' : Axioma (?)" : "Ac re vera, post suppressa tam multa coemeteria ecclesiastica, accidere debuit ut ad locum sepulturae multo minus attenderetur."—*Periodica,* XVI (1927), 65.

[58] "Dicemus igitur, hodierno iure tumulationem et funus ita esse separata ut sine alio indicio non possis unum ex altero inferre . . . et potius, attentis praesentibus moribus, tumulationem ut connaturale complementum habeas funeris quam ex tumulo velis regere funus."—*Ibid.,* pp. 65–66.

[59] Kerin, *The Privation of Christian Burial,* 110.

the meaning of the words employed.[60] The opponents of their teaching who maintain that there has been no change in the law, and therefore hold that the canons are to be judged according to the older law and the interpretations of it as found in the writings of the approved authors, must at least admit the new emphasis on the distinction between funeral and burial, and the new and explicit method employed in the determination of the funeral church and the consequences of that method of determination.[61]

In the subsequent discussion the various terms will be employed as they are understood by Maroto and Vermeersch. "*Sepultura ecclesiastica*" means the transfer of the body to the church, the exequies held therein, and the final interment. "*Sepultura*" signifies the act of interring or the interment itself. The right to ecclesiastical burial implies the right to the three acts; the right to burial implies the right to be placed in a tomb, whether this is in a parochial cemetery, or in a cemetery that has been selected by the deceased, or in a family plot. The funeral differs from and does not depend upon the burial. The right to conduct a funeral, the "*ius funerandi,*" is no longer determined by the right to inter the body, the "*ius tumulandi.*" With the help of these conclusions it will be possible to determine the meaning of the "funeral church."

B. The Meaning of the Term "Funeral Church"

Canon 1215 states: "Nisi gravis causa obstet, cadavera fidelium, antequam tumulentur, transferenda sunt e loco in quo reperiuntur, in ecclesiam ubi funus, idest totus *ordo exsequiarum* quae in

---

[60] Maroto, "De Axiomate 'Ubi tumulus ibi funus'.": ". . . Nec opponant adversarii in novo Codice generatim retineri veterem disciplinam de sepultura ecclesiastica et de re funeraria, et ideo novos canones ex veteris iuris auctoritate aestimandos esse. At id recte diceretur si constaret in novis canonibus ius vetus ex integro referri; constat autem e converso plurimas gravioresque hac in re immutationes esse allatas; inde, prout habetur in c. 6, n. 3, canones qui ex parte tantum cum veteri iure congruunt, qua congruunt, ex iure antiquo aestimandi sunt; qua discrepant, sunt ex sua ipsorum sententia diiudicandi."—*Apollinaris,* I (1928), 265.

[61] Coronata, *De Locis et Temporibus Sacris,* nn. 186, 202; DeMeester, *Compendium,* III, nn. 1196, 1200; Cocchi, *Commentarium,* V, nn. 59–63; Wernz-Vidal, *Ius Canonicum,* IV, Pars I, n. 592.

probatis liturgicis libris describuntur, persolvatur." What is the meaning of the term "*funus*" in this canon? The answer to this question must be found in the answer to another question: what is the meaning of the term "*exsequiae*" in the same canon? If the Code of Canon Law gives the term "*exsequiae*" an exact meaning, a definition both of the term "*funus*" and of the term "funeral church" can be obtained. It seems to the writer that the Code does use the term "*exsequiae*" in a very precise manner, that is, to designate all the liturgical actions celebrated in the church.

Canon 1204 declares that ecclesiastical burial consists in the transfer of the body to the church, the exequies celebrated over the body in the church, and the interment of the body in a place rightly set aside for the burial of the faithful departed.[62] There are three distinct acts. The second, namely, the exequies celebrated over the body in the church, merits attention here. It is this element that the subsequent canons reiterate. It must be noted especially that the canon emphasizes the distinction between the transferral *to* the church, the exequies celebrated *in* the church, and the deposition *not in* the church, *but in* a place set aside rightly for the burying of the faithful departed. This is the first instance of the use of the word "*exsequiae*," and it is used in reference to the action in the church.

Canon 1230, §§ 1, 2, states that the proper pastor of the deceased has not only the right but also the duty, except in a grave case of necessity, to receive the body at the home himself or through his delegate, to accompany it to his own church, and to perform the exequies there; that, if the person died in another parish and the body can be brought readily to the church of the proper parish, it is, even in that case, the right of the proper pastor to receive the body at the home, to accompany it to his own church, and to perform the exequies there.[63] In the third

---

[62] "Sepultura ecclesiastica consistit in cadaveris translatione ad ecclesiam, exsequiis super illud in eadem celebratis, illius depositione in loco legitime deputato fidelibus defunctis condendis."

[63] C. 1230, §§ 1, 2: "Proprius defuncti parochus non solum ius sed etiam officium habet, excepto gravi necessitatis casu, levandi per se vel per alium cadaver, illud comitandi ad suam ecclesiasm paroecialem ibique exsequias persolvendi . . . ; Quod si mors acciderit in loco alienae paroeciae, et

paragraph of canon 1230, the Code declares that, if the church of the funeral is a church of the regular clergy, or another church exempt from the jurisdiction of the pastor, the pastor receives the body at the home and escorts it to the church, but the rector of the church celebrates the exequies.[64] The fourth paragraph of canon 1230 rules that, if the church of the funeral is not exempt from the jurisdiction of the pastor, the celebration of the exequies belongs, not to the rector of the funeral church, but to the pastor in whose territory the funeral church is situated, provided that the deceased was a subject of the pastor.[65] Finally, paragraph seven of canon 1230 states that, if the body is sent to a place in which the deceased did not have a proper parish, or in which there was not a funeral church which he had legitimately selected, the rights to receive the body, to perform the exequies, and to conduct the body to the place of burial, belong to the cathedral church of the respective town; but that if there is not a cathedral church there, the same rights belong to the church of the parish in which the cemetery is situated, unless there is a custom to the contrary, or unless the diocesan statutes ordain otherwise.[66]

It may be noted that in this canon there is a reference to four rights: the right to receive the body, the right to escort the body to the funeral church, the right to perform the exequies in the church, and the right to conduct the body to the place of burial. The right to perform the exequies in the church is to be exer-

---

cadaver ad ecclesiam propriae paroeciae commode asportari possit, parochi proprii est . . . illud levare, comitari ad suam ecclesiam ibique exsequias peragere."

[64] " Si ecclesia funeris sit ecclesia regularis, aliave exempta a iurisdictione parochi, parochus . . . cadaver levat ac deducit ad ecclesiam; sed exsequias rector ecclesiae celebrat."

[65] " Si vero ecclesia funeris non sit exempta a iurisdictione parochi, celebratio exsequiarum . . . pertinet non ad rectorem ecclesiae funerantis, sed ad parochum in cuius territoria ecclesia sita est, dummodo defunctus parocho subiectus fuerit."

[66] " Si cadaver mittatur ad locum ubi nec defunctus propriam paroeciam habebat, nec ecclesia funeris legitime fuerat electa, ius levandi cadaver, peragendi exsequias . . . et cadaver ad sepulturam deducendi, pertinet ad ecclesiam cathedralem eiusdem loci; quae si desit, ad ecclesiam paroeciae in qua coemeterium situm sit, nisi aliud ferant loci consuetudo aut dioecesana statuta."

cised after the first two rights have been exercised and before the right to conduct the body to the place of burial will be exercised. It may be noted also that the term "*exsequiae*" is always used in reference to an action that occurs in the church after the body has been brought to the church and before the body is taken from the church to the cemetery.

Canon 1215 rules that before the body is interred, it is to be brought from the place in which it rests into the church, where the funeral, that is the whole order of the exequies which are described in the liturgical books, is to be performed. This canon implies that the rights mentioned in canon 1230 are to be exercised, i.e., the right to receive the body and to escort it from the place in which it rests to the funeral church, the right to perform the exequies over the body in the church, and the right to conduct the body to the place of burial.

The transferral to the church of which the Code speaks in canon 1215 corresponds to the act of receiving of the body and the escorting of it to the church, as described in canon 1230. Especially, the exequies mentioned in canon 1215 correspond to the exequies celebrated in the church as described in canon 1230. It is quite clear, therefore, that the proper meaning of "*exsequiae*" in canon 1215 is the action celebrated in the church after the body has been brought to it. The Code thus gives an exact meaning to the term "*exsequiae.*" Thus, the term "*funus*" in canon 1215 seems to signify in the mind of the legislator the whole order of the actions described in the liturgical books as to be celebrated in the church. The "funeral church" may be understood, therefore, as the church in which the exequies are celebrated.

Canon 1231, §§ 1, 2, further confirms this conclusion. The first paragraph declares that, after the exequies have been completed in the church, the body is to be entombed in the cemetery of the funeral church with the ceremonies prescribed by the liturgical books, unless the body is to be taken to some other cemetery in accordance with canons 1228 and 1229.[67] The funeral church

[67] "Expletis in ecclesia exsequiis, cadaver tumulandum est ad normam librorum liturgicorum in coemeterio ecclesiae funeris, salvis praescriptis can. 1228, 1229."

therefore is already definitely specified before there is any consideration of the interment. This is clear from thc fact that the body is to be interred according to the prescriptions of the liturgical books in the cemetery of the funeral church. The funeral church is, therefore, juridically distinct from the church of the place where a person is buried. Of course, one may be buried in the cemetery of the funeral church and, indeed, one must be buried there, unless he has chosen a cemetery for his burial or possesses a family plot. However, the funeral church and the burial church are juridically not one and the same. The funeral church mentioned in canon 1231 is clearly the church in which the exequies are celebrated, and the exequies or the funeral are the ceremonies and prayers that are celebrated in the church prior to the interment.

Canon 1231, § 2, records the general rule that the priest who conducts the exequies in the church has not only the right but also the duty, except in a case of grave necessity, to accompany the body to the place of burial.[68] Again, there is offered here a contrast between the conducting of the exequies and the conducting of the body to burial. There would be no necessity of expressing the right involved here, if the performance of the exequies and the conducting of the body to the place of burial were identical. The determination of the right would already have been made in Canon 1230. Canon 1231, § 2, would be just a repetition of canons 1230, §§ 1, 3, 4, if the terms of the two canons designated synonymous rights.[69]

Under the ordinary law, the three possibilities as to clerics given the right of conducting the funeral are, the pastor of the parish church,[70] either in his own church or in a church subject

[68] "Qui exsequias in ecclesia peregit, non solum ius, sed etiam officium habet, excepto gravi necessitatis casu, comitandi per se vel per alium sacerdotem cadaver ad locum sepulturae."

[69] C. 1230, § 1: "Proprius parochus defuncti . . . ius habet . . . ibique in ecclesia exsequias persolvendi"; c. 1230, § 3: "sed exsequias rector ecclesiae funeris celebrat"; c. 1230, § 4: "Si vero ecclesia funeris non sit exempta a iurisdictione parochi, celebratio exsequiarum . . . pertinet non ad rectorem ecclesiae funerantis, sed ad parochum in cuius territorio ecclesia sita est, dummodo defunctus parocho subiectus fuerit."

[70] C. 1230, § 1.

to him when the one to be buried is his subject,[71] or the rector of a church which is exempt from the jurisdiction of the pastor,[72] or the rector of a church which is subject to the pastor in the event that the deceased is not a subject of the pastor.[73] The right to conduct the exequies is granted in appropriate cases to these by canon 1230. Why should there be a repetition of the concession of this right in canon 1231, § 2? Obviously there would be a repetition if the right to conduct the exequies signified the right to conduct the body to burial.

Under this hypothesis the only new idea that would be found in canon 1231, § 2, would be that of the obligation to conduct the body to burial. But even this obligation would, in the hypothesis, depend on canon 1231 in only two instances, that is, when the funeral church is a church exempt from the jurisdiction of the pastor,[74] and when the funeral church is one subject to the pastor but the deceased was not subject to the pastor,[75] since the obligation as affecting the pastor would have been expressed in canon 1230, § 1. Hence, if the right to perform the exequies in the church and the right to conduct the body to burial are identical, the canon should contain only an expression of the obligation for the rectors of the funeral church to conduct the body to burial in the two instances described.

The canon, however, refers to more than the obligation imposed on the above-mentioned rectors to conduct the body to burial. It rules that those who have conducted the exequies in the church have the right and the obligation to conduct the body to the place of burial. This it does since the right and the obligation to conduct the body to the place of burial have not been given to or imposed on anyone in the preceding canons, but the right and the

---

[71] C. 1230, § 4.

[72] C. 1230, § 3.

[73] C. 1230, § 4.

[74] "Si ecclesia funeris sit ecclesia regularis aliave exempta a iurisdictione parochi, parochus . . . cadaver levat ac deducit ad ecclesiam; sed exsequias rector ecclesiae celebrat."—Canon 1230, § 3.

[75] "Si vero ecclesia funeris non sit exempta a iurisdictione parochi, celebratio exsequiarum . . . pertinet non ad rectorem ecclesiae funerantis, sed ad parochum in cuius territorio ecclesia sita est, dummodo defunctus parocho subiectus fuerit."—Canon 1230, § 4.

obligation to perform the exequies have been given to and imposed on various priests in canon 1230. Since in canon 1231, §§ 1, 2, there is the first mention then of the right to conduct the body to burial, mention of this right is obviously not contained in the right to perform the exequies in the church.

According to the canons, therefore, the term "*exsequiae*" has a definite meaning. It signifies the action in the church which takes place after the body has been brought to the church and before the body is taken from the church to the cemetery. It seems to the writer that this must be taken as its meaning in canon 1215. It was seen that canon 1215 declares that the body is to be brought from the place in which it rests into the church where the funeral, that is, the whole order of the exequies which are described in the liturgical books, is to be performed. The exequies, according to the Code, are the liturgical actions which occur in the church. The meaning of the term "*funus*," as it is used in the Code of Canon Law, is therefore clear. The "funeral" may be defined as the whole order of the exequies which occur in the church. Moreover, the "funeral church" may be defined as the church in which the exequies occur, or as the church in which occur all the actions which in connection with a funeral are to be celebrated in the church.

ARTICLE III. THE MEANING OF "EXSEQUIARUM ORDO" IN THE ROMAN RITUAL

It has been maintained that the Code of Canon Law intends the word "funeral" to mean the exequies celebrated in the church and that, therefore, the phrase "*totus ordo exsequiarum*" in the meaning of the Code must be rendered "the whole order of the ceremonies which are described in the liturgical books as occurring in the church."[76] Upon examination the Roman Ritual is found to have as a caption for the third chapter of Title VI the phrase "*Exsequiarum ordo.*" When the content of this chapter of the Ritual is considered, it is found to contain the ceremonies which

[76] C. 1215: ". . . cadavera fidelium, antequam tumulentur, transferenda sunt e loco in quo reperiuntur, in ecclesiam, ubi funus, idest totus ordo exsequiarum quae in probatis liturgicis libris describuntur, persolvatur."

are performed at the home of the deceased, in the church and at the cemetery. If the phrase "*Exsequiarum ordo*" were to be identified with the phrase of canon 1215, namely, "*totus ordo exsequiarum quae in probatis liturgicis libris describuntur,*" then the term "*funus*" could not simply be understood as the exequies which occur in the church, but as including all the ceremonies which are performed at the home, in the church, and at the cemetery.

In the present article an attempt will be made to show that the phrase "*totus ordo exsequiarum*" of canon 1215 has a more specific meaning than the phrase "*Exsequiarum ordo*" in the Roman Ritual. In doing this the writer will seek to show that, since the "*Exsequiarum ordo*" is nothing more than the caption of a chapter of the Ritual, it is only a general term referring to all the rites of Christian sepulture contained therein. A chapter heading is not self-explanatory, nor can it be considered as a term that has a specific meaning until it has been used or embodied in a definitive statement. But nowhere in the chapter under consideration is the phrase "*Exsequiarum ordo*" used to refer to any of the particular ceremonies connected with a Christian funeral and burial. "*Exsequiarum ordo*" remains, then, only a chapter heading and cannot be used as a defined term with a specific meaning. It is quite otherwise with the canonical phrase "*totus ordo exsequiarum.*" The Code does not use this term to refer specifically to the ceremonies performed in the home, or to those performed on the occasion of the procession to the church, or to those performed on the occasion of the burial, but simply to the rites that take place in the church. A detailed examination of the Code and of the Ritual follows. From this examination the meaning of the phrase "*ordo exsequiarum*" in the Code as distinct from the meaning of the chapter heading "*Exsequiarum ordo*" in the Ritual should be apparent.

The third chapter of Title VI of the Roman Ritual has as its heading the phrase "*Exsequiarum ordo.*" Under this general heading there are found nineteen numbers. The last five of these numbers refer to the prayers to be said after the corpse has been interred,[77] to some general norms regarding the recitation of the Divine Office and the celebration of the Requiem Mass,[78] and to the manner of celebrating the ceremonies in the event that a deacon has permission to act as the celebrant of the ceremonies.[79]

As for the rest of the chapter, the first two numbers describe the processions from the church to the home and from the home to the church. In the second number are contained the prayers and rites to be performed on the occasion of removing the body from the home and during the procession from the home to the church.

The third number contains the ceremonies which are to be conducted on the reception of the body at the door of the church and on its transfer to the position in the church which it will occupy during the services. The fourth and fifth numbers of this chapter contain instructions on the chanting of the Divine Office; the sixth number records that during the recitation of the lauds of the Divine Office the priest and his ministers prepare themselves to celebrate the Requiem Mass. The seventh, eighth, ninth, and tenth numbers contain the prayers and ceremonies of the Absolution over the deceased person.

The eleventh to the fourteenth number inclusive present the prayers and the ceremonies to be performed as the body is carried from the church to the cemetery and as it is actually interred.

Canon 1215 [80] states that the bodies of the faithful are to be transferred to the church from the place in which they are resting at the time. As indicated above, the first two numbers of the chapter entitled "*Exsequiarum ordo*" deal expressly with the rites and prayers to be performed on the occasion of the transfer of the body to the church. Secondly, canon 1215 declares that the bodies are to be transferred to the church, where the funeral, that is, the whole order of the exequies (*totus ordo exsequiarum*),

---

[77] Rituale Rom., tit. VI, c. 3, *Exsequiarum ordo,* n. 15.

[78] *Ibid.,* nn. 16–18.

[79] *Ibid.,* n. 19.

[80] "Nisi gravis causa obstet, cadavera fidelium, antequam tumulentur, transferenda sunt e loco in quo reperiuntur, in ecclesiam, ubi funus, idest totus ordo exsequiarum quae in probatis liturgicis libris describuntur, persolvatur."

is to be celebrated. The third to the eleventh number inclusive of the chapter in the Ritual, as it has been seen, present the rites which are celebrated in the church. Thirdly, the canon commands that the transfer of the body to the church and the celebration of the exequies are to occur before the bodies are interred. Clearly, the eleventh to the fourteenth number of the "*Exsequiarum ordo*" of the Ritual contains the rites to be celebrated at the interment.

Canon 1215 in its three parts displays a basic outline of all the rites and ceremonies contained in the chapter entitled "*Exsequiarum ordo.*" It distinguishes clearly the transfer to the church, the exequies celebrated in the church, and the interment. The "*Exsequiarum ordo*" presents the rites that are celebrated as each of these three actions occurs. It is indeed of importance to note how general the meaning of the heading "*Exsequiarum ordo*" is in relation to the term "*ordo exsequiarum*" as occurring in canon 1215.

It is especially in canons 1230 and 1231, which treat directly of the ceremonies of Christian burial, that the contrast between the term "*ordo exsequiarum*" of canon 1215 and the chapter heading "*Exsequiarum ordo*" which is the title of a chapter in the Ritual can be seen most clearly.

Canon 1230, § 1,[81] states that the proper pastor of the deceased has the right and the duty "*levandi cadaver, illud comitandi ad suam ecclesiam paroecialem, ibique exsequias persolvendi.*" The socalled "*levatio*" or the reception of the corpse refers to the first of the liturgical acts which is described in the second number of the chapter entitled "*Exsequiarum ordo.*" The escorting of the body to the church is described in the first and second numbers of the same chapter. Likewise, the exequies celebrated "*ibique*" (*in ecclesia paroeciali*) are presented in the third to the tenth number inclusive of this chapter of the Roman Ritual.

In the several paragraphs of canon 1230[82] there is a constant

---

[81] "Proprius defuncti parochus non solum ius sed etiam officium habet, excepto gravi necessitatis casu, levandi per se vel per alium cadaver, illud comitandi ad suam ecclesiam paroecialem ibique exsequias persolvendi. . . ."

[82] § 2: "Quod si mors acciderit in loco alienae paroeciae et cadaver ad ecclesiam propriae paroeciae commode asportari possit, parochi proprii est

reference to the possession of the three rights. In distinguishing the three rights the Code directly points to distinct parts of the chapter of the Roman Ritual entitled "*Exsequiarum ordo.*" It is quite evident then that the heading "*Exsequiarum ordo*" denotes a more general term than any of the terms used in canon 1230, namely, the reception of the body, the escorting of the body to the church, and the performance of the exequies in the church. In fact, the "*Exsequiarum ordo*" of the Ritual contains the ceremonies to be performed on all three occasions.

Canon 1231, § 1, states[83] that, after the exequies have been celebrated in the church, the body is to be interred in the cemetery of the same church with the ceremonies prescribed by the liturgical books. The ceremonies prescribed by the Roman Ritual for the interment are found in the eleventh to the fourteenth numbers inclusive of the chapter entitled "*Exsequiarum ordo.*" The canon clearly points to the necessity of interring the body with the prescribed ceremonies after the "*exequies*" celebrated in the church have been completed.

The second paragraph of canon 1231[84] declares that the priest who conducted the exequies in the church has the right and duty to accompany the body to the place of burial. This law also marks the difference between the celebration of the exequies in the church

---

. . . , illud levare, comitari ad suam ecclesiam ibique exsequias peragere." § 3: "Si ecclesia funeris sit ecclesia regularis aliave exempta a iurisdictione parochi, parochus . . . cadaver levat ac deducit ad ecclesiasm, sed exsequias rector ecclesiae celebrat." § 4: "Si vero ecclesia funeris non sit exempta a iurisdictione parochi, celebratio exsequiarum . . . pertinet . . . ad parochum in cuius territorio ecclesia sita est. . . ." § 5: ". . . indeque, si de religiosis agatur iurisdictioni parochi non obnoxiis, ad propriam religiosae domus ecclesiam vel oratorium deducit et exsequias peragit cappellanus. . . ." § 7: ". . . ius levandi cadaver, peragendi exsequias . . . pertinet ad ecclesiam cathedralem eiusdem loci."

[83] "Expletis in ecclesia exsequiis, cadaver tumulandum est ad normam librorum liturgicorum in coemeterio ecclesiae funeris, salvis praescriptis can. 1228, 1229."

[84] "Qui exsequias in ecclesia peregit, non solum ius, sed etiam officium habet . . . comitandi per se vel per alium sacerdotem cadaver ad locum sepulturae."

and the rite of the interment. It grants, moreover, to the priest who conducted the exequies in the church the right to accompany the body to the place of burial. The canon, therefore, indicates a fourth right distinct from the rights to receive the body, to escort the body to the church, and to perform the exequies in the church. The fourth right is exercised obviously through the execution of the prescriptions of the Ritual as they are presented in the eleventh to the fourteenth number inclusive of the chapter entitled "*Exsequiarum ordo.*"

From this study of the relationship of the Roman Ritual to the Code of Canon Law it is evident that the heading in the Roman Ritual, namely, "*Exsequiarum ordo,*" has a more general meaning than the term "*ordo exsequiarum,*" which is used in canon 1215. The heading refers to all the ceremonies, whether they are celebrated at the home, in the church, or at the cemetery. On the other hand, the Code has given a specific meaning to the term "*exsequiae*" in canon 1230. In its use of that term it designates only the liturgical actions which occur in the church. Consequently, from the fact that the Code has given a specific meaning to the term "*exsequiae*" in canon 1230, it is logical to infer that the legislator desires the same meaning to attach to the word when it is used in canon 1215.

It becomes evident, then, how the words of canon 1215, "*totus ordo exsequiarum quae in probatis liturgicis libris describuntur,*" must be understood. Since the term "*exsequiae*" indicates the liturgical actions which occur in the church, the complete phrase must be rendered "the whole order of the liturgical actions which are described in the liturgical books as occurring in the church." The actions which take place in the church are described in the third to the tenth numbers of the chapter of the Ritual entitled "*Exsequiarum ordo.*" The principal liturgical actions which are described in these numbers are the celebration of the Requiem Mass and the ceremony of the Absolution over the body of the deceased.

It seems then that the definition of the term "*funus,*" as used in canon 1215, is clear. It is the whole order of the liturgical actions celebrated in the church that is described in the third to the tenth number inclusive of the chapter of the Ritual which is entitled "*Exsequiarum ordo.*" It may be said to consist principally in the celebration of the Requiem Mass and of the Absolution over the body of the deceased person.

Beste is of the opinion that by the words "*funus*" and "*exsequiae*" the funeral rites celebrated over the body in the church are to be understood.[85] Sipos declares simply that the parts of the funeral (*funus*) are the office of the dead, the Requiem Mass, and the Absolution.[86] Vermeersch-Creusen state most explicitly that the whole order of the exequies prescribed by the Roman Ritual is composed of three parts: first, the transfer of the deceased to the funeral church from the place where the body rests; secondly, the office of the dead, the Requiem Mass or at least the prayers of the Absolution; thirdly, the accompaniment of the deceased from the funeral church to the place of the burial. They add that, on the contrary, the exequies in canon 1215 designate the ceremonies and liturgical prayers which are performed in the church before the body is conducted to the sepulcher.[87]

From this understanding of the meaning of the terms, "*funus,*" "*exsequiae,*" "*ordo exsequiarum*" and "*Exsequiarum ordo,*" which has been gained from the consideration of the canons and the Roman Ritual, it can be concluded that the terms, "*funus,*" "*exsequiae,*" and "*ordo exsequiarum*" have the same specific meaning which differs from that of the heading in the Ritual, that is, "*Exsequiarum ordo.*" Furthermore, since the funeral consists principally of the Requiem Mass and the ceremony of the Absolution over the body of the deceased, a more specific

---

[85] *Introductio in Codicem,* ad c. 1223, § 1.

[86] *Enchiridion Iuris Canonici* (Pécs: Ex Typographia "Haladás R. T.," 1926), § 150, n. 4.

[87] "Totus exsequiarum ordo ad normam tituli VI Rit. Rom. tribus constat: delatione defuncti e loco ubi reperitur in ecclesiam funeris; officio defunctorum, Missa exsequiali aut saltem precibus absolutionis; deductione defuncti ab ecclesia funeris ad locum sepulturae. Contra, in can. 1215 exsequiae designant caerimonias et preces liturgicas quae in ecclesia peraguntur, antequam cadaver ad tumulum deducatur."—*Epitome,* II, n. 526.

definition of the " funeral church " can be formed. It is to be defined, not as the church from which the procession starts to the home, nor as the church in whose cemetery the rite of interment is performed, but simply as the church in which the Requiem Mass and the Absolution over the body of the deceased occur.

CHAPTER IV

THE FUNERAL CHURCH ACCORDING TO THE ORDINARY LAW

The funeral church, it was learned, is the church in which especially the Requiem Mass and the Absolution over the body of the deceased occur. To this church the body is to be transferred before it is interred. Canons 1216–1218 contain the ordinary law governing the determination of the funeral church; canons 1219–1222 contain special law for certain classes of persons in the same matter, and canons 1223–1227 the law on the choice of the funeral church. The first group of canons will be considered in the present chapter.

ARTICLE I. THE FUNERAL CHURCH OF THE PERSON WHO DIES IN HIS PROPER PARISH

Canon 1216, § 1: **Ecclesia in quam cadaver pro funere transferri debet ex iure ordinario est ecclesia propriae defuncti paroeciae, nisi defunctus aliam funeris ecclesiam legitime elegerit.**

§ 2: **Si defunctus plures habuerit paroecias proprias ecclesia funeris est ecclesia paroeciae in cuius territorio decessit.**

In the first paragraph of this canon there is found the ordinary law in regard to the funerals of all Catholics. The canon ordains that the church to which the body ought to be transferred for the funeral is the church of the proper parish of the deceased, unless he has chosen legitimately another funeral church. It lists therefore two possible funeral churches, the parish church and the church chosen by the deceased. Since a special chapter will be devoted to a consideration of the right to select the funeral church and the conditions governing the exercise of that right, more elaborate treatment of the funeral church specifically selected will be found there.[1] However, the fact that one has a right to choose the funeral church must always be borne in mind when any statements are made in this section in regard to the rights of the church of the proper parish.

The proper value of the qualifying clause, then, having been conceded, it may be said that the canon states the common law governing the funerals of all Catholics. The canon uses the phrase, "*ex iure ordinario.*" Ecclesiastical law can be regarded from different viewpoints. By reason of its obligatory force, it is called common law or singular law, in so far as it establishes either a norm that is to be usually observed, or an exception from the ordinary rule respectively. The *ordinary* law of this canon is synonymous with the *common* law.[2] The word *ordinario* implies that there can be exceptions to the law. Thus, Beste says that it is so called because a particular law confirmed by the Holy See, an apostolic privilege, customary law, and also the legitimate choice of the deceased can detract from its usual force.[3] The legitimate choice of the deceased[4] and the special laws found in the Code as affecting certain classes of persons[5] will be discussed in later chapters.

Canon 1216 commands, then, that ordinarily the body of the deceased is to be transferred for the funeral to the church of the proper parish of the deceased. The proper parish of the deceased is determined by the Code. A person obtains his proper pastor or Ordinary by reason of his domicile or quasi-domicile.[6]

---

[1] Cf. *infra,* p. 103.

[2] Coronata, *De Locis et Temporibus Sacris,* n. 164; nota 1; "Sepultura ex iure ordinario seu communi . . ."—Cocchi, *Commentarium,* V, n. 57; "Ex iure ordinario, dice il canone, ossia per diritto commune . . ."—Rossi, *Sepultura Ecclesiastica,* n. 46.

[3] "Dicitur 'ex iure ordinario,' quia iuri, quod hoc canone paroeciae agnoscitur, derogare potest vel ius particulare a S. Sede firmatum, vel privilegium apostolicum, vel ius consuetudinarium, vel etiam electio ipsius defuncti, dummodo de tali contrario iure omnino constet."—*Introductio in Codicem,* Commentary on canon 1216.

[4] Cf. *infra,* p. 103 ff.

[5] Cc. 1219–1222; cf. also pp. 152–190.

[6] C. 94, § 1.

The proper pastor of the wanderer (*vagus*) as well as of the person who has only a diocesan domicile or quasi-domicile is the pastor of the place in which each of these actually dwells.[7]

Domicile is acquired by residence in any parish or quasi-parish, or at least in a diocese, a vicariate apostolic or a prefecture apostolic. This residence must either be joined with the intention to stay there forever unless something calls one away, or actually extend over ten complete years.[8] Quasi-domicile is obtained either by residence in a parish or a diocese, with the intention to stay there for at least the greater part of the year unless something calls one away, or by actual residence in the parish or the diocese for the greater part of the year.[9] The domicile or quasi-domicile is called parochial, if either of these exists in a parish or quasi-parish; diocesan, if either of these exists in a diocese, a vicariate or a prefecture apostolic, but not in a parish or a quasi-parish.[10]

There are several persons for whom the Code establishes a legal or necessary domicile. This kind of domicile, distinct from that called voluntary, is the domicile necessarily acquired from the disposition of the law by those persons who are not *sui iuris* by reason of a bond with the persons to whom they are subject. A wife who is not legitimately separated from her husband retains his domicile; an insane person possesses that of his guardian; a minor, that of the person to whom he is subject.[11] After the completed seventh year of age, a minor, that is, a person who has not completed twenty-one full years of age, can obtain his own quasi-domicile.[12] Likewise, a wife, although not legitimately separated from her husband, can establish her own quasi-domicile; if she is legitimately separated from him, she can acquire even her own domicile.[13] Yet, even if she is maliciously deserted by her husband, she cannot acquire a domicile distinct from that of her

[7] C. 94, §§ 2, 3.
[8] C. 92, § 1.
[9] C. 92, § 2.
[10] C. 92, § 3.
[11] C. 93, § 1.
[12] C. 93, § 2.
[13] C. 93, § 2.

husband unless she has obtained from the ecclesiastical judge a decree of perpetual separation or of a separation for an indefinite period of time.[14] It should be noted also that the insane person cannot acquire by himself a domicile or quasi-domicile, but is totally dependent on their possession by the guardian.[15]

There is a question among canonists whether the wife, the insane person and the minor share in the quasi-domicile of those to whom they are subject. De Meester [16] and Ojetti (1862–1932) [17] hold that the Code completely eliminated the idea of a necessary or legal quasi-domicile, while Wernz (1842–1914)-Vidal (1867–1938),[18] Maroto (1875–1937) [19] and Beste [20] maintain that the legal quasi-domicile of those to whom they are subject is obtained by the wife, the minor and the insane person respectively. Vermeersch-Creusen [21] realize that the Code in itself does not mention the legal quasi-domicile, but admit at least that the quasi-domicile of the guardian or husband, when either of these does not have a domicile, will become the legal quasi-domicile of the minor, of the

---

[14] *AAS,* XIV (1922), 526.

[15] " Num vero eo ipso (incidendo in insaniam) etiam proprium domicilium et quasi-domicilium, si quod habuerit ante mentis alienationem, amittat, non constat. Ex can. 95 potius negandum videtur."—Beste, *Introductio in Codicem,* Commentary on canon 93, § 2.

[16] *Compendium,* I, n. 318.

[17] *Commentarium in Codicem Iuris Canonici* (4 vols., Romae: Universitas Gregoriana, 1927–1931), II, n. 50, nota 40.

[18] *Ius Canonicum,* II, n. 12.

[19] *Institutiones Iuris Canonici ad Normam Novi Codicis* (2 vols., Vol. I, 3 ed., Romae, 1919–1921), I, n. 413 (hereafter this work will be cited *Institutiones*).

[20] " Ratio est, quod haec participatio intactam servat auctoritatem a Codice admissam in protectionem eorum qui non sunt sui iuris, et quod in iure domicilium et quasi-domicilium voluntaria passim aequiparantur, neque ulla videtur solida ratio cur id negandum sit domicilio et quasi-domicilio necessariis."—*Introductio in Codicem,* Commentary on canon 93, § 2.

[21] " Attamen, deficiente domicilio viri vel eius cuius potestati subsunt, si personae protectae proprio quasi-domicilio careant, ne vagae dicendae sint, tunc applicando analogiae, quod c. 20 permittitur, dicemus ab iis quasi-domicilium viri, curatoris, etc. participari."—*Epitome,* I, n. 214. Cf. also Coronata, *Institutiones,* I, n. 125, nota 2.

insane person, and of the wife. Costello[22] favors the opinion which denies the existence of a legal quasi-domicile, yet he admits the solid probability of both opinions.

Domicile and quasi-domicile are lost by the departure from a place with the intention of not returning, except in the case of a legal or a necessary domicile and quasi-domicile. Since the law provides a necessary domicile for certain classes of persons, it is not within the capacity of these, namely, minors, married women and the insane, to lose it by leaving the place with the intention of not returning. It is only when the reason for their subjection substantially changes that the legal domicile or quasi-domicile is lost. And even then it may become a voluntary domicile until it is clear that it has been abandoned.[23]

It is difficult to determine how many domiciles a person may have at the same time. As a conclusion to his study, Costello affirms that it would seem quite probable that a person could have three or, at most, four domiciles at the same time.[24]

Of course two quasi-domiciles are possible to wives and minors who share in the legal quasi-domicile of those to whom they are subject. Whether other persons can have two quasi-domiciles is disputed. Many authors hold that a person having acquired a

---

[22] *Domicile and Quasi-Domicile,* The Catholic University of America Canon Law Studies, n. 60 (Washington, D. C.: The Catholic University of America, 1930), p. 177.

[23] " Although this necessary domicile as such ceases upon the cessation of the fact upon which it was founded, it is presumed to have passed into a voluntary domicile unless it is clear that it has been definitely abandoned. Thus, e.g., a son upon reaching his majority loses his necessary domicile as a necessary domicile, but he is presumed to retain it as a voluntary domicile until it is clear that he has given it up."—Costello, *Domicile and Quasi-Domicile,* p. 166.

[24] *Domicile and Quasi-Domicile,* p. 153; ". . . cum enim ad fovendum domicilium satis sit commoratio trium vel quattuor mensium quotannis, si quis revera haberet tres vel quattuor domus instructas et alternative eas habitaret, in singulis locis domicilium retinere dicendus esset."—Chelodi, *Ius de Personis iuxta Codicem Iuris Canonici* (2. ed., Tridenti, 1927), n. 92, p. 165, nota 1 (hereafter cited as *Ius de Personis*); Woywod, *A Practical Commentary on the Code of Canon Law* (2 vols. [Vol. I, Sixth Printing, 1941; Vol. II, Seventh Printing, 1943], New York: Joseph F. Wagner, 1941–1943), I, 41.

quasi-domicile in one place may leave that place intending to return, and if he stays for the greater part of the year in the other place he acquires there a quasi-domicile, while the other was not lost inasmuch as he intends to return.[25] It is rarely taught that the fact of his stay for the greater part of the year in the new place shows his intention not to return to the first quasi-domicile.[26]

The proper parish is obtained by the possession of domicile or quasi-domicile, whether voluntary or necessary.[27] The opinion that once held the parish of quasi-domicile not to be the proper parish was undermined by the response of the Sacred Congregation of the Council. The Provincial Synod of Armagh in Ireland, held in 1908, had decreed that on the death of any person outside the limits of his proper parish, the priest of his domicile had the right to three-fourths of the offerings made on the occasion of the funeral, no matter where the funeral was celebrated, and that one-fourth belonged to the priest of the place where the death occurred, who moreover was to see to it that a Mass was celebrated for the soul of the deceased. The meaning of the terms, "his proper parish," and "domicile" as contained in this decree, was obscure for a few priests. Some contended that because domicile alone was mentioned, the legislators intended to exclude quasi-domicile, and that consequently "his proper parish" signified only the parish in which one had a domicile. After the publication of the Code of Canon Law, others thought that the pastor of the quasi-domicile could not acquire a right to the funeral offerings unless the person newly arrived in his parish had actually lived in the parish for the greater part of the year.

---

[25] Costello, *Domicile and Quasi-Domicile,* p. 156; "Si quis ergo, acquisito in loco aliquo quasi-domicilio ad locum alium se conferat ut ibi per maiorem partem anni partem commoretur, cum animo tamen postea ad priorem locum revertendi, hoc in loco certo quasi-domicilio conservat (c. 95); in illo vero acquirit ex c. 92, § 2."—Maroto, *Institutiones,* I, n. 413; Chelodi, *Ius de Personis,* n. 92, p. 166, nota 4.

[26] Cf. however, De Meester, *Compendium,* I, n. 318.

[27] "Domicilium autem fictitium seu legale necessarium, ut domicilium verum habitationis quod ad funera habendum est, salvo semper iure electionis, ita e.g. paroecia uxoris vi domicilii fictitii est paroecia viri"—Coronata, *De Locis et Temporibus Sacris,* n. 164.

To settle these contentions, the Bishop of Ardagh presented the dispute to Rome. The Sacred Congregation of the Council, in its remarks, asserted: "What was established in the old law by not a few decisions of the Sacred Roman Congregations . . . and was held as the common opinion is plainly stated in the Code of Canon Law in canon 94, § 1: 'A person acquires his own pastor and Ordinary through either domicile or quasi-domicile.' Hence, wherever in Title XII of Book III there is mention of the *proper* [one's own] pastor and the *proper* [one's own] parish, beyond a doubt the quasi-domicile also is included. . . . No distinction is made between a parish in which a person has actually lived for the greater part of the year and one in which he has just begun to live, with the intention, however, of remaining there if nothing calls him away; for in both cases his proper parish is obtained by quasi-domicile."[28] To the question proposed, namely, "Whether after the Code of Canon Law, the parish of the quasi-domicile is also in the proposed case the proper parish of the deceased for the purpose of receiving funeral fees," the Sacred Congregation replied at its plenary session on June 9, 1923; "In the affirmative."[29]

In rendering this response, the Sacred Congregation had both kinds of quasi-domicile explicitly before it for consideration, so both are included in its provision. Hence the parish of quasi-domicile, whether the quasi-domicile is acquired by residence and intention or by mere residence alone, is the proper parish of a

[28] "Quod etiam in vetere iure crebris SS.RR. Congregationum resolutionibus . . . et communi doctrina firmabatur, in Codice iuris canonici can. 94, § 1, apertissime edicitur: 'Sive per domicilium sive per quasi-domicilium *suum* quisque parochum et Ordinarium sortitur.' Igitur ubicumque in Tit. XII lib. III mentio occurrit parochi *proprii* et paroeciae *propriae,* procul dubio venit et quasi-domicilii paroecia; . . . Nec ulla distinctio fit paroeciae in qua quis reapse commoraverit per maiorem anni partem aut in qua commorare tantum incoeperit cum animo tamen ibi sic manendi si nihil avocet; nam in utroque casu per quasi-domicilium paroecia propria obtinetur."—*AAS,* XVII (1925), 509; reported in Bouscaren, *The Canon Law Digest,* II, 355.

[29] "Sacra Congregatio Concilii . . . ad propositum dubium; 'An, post datum Codicem iuris canonici etiam paroecia quasi-domicilii sit paroecia propria defuncti ad effectum percipiendi emolumenta funeraria in casu,' respondendum censuit: Affirmative."—*AAS,* XVII (1925), 510.

deceased person.[30] It is interesting to note that the Sacred Congregation remarked that wherever in Title XII of Book III of the Code there is mention of the proper parish, there is understood also the parish of the quasi-domicile.[31]

A parish may be defined as a determined group of the faithful to which there is assigned a special church, and over which there is a special rector as a proper pastor for the necessary care of souls.[32] A parish is said to be territorial, when the faithful are subject to the pastor by reason of the territory in which they live; personal, when the reason for the subjection of the faithful to the pastor is not founded on territory but on some purely personal quality; mixed, if the parishioners are determined both by the territory and by a personal quality at the same time, so that if either of these is not present, a person is not judged to be affiliated with such a parish. The personal quality depends very often on a difference of language or nationality; hence, the parish is often called a national parish.[33]

Woywod (1880–1941) [34] and Beste [35] maintain that national

---

[30] Cf. "Funeral Offerings—Important Decision of the Congregation of the Council on the Celebrated Armagh Statute"—J. Kinane, *Irish Ecclesiastical Record* (Dublin, 1864–), 5 Series, XXVI (1925), 518–522.

[31] *AAS,* XVII (1925), 509.

[32] Cf. c. 215; Fanfani, *De Iure Parochorum,* n. 1.

[33] Cf. Fanfani, *De Iure Parochorum,* n. 3; Beste, *Introductio in Codicem,* Commentary on canon 216.

[34] *A Practical Commentary on the Code of Canon Law,* I, 84.

[35] "Ultima haec species paroeciarum praesertim in usu est apud nos, ubi erectae sunt paroeciae mixtae polonorum, italorum, gallorum, etc."—Beste, *Introductio in Codicem,* Commentary on canon 216, § 4; Anonymous, "National Pastors and Assistance at Marriage": "It does indeed seem that some national parishes are strictly personal without any territorial limits. On the other hand, it seems that in most cases the national parishes of this country are erected for the faithful of the respective nationalities settled in the particular districts. . . . Now the territorial limits of these parishes mutually separating them are sufficient to render those parishes 'distinct territorial parts' with their proper pastor. The same applies even if there is but one parish of a given nationality in a city or town. . . . It is therefore difficult to escape the conviction that most national parishes in this country enjoy sufficiently definite territorial limits to fulfill the requirements of canon 216, § 1, and that they are territorial parishes."—*The American Ecclesiastical Review* (Philadelphia, 1889–), LXXX (1929), 88–94 (here-

parishes in the United States are canonical parishes. The jurisdiction which the pastor possesses is both personal, in that it extends to people of the same language other than English, and territorial, inasmuch as it is restricted to the faithful residing in a certain territory, which may be more extensive than the limits of the strictly territorial parish or even of several of them. The pastor of the purely territorial parish enjoys complete pastoral jurisdiction over the entire territory subject to him, and for this reason over all the people who dwell within the parish limits, except over those who choose to belong to the national parish. The pastor of the national parish possesses pastoral jurisdiction only over the members of a given national group within the determined territory of the national parish.[36] However, the children born in America of parents who are not Americans and who speak a language other than English, upon becoming emancipated, are not obliged to join the parish to which the parents belong, but have the right to join the parish in which the English language is used. Catholics who were not born in America but who know English have the right to become members of the church where the English language is spoken, and cannot be obliged to subject themselves to the jurisdiction of the rector of the church which was established for the people who speak the language of their own country. The English-speaking parish with which they may affiliate is that American territorial parish in which these foreign immigrants and their children have their domicile.[37]

The theory which Augustine held in regard to the administra-

---

after this periodical will be cited *AER*). Cf. Augustine, *The Pastor According to the New Code of Canon Law* (2. ed., St. Louis: B. Herder Book Co., 1924), pp. 56–58; *Canonical and Civil Status of Catholic Parishes* (St. Louis: B. Herder Book Co., 1926), p. 75.

[36] "A conflict need not arise; for even though the national parish is within the territory of an English-speaking parish, the pastor of the former is restricted in his ministrations to the faithful of the respective nationality who have not yet joined the English-speaking parish."—"National Pastors and Assistance at Marriage."—*AER*, LXXX (1929), 88–94.

[37] Cf. the letter of the Most Rev. A. G. Cicognani, Archbishop of Laodicea, Apostolic Delegate to the United States, of February 17, 1938, which contains also the private declaration of the Sacred Congregation of the Council, of January 15, 1938—cited in Bouscaren, *The Canon Law Digest,* II, 78–80.

tion of baptism cannot, in the writer's opinion, be maintained. His case is the following: an Italian family moves into a district in which there exist a purely territorial parish, and two national churches, the one Italian, the other German; before the family affiliates with the Italian or the purely territorial parish, a child is born. Augustine acknowledged to the pastor of the German parish a right to baptize this child.[38] The writer believes that the pastor of the German parish does not possess any such right over Italians, even if the pastor speaks English, or the pastor and the Italian family speak English. At all times the jurisdiction of pastors of national parishes, even if they had clearly defined territorial limits, was recognized as restricted to the faithful of the respective nationality.[39]

The Italian family belongs, then, to either the Italian or the English parish. The Italian pastor has the right to baptize the child if the parents are immigrants and do not speak the English language, since the Italian parish is founded for such persons. However, it seems that he does not have the right if they are Italian immigrants who speak English, or are descendants of Italian parents who likewise speak English. It does not rest with either the one or the other of the pastors to decide to which parish such persons belong. These have a right to choose the parish of which they will become members. Until they exercise that right, the purely territorial parish enjoys the favor of the law.

Of course, the parents may choose to become members of the Italian parish at the time they bring the child to that church for baptism. Their presentation of the child for baptism to the pastor of the territorial parish could be legitimately interpreted as a sign on the part of the parents that they wished to join that particular parish in preference to their own national church.[40] The mere fact, however, that there is an Italian parish in the district into which they have moved does not mean that these new arrivals belong to it. If they had been at one time parishioners of the

---

[38] *The Pastor According to the New Code of Canon Law,* pp. 56-57.

[39] *AER,* LXXX (1929), 93.

[40] Cf. Waldron, *The Minister of Baptism,* The Catholic University of American Canon Law Studies, n. 170 (Washington, D. C.: The Catholic University of America Press, 1942), p. 100.

Italian parish, or if they be children of parishioners of that parish, they would continue to belong to that parish until they had chosen to belong to the purely territorial parish. Hence it appears to the writer that the pastor of the purely territorial parish has the right to baptize in this case, unless the Italian family does not wish to surrender its affiliation with the Italian parish.

It may be of some assistance to summarize the considerations in regard to the determination of the proper parish. Most of the parishes in the United States are territorial parishes. For those who have a domicile or a quasi-domicile or who are travellers, the proper parish in relationship to funerals is that of the domicile or the quasi-domicile of the deceased. Those who have several domiciles or quasi-domiciles will have several proper parishes, one in each place where the individual domicile or quasi-domicile is established. For those who belong to a national parish, the proper parish will be the determined national parish. The proper parish of wanderers (*vagi*) is that in which they happen to be at the time they die. For those who have only a diocesan domicile, the proper parish is also that in which they are dwelling at the time of death. The wife not legitimately separated from her husband has as her proper parish the parish of her husband, yet she can have her own proper parish by the acquisition of a quasi-domicile. If she is legitimately separated, she also possesses her own proper parish by reason of her domicile. The minor still an infant has as his only proper parish that of his parents or guardians; after he has passed beyond infancy he may acquire his own proper parish by reason of his acquisition of a quasi-domicile. For the insane, the proper parish is that of the guardian.

The legislator in canon 1216 presents two possibilities in reference to the determination of the funeral church by the place in which the deceased was living at the time of death. First he considers the funeral church for the person who possesses a single proper parish and dies within its limits. Then the funeral church to which the body is to be transferred is the proper parish church of the deceased. It is here the exequies will be held. Secondly, he considers the funeral church for the person who possesses several proper parishes and dies within the limits of one of them. The funeral church in this case is the parish church in whose territory he dies. It is important to remember that the parish church of the quasi-domicile has the same standing as the parish church of the domicile. There is no reason to say that the body must be transferred to the parish church of the domicile in the event that death occurs in the parish of quasi-domicile, even though the body can be transported easily to the parish church of the domicile.[41] Since all the titles by which any one is said to have a proper parish are entirely equal, none of them prevails over the other.[42]

A special difficulty arises in regard to the national parish. Certainly it has the right to be the funeral church for all those who have been members of it and dwell within its limits. Obviously, too, the purely territorial parish cannot exercise the right of conducting their funerals, unless it has been chosen as the funeral church. The national church will be the funeral church for the descendants of the parishioners unless they have chosen to become members of the purely territorial parish in which they dwell. It appears to the writer that the national parish will have the right to conduct the funerals of all those who may have come lately from another nation and do not speak English. In practice, they will naturally gravitate to the national church and become members of that parish. The number of such people, due to immigration restrictions, is constantly growing smaller.

In regard to all others, that is, those who come into the district from another district in the United States, according to the writer's opinion, the purely territorial parish has the right to conduct the funeral unless these people have signified in some way or other their intention to belong to the national parish. This indication of affiliation may happen by means of a formal enrollment on the list of parishioners or by any other means sufficient to justify a judgment that affiliation has occurred, such as attendance at Mass in the church of the national parish or a reception

---

[41] Cf. *supra*, p. 82.

[42] " Nota insuper hos omnes titulos, quibus aliquis propriam habere dicitur, inter se omnino aequales esse, nec unum alteri praevalere, ita ut e.g. si quis alicubi habuerit quasi-domicilium et alibi domicilium decesserit autem in loco quasi-domicilii, ibi est ecclesia propriae paroeciae, licet paroeciae domicilii ecclesia forte propior sit."—Coronata, *De Locis et Temporibus Sacris*, n. 165.

of the sacraments there over a protracted period of time.

In practice, there may be diocesan customs or statutes which determine more definitely the basis for membership in such parishes, e.g., the nationality of the father or of the mother. Actual membership in the national parish will depend then on whether either of these is a parishioner or has chosen to become a member of the national parish when his or her family came into a new district. Thus, if a man of English descent marries an Italian woman even in her national parish, it would appear very reasonable, even apart from the consideration of the local custom or of the particular diocesan statute, that the family would be members of his territorial parish. If the husband were an Italian and belonged to a national parish, it would appear very reasonable also that the family would belong to the national parish. The opposite conclusions to these conditions may be drawn, if the affiliation is based on the nationality of the wife and mother. It seems necessary in all cases to investigate the local conditions before a final decision can be made.

In regard to wanderers (*vagi*) and those possessing only a diocesan domicile, even though they are of a nationality for which there is a church in the territory in which they die, the funeral church seems to be the parish church of the territorial parish, and not that of the national parish, unless they had indicated in some way their affiliation with the national parish, or are only late arrivals from another nation and incapable of speaking English. This last class, as has been said, will be found rarely.

Thus has canon 1216 determined the funeral church for the parishioner who has died in his proper parish. Containing the ordinary law, it accents too the position of the proper parish church. Even more so does canon 1217, which states: *In dubio de iure alius ecclesiae, ius propriae ecclesiae paroecialis semper praevalere debet.*

In the early fifteenth century, Panormitanus (1386–1453) remarked that, since the right of burying parishioners was a parochial right, the pastor had by presumption of law the right of burying in his church all who died within the confines of his parish. He declared further that, if anyone other than the pastor claimed to have the right to bestow burial, or asserted that the deceased person was to be buried in a church other than the parish church, he had to prove that there existed a law or a special concession which gave him the right to interfere, or which gave to the other church the right to bestow burial.[43] He concluded that the right of the pastor then would yield only to the proof that the deceased had actually chosen a place of burial or had a family tomb. Panormitanus based his reasoning, of course on the old principle found in the Decretals, namely, one is to be buried in that church in which he was accustomed to hear Mass and to receive the sacraments.[44] The study of the decisions of the Roman Congregations, given from the last quarter of the sixteenth century to the promulgation of the Code in favor of the parochial church, brought the position of the parochial church and its right into sharp relief.[45]

Canon 1217 repeats the old law. The parochial church enjoys the favor of the law.[46] Its right to be the funeral church ought to prevail always in any doubt concerning the right of another church. An exception to the exercise of its right, if there be any asserted, must be proved, not presumed.[47]

This prerogative of the parochial church is one of the parochial rights. In several cases considered by the Sacred Congregation of the Council since 1918, the Sacred Congregation has continued to maintain this right as parochial. Cases in which the invalid selection of the funeral church,[48] a custom contrary to the Code,[49] and the assumption that the choice of a cemetery for burial included the selection of the church within whose limits the cemetery was located as the funeral church [50] were involved, were settled in favor of the proper parish church of the deceased.

---

[43] Cf. *supra*, p. 21.

[44] Cc. 1, 6, 8, 10, X, *de sepulturis*, III, 28.

[45] Cf. *supra*, pp. 28 ff.

[46] ". . . hinc propria defuncti paroecia gaudet favore iuris."—Cocchi, *Commentarium*, V, n. 57.

[47] Beste, *Introductio in Codicem*, Commentary on canon 1217.

[48] S. C. C., *Dianen.*, 9 iul. 1921—*AAS*, XIII (1921), 534; reported in Bouscaren, *The Canon Law Digest*, I, 573.

[49] S. C. C., *Gallipolitana*, 25 maii et 15 nov. 1930—*AAS*, XXV (1933), 155; reported in Bouscaren, *The Canon Law Digest*, I, 576.

[50] S. C. C., *Apuana*, 12 nov. 1927—*AAS*, XX (1928), 142; reported in Bouscaren, *The Canon Law Digest*, I, 578–580.

Canon 1217 refers to the case of doubt concerning the right of another church. If there is a clear choice of a funeral church, proved according to the norms of law,[51] one cannot still insist on the parish church as the funeral church. The presumption which stands for the proper parish church as the funeral church for all the parishioners must give way to the truth. To justify the presumption in favor of the parish church, the doubt concerning the right of the other church must be of a probable and positive character, whether as a doubt of law or as a doubt of fact; otherwise the right of the parish cannot prevail.[52] It is precisely in the case in which there is alleged the supposed choice of a church other than the proper parish church as the funeral church that the principle enunciated in this canon will be of greatest service. If there is a doubt concerning the right to conduct the funeral among several proper parish churches, the principle does not apply, but the doubt must be solved by the principle already given in canon 1216, § 2, or by the principles of canon 1218, which are about to be considered.[53]

ARTICLE II. THE FUNERAL CHURCH OF THE PERSON WHO DIES OUTSIDE HIS PROPER PARISH

The Code in canon 1218 determines the funeral church in the event that death occurs while the individual is outside his proper parish. In the historical section it was seen that ever since its promulgation the decretal of Pope Boniface VIII (1294–1303) had governed till the promulgation of the Code the determination of the place of the funeral in this case. It had declared that if the person who had a domicile in a city, and sometimes went to a country place for recreation or indulgence in rural pursuits, were to die there without having chosen a place of burial, he was to be buried, not in the church of the country place, but in his parish church or rather in that church in which there long existed a tomb of his ancestors, provided that the body could without

---

[51] Cf. *infra*, pp. 103–120.

[52] Wernz-Vidal, *Ius Canonicum*, IV, Pars I, n. 600; Cappello, *Summa*, II, n. 722; Coronata, *De Locis et Temporibus Sacris*, n. 166.

[53] Cappello, *Summa*, II, n. 722.

danger be transported to that church.[54] Up to the promulgation of the Code, there was no determination by the Canon Law of the circumstances which could be considered as rendering such a transfer dangerous.[55] Among the commentators on the law, some held that the transfer had to be considered dangerous if a journey of one day were required to transport the body to the parish church of the deceased, while others left the determination regarding the presence of the danger to the judgment of a prudent man.[56]

A study of canon 1218 will indicate, on the one hand, that for the funeral the parish church is favored over all churches save that church which has been chosen legitimately by the deceased. On the other hand, the canon regulates more precisely than does the old law the circumstances which render the transfer to the parish church unnecessary, and makes it the business of each Ordinary to establish for his territory a norm by which it may be judged whether the transfer of the body to the parish church is burdensome or not. It also regulates the part the relatives may play in choosing the funeral church when the deceased has died outside his proper parish.

In the first paragraph of this canon, the legislator enacts the general rule in regard to the determination of the funeral church for the person who dies outside his proper parish. In this canon it is asserted that the body is to be transferred for the funeral to the deceased's nearest parochial church, if it can be transported to this church easily on foot; that, if it cannot, the body is to be transferred to the church of the parish in which the person died.

§ 1. **Licet mors acciderit extra propriam paroeciam, cadaver tamen in ecclesiam paroeciae propriae quae vicinior sit, ob funus transferendum est, si ad eam commode pedestri itinere asportari possit; secus in ecclesiam paroeciae in qua mors accidit.**

Death may occur while one is outside the boundaries of one's proper parish. Notwithstanding that fact, the Code still requires that the body be transported to the proper parish church. The

[54] C. 3, *de sepulturis,* III, 12, in VI°.

[55] Cf. *supra,* pp. 37–39.

[56] Cf. *supra,* pp. 37–39.

right of the proper parish to conduct the funeral of its parishioners is not lost *per se* when one of them dies outside its limits. The right is lost under two separate conditions, either of which suffices for the purpose. The first condition, which will be treated at some length in this article, is that the body cannot be transferred conveniently on foot to the church of a proper parish. The second condition, with which there is already some familiarity in the mind of the reader based on the foregoing, is that mentioned above,[57] namely, if the deceased has chosen as a funeral church a church other than his proper parish church. This condition always affects the right of the proper parish church to conduct the funeral. It was seen that it does so even if the parishioner has a single or several proper parishes and dies in one of them. *A fortiori* the selection of a funeral church will always determine the funeral church also in the event the parishioner dies outside his parish.[58]

In maintaining the right of the parish church to conduct the funeral of parishioners whether they die inside or outside the parish limits, except in the case of the choice of another, the Code agrees with the decretal of Pope Boniface VIII. However, that decretal further ordained that the body was to be transferred to the church in which there was an ancestral tomb, if there were such, rather than to the parish church. However, any precedence as a funeral church enjoyed by the church in which the ancestral tomb existed over the church of the proper parish by virtue of this decretal has been eliminated by the Code. In fact, not a trace of a right to be the funeral church of the church in which the ancestral tomb exists can be found in the Code.

The legislator in canon 1218 commands the body to be brought for the funeral to the deceased's nearest parochial church, should death occur outside the proper parish. Obviously, if the deceased had only a single proper parish, the body is to be transferred for the funeral to this church,[59] if it can be done easily on foot. If it cannot be so transferred, it is to be brought to the church of the parish in which death occurred.

57 Cf. *supra*, p. 76.

58 Cf. Coronata, *De Locis et Temporibus Sacris*, n. 167.

59 Rossi, *Sepultura Ecceslìastica*, n. 52.

The regulation of the Code covers more explicitly the case in which the deceased had several proper parishes and died outside the limits of all of them. The legislator rules, of course, that the body is to be transferred for the funeral "*in ecclesiam paroeciae propriae quae vicinior sit.*" Authors are not in agreement over the meaning of the clause, "*quae vicinior sit.*" The word, "*quae,*" can refer *per se* to "*ecclesiam*" or to "*paroeciae.*" If it refers to "*paroeciae,*" this part of the sentence must be translated "into the church of the nearer proper parish." If, on the contrary, it refers to "*ecclesiam,*" the meaning is that the body must be transferred "into the nearer proper parish church." A case in which the parish is nearer, but the church is farther away, and vice versa, can be readily imagined.

Coronata[60] maintains that "*quae*" refers to "*paroeciae.*" According to his interpretation, if one died a block south of his domiciliary parish whose church is a mile away at the far north end of the parish, and two blocks from his parish of quasi-domicile, whose church is only five blocks away, the body is to be transferred to the parish church of his domicile, because he died nearer to that parish. For his opinion, Coronata argues from the seeming parity with the second part of the same paragraph, where the same pronoun evidently is to be referred to the parish and not to the church.[61] He also states that his interpretation agrees with the rules of grammar which teach that the relative pronoun must be referred to the nearer word, or "*paroeciae*" in this instance.

However, it must be said that it is practically impossible to assent to such an interpretation, if the context and the end of the law are considered.[62] The context of canon 1218 emphasizes the transfer of the body for the funeral into a church, as is clear from the phrases, "*in ecclesiam,*" "*ad eam,*" and again, "*in ecclesiam.*" It is the church which is of prime interest. The end of the law obviously is to safeguard the right of the proper parish. How-

[60] *De Locis et Temporibus Sacris*, n. 167.

[61] ". . . secus in ecclesiam paroeciae in qua mors accidit."

[62] "Perspecto textu et contextu Codicis et fine legis attento, opinamur vocem esse referendam praesertim ad ecclesiam, ita ut haec principaliter, paroecia secundario spectanda sit."—Cappello, *Summa*, II, n. 723.

ever, if the body must always be transferred to the church of the nearer proper parish instead of the nearer proper parish church, it may happen frequently that neither proper parish will conduct the funeral since the church of the nearer parish may often lie beyond the distance within which the body can be brought to this church conveniently and on foot. The right of the proper parish—and it must be remembered that all proper parishes are of equal right—will always be protected as much as possible, if the body is required to be brought always to the deceased's nearest parochial church. Moreover, there does not seem to be a parity between the phrases "*quae vicinior sit*" and "*in qua mors accidit,*" because "*quae*" can modify "*ecclesiam*" or "*paroeciae,*" and "*in qua*" can refer only to "*paroeciae.*"

The rules of grammar do not necessarily strengthen Coronata's position. In fact, in this instance they rather favor the other opinion. It is true that in order to avoid any misunderstanding the relative pronoun is ordinarily placed as close as possible to the noun to which it refers. However, when it is placed after two nouns, it is not infrequently made to refer to the noun which is more remote, but which at the same time is the more important or which is in the foreground of interest.[63] In this canon, it is "*ecclesia*" which is the more remote of the nouns but, at the same time, the far more important. If the legislator intended a reference to "*paroeciae,*" would he not have said simply, "*in ecclesiam paroeciae propriae vicinioris*"? Hence, to the writer it appears that canon 1218 enacts a rule that continues to safeguard better the right of the proper parish and one that is more practical, if it is understood to command that when death occurs

[63] "Das Relativ schliesst sich in seiner Stellung, ebenso wie im Deutschen, naturgemäss möglichst an das Nomen an, auf welches es sich bezieht, um Missverständnisse zu vermeiden. Indes wird es nicht selten nach zwei genannten Nomen an das zwar ferner stehende aber wichtigere und im Vordergrunde des Interesses stehende Nomen angeschlossen. Von "Flüchtigkeit" oder "stilistischer Ungewandtheit" wird man in solchen Fällen kaum reden dürfen. So Caes, B. G. 7, 59, 2 *Bellovaci* defectione Aeduorum cognita, *qui* iam ante erant per se infideles . . . aperte bellum parare coeperunt."—Kühner-Stegmann, *Ausführliche Grammatik der lateinischen Sprache* (2. ed., 2 vols., Hannover, 1912-1914), II, 1 and 2, p. 286.

outside the proper parish the body is to be transferred for the funeral to the nearer parochial church of the deceased.[64]

Whenever death occurs outside the proper parish, the body is to be transferred for the funeral to the nearer parochial church of the deceased, if the body can be transferred to this church easily on foot. The contrast between the old law and the law of the Code will be immediately apparent if the two conditions are juxtaposed. The decretal of Pope Boniface reads: "*Dummodo* [*defunctus*] *ad ipsam* [*ecclesiam*] *absque periculo valeat asportari*"; the law of the Code: "*. . . si ad eam commode pedestri itinere asportari possit.*" The phrase "*pedestri itinere*" is new in the present law.

The word "*commode*" demands that the transferral of the body occur without difficulty or inconvenience. It appears to be a positive statement of the phrase in the old law, i.e., "*absque periculo.*" In itself, then, it does not seem to be more enlightening as to the determination of the conditions under which the transferral is to be made than was the old law. Prior to the promulgation of the Code, some authors felt that the transfer ought to be considered dangerous, if it required a day's journey; others left the determination regarding the presence of the danger to the judgment of a prudent man.[65]

To Rossi, "*commode*" signifies that it should be possible to transfer the body without burdening excessively the relatives or the mourners with the expenses of the transportation to the church.[66] Certainly, it may very well have this meaning. Many (+1922), in commenting on the pre-Code law, felt that consideration should be given to the expenses that would necessarily be incurred by the relatives when judgment would be rendered in regard to the meaning of "*absque periculo.*"[67]

Yet, in the present law the word is used in conjunction with

---

[64] Woywod, *A Practical Commentary on the Code of Canon Law,* II, 36; Cocchi, *Commentarium,* V, n. 57.

[65] Cf. *supra,* pp. 37–39.

[66] ". . . commode, cioè senza gravare delle spese di trasporto i parenti a dolenti di defunto, il che si rileva dal § 3 del canone 1218"—*Sepultura Ecclesiastica,* n. 52.

[67] Cf. *supra,* p. 38.

the phrase, "*pedestri itinere.*" This term indicates that the transfer of the body should occur not by railroad nor by automobile, but only and entirely on foot, and by a journey which is ordinarily not too burdensome to good health.[68] The words "on foot" are to be understood literally, since the transferral to the church ought to be carried out in procession according to the Roman Ritual.[69] Hence it refers to those who accompany the body. When "easily" then is used in conjunction with "on foot," it signifies first that regard must be paid to the streets through which the procession must necessarily pass on foot.[70]

To judge whether the transferral is inconvenient, the prime question is not whether the expenses for the relatives will be too heavy, although this may be a consideration, but whether the streets are such that a procession on foot can be carried out as the Ritual prescribes. Further, a procession on foot which would begin five miles away from the church, or which would last for two hours, could hardly be described as convenient. Such a distance would tax the strength of all in the procession. Further, all the morning hours would be spent by the priest and the other members of the cortège in going to the house in procession to receive the body and in returning in procession to the church to conduct the exequies, as they should do according to the Ritual. Such a procession could not be said to be conducted easily, even though the distance were not great, if it would have to be made quite circuitously, in order to avoid hills or narrow streets, or certain sections of an industrial city where commerce or traffic is heavy.

To obviate any debate which might arise concerning the nature of an inconvenient transferral, the Code in the second paragraph of canon 1218 declares that it is the business of the local Ordinaries to determine for their territories the circumstances which render such a transferral inconvenient.[71]

---

[68] Cappello, *Summa,* n. 723.

[69] Rituale Rom., tit. VI, c. 3, *Exsequiarum ordo,* n. 1; cf. Cocchi, *Commentarium,* V, n. 57; Rossi, *Sepultura Ecclesiastica,* n. 52; Coronata, *De Locis et Temporibus Sacris,* n. 168.

[70] Coronata, *De Locis et Temporibus Sacris,* n. 168.

[71] Canon 198, § 1: "In iure nomine Ordinarii intelliguntur, . . . praeter Romanum Pontificem, pro suo quisque territorio Episcopus residentialis,

§ 2: **Ordinarii est pro suo territorio, inspectis peculiaribus circumstantiis, distantiam aliaque adiuncta designare, quae translationem cadaveris ad ecclesiam funeris aut locum sepulturae incommodam redeant; et si paroeciae ad diversas dioeceses pertineant, designatio attenditur Ordinarii dioecesis in qua defunctus supremum diem obiit.**

After having considered the peculiar circumstances in his territory, the local Ordinary is to designate the distance and other related details which render burdensome the transferral of the corpse to the funeral church or to the place of burial.[72] This designation can be established by diocesan law or by special decree.[73] From a consideration of the words of the canon, it seems that the designation ought to be made once for all, but if the law or decree has not been issued, nothing forbids the local Ordinary to determine whether the circumstances render the transferral inconvenient in individual cases.[74] However, Coronata asserts that if the local Ordinary makes this determination only as each individual case occurs, a practice will arise which seems to him not exactly in conformity with the Code, since a norm established in this way can open the way to the resentment of his subjects and a display of favoritism on the part of the local Ordinary.[75]

The local Ordinary, among the other circumstances, is required to determine the distance which renders the transferral burdensome. Whereas among the commentators on the pre-Code law

---

Abbas vel Praelatus nullius eorumque Vicarius Generalis, Administrator, Vicarius et Praefectus Apostolicus, itemque ii qui praedictis deficientibus interim ex iuris praescripto aut ex probatis constitutionibus succedunt pro regimine. . . ."

[72] ". . . quae determinatio erit authentica, eidemque standum erit ad iuris effectus, adversus quam tamen, si esset erronea, daretur locus recursui ad S. Concilii Congregationem, imo illa designatio subiecta esset mutationi in futurum ob circumstantiarum variationem."—Blat, *Commentarium Textus Codicis Iuris Canonici* (6 vols., Romae: "Collegio Angelico," 1921–1927 [Lib. III, *De Rebus*, Romae: "Collegio Angelico," 1923]), III, Pars II–VI, n. 76 (hereafter this work is cited *Commentarium*).

[73] Cappello, *Summa*, n. 724.

[74] Cappello, *loc. cit.*

[75] *De Locis et Temporibus Sacris*, n. 168.

it was a frequent opinion that a day's journey would render a transfer inconvenient, the distance sufficient to meet this requirement is lessened very much by the Code.[76] As has been remarked above, when one speaks of a procession on foot, attention must to be paid to the length of the streets through which the procession must pass. It seems almost too obvious to say that the distance from the place where the body is reserved previous to the procession to the funeral church must not be measured as the crow flies, but that the whole route of the procession must be considered. One could easily conceive of a person dying in a hilly country, one mile by air route from his proper parish church, and yet three miles from it if the length of the streets through which the procession must pass is measured.[77]

Cappello[78] records that many authors judge that a distance of one or two kilometers from the place where the body is reserved to the funeral church makes the transferral inconvenient. He rather agrees with the few who think that three kilometers[79] is not too far, if other conditions are perfect. Cocchi notes that the distance specified in the Archdiocese of Genoa is of three kilometers.[80] In this country, where there has been a custom of not holding the procession from the home to the church, the determination of the distance in the majority of cases has not yet been made. Beste asserts that, as long as that determination is lacking, it is permissible to follow the local custom.[81]

---

76 ". . . attendendum est autem in hac re ad mores quarundam regionum."—Cocchi, *Commentarium,* V, n. 57; Augustine, *A Commentary on the New Code of Canon Law* (8 vols., St. Louis: Herder, 1931-1938 [Vol. VI, 3 ed., *Administrative Law,* 1936]), VI, 119 (hereafter this work is cited *A Commentary on Canon Law*).

77 Cf. Coronata, *De Locis et Temporibus Sacris,* n. 168, nota 1; "In distantia aliisque circumstantiis perpendendis circa exsistentiam incommodi necne, plura practice sunt attendenda praesertim asperitas viarum."—Cappello, *Summa,* II, n. 724.

78 *Loc. cit.*

79 A kilometer is five eighths of a mile; hence, about two miles.

80 "In Archidioecesi Genuensi iter commodum pedestre statutum est quod sit infra distantiam trium chilometrorum."—*Commentarium,* V, no. 57.

81 "Apud nos determinatio distantiae plerumque nondum facta est et ideo, in eius defectu, sequi licet consuetudinem."—Beste, *Introductio in Codicem,* Commentary on canon 1218, § 2.

Not only the distance, but also other circumstances are to be weighed before one forms a judgment as to what conditions will render the transferral inconvenient. The peculiar circumstances of places and persons, which vary so much if a mountainous or a level region, an industrial or a farming community, a wealthy or a poverty-stricken group, are under consideration, will evidently lead to the formation of different norms of action. Blat [82] gives consideration also to the seasons of the year and the causes of death. And although it may be thought by some [83] that the amount of expense involved is too insecure and uncertain a basis for forming a criterion in this matter, it must be admitted with Cocchi [84] and Rossi [85] that it is one of the more important circumstances relevant to his judgment and therefore to be considered by the local Ordinary.

Parishes may lie along the boundaries of dioceses; in fact, parishes belonging to different dioceses may often be contiguous. Members of a parish in one diocese may die in a neighboring parish which is in another diocese. The Code commands that, in case the parishes belong to different dioceses, the designation of what constitutes an inconvenient transferral as indicated by the Ordinary of the diocese where the death occurred is to be the norm for determining which church will be the funeral church.

Canon 1218, § 3: **Licet translatio ad ecclesiam funeris aut ad locum sepulturae incommoda sit, semper tamen integrum est familiae, heredibus aliisve quorum interest, cadaver illuc deferre, susceptis translationis expensis.**

To the family, the heirs, and to others who are interested, the canon gives the right to transfer the body to the funeral church or to the place of burial as long as they pay the expenses, even though the transferral of the body to either of these is inconvenient. The first paragraph of this canon states that if the

---

82 *Commentarium,* III, Pars II–VI, n. 76.

83 Coronata, *De Locis et Temporibus Sacris,* n. 168, nota 1.

84 *Commentarium,* V, n. 57.

85 *Sepultura Ecclesiastica,* n. 52.

transferral to the nearer proper parish church would be inconvenient, the body ought to be transferred to the church of the parish where the death occurred. This third paragraph, in the circumstances noted in it, withdraws from the church where death occurred the right to conduct the funeral. Hence, if there are several proper parish churches and it is inconvenient to transfer the body to any of them, it must be left to the relatives to determine to which of the churches of these several parishes the body will be transferred. None of the churches of the proper parishes has an absolute right to be called the particular funeral church in this case, since it is inconvenient to transfer the body to any of them. Neither has the church of the parish where death occurred a right to be called the particular funeral church, since the relatives are given complete discretion, as long as they pay the expenses, to transfer the body to a funeral church, which may be any one of the churches of the several proper parishes. They may even select the proper parish church that is the farthest away, for the Code rules that the body is to be transferred to the nearer proper parish church only if it can be transported there easily in procession.[86] If the relatives do not care to pay the expenses or are not interested in the transferral of the body for the funeral to one of the churches of the proper parishes, the body should be transported to the church in the parish in which the death occurred.

The terms used in regard to those to whom the right is given are so general that no one seems to be excluded from transferring the body to the funeral church as long as he pays the expenses. " Family " includes the immediate kindred; the " heirs," those who receive any of the property of the deceased. " Those who are interested " may be those persons who are related in any degree of consanguinity or affinity, the friends of the deceased, confraternities, burial societies, other pious unions, county welfare boards, city poor commissions, in fact any moral person, whether ecclesiastical or civil.[87]

---

[86] Cf. Cocchi, *Commentarium,* V, n. 57: " Si paroeciae propriae sint plures, familia vel heredes aliive possunt ex eisdem unam vel alteram pro lubitu eligere, in quam defunctus sit transferendus."—Cappello, *Summa,* II, n. 724.

[87] Cf. Cappello, *Summa,* II, n. 724.

The rule which the local Ordinary constitutes as a norm for determining whether or not a transfer is inconvenient is also subject to the provision of this third paragraph. On the other hand, when the transfer of the body to a single proper parish church, or to the nearer proper parish church in case there are several, is convenient, it is not within the power of the interested persons to decide whether or not they will transfer the body to the proper funeral church designated by the common law. The right of the proper parish church to conduct the funeral is established. The fact that the relatives will pay the expenses for the transfer of the body to a church of their own choosing or to the church where the family burial lot is located does not give them the license to disregard the right of the proper parish.

Canon 1218, then, determines the funeral church for the person who has died outside his proper parish. First, the deceased who has one proper parish is to be transferred for the funeral to the church of this parish if transferral on foot according to the Ritual can be easily made. Even if it cannot, the interested persons have the right to transfer the body to that church, as long as they pay the expenses. If the relatives or others do not care to exercise their right, the body is to be transferred to the church of the parish in which the person died. Secondly, he who has several proper parishes, but dies outside the limits of all of them, is to be transferred for the funeral to his nearest parish church, if this transferral can be made conveniently. If it cannot, his relatives or any others interested in him may transfer the body to any one of his parish churches they may select, provided, of course, that they have undertaken to pay the expenses. If they are not interested in having the body transferred to any of those churches, or in assuming the expenses, the body is to be brought for the funeral to the church of the parish in which the deceased died.

The following diagram may be of some assistance for remembering the diverse provisions of canons 1216–1218 in regard to the determination of the funeral church.

<table>
<tr><th colspan="3">IF THE DECEASED</th><th>THE FUNERAL CHURCH IS</th></tr>
<tr><td colspan="3">1. Had only one proper parish and died in it</td><td>The parochial church</td></tr>
<tr><td colspan="3">2. Had several proper parishes and died in one of them</td><td>The parochial church of the parish where he died</td></tr>
<tr><td rowspan="4">3. Died outside the one proper parish or several proper parishes.</td><td colspan="2">A. Either he had a single proper parish and the body can be transferred easily in a funeral procession</td><td>The parochial church of his proper parish</td></tr>
<tr><td colspan="2">B. Or he had several proper parishes to whose churches he can be transferred easily in a funeral procession</td><td>His own parochial church nearest to the place of death</td></tr>
<tr><td rowspan="2">C. Or he died so far from his proper parish or proper parishes that the transfer is inconvenient</td><td>1. If his relatives transport the body</td><td>The parochial church of the proper parish which the relatives select</td></tr>
<tr><td>2. If they do not care to transport the body</td><td>The parochial church of the parish where the person died</td></tr>
<tr><td colspan="3">4. Was a wanderer (had neither a domicile nor a quasi-domicile) or a person who had only a diocesan domicile or quasi-domicile.</td><td>The parochial church of the parish where the person died</td></tr>
</table>

CHAPTER V

THE FUNERAL CHURCH SPECIFICALLY SELECTED

To the entire ordinary law in regard to the funeral church, the Code places the condition, "*nisi defunctus aliam funeris ecclesiam legitime elegerit.*" The free choice of burial on the part of the faithful is of ancient institution, being regarded from the time of Pope St. Gregory the Great (590–604) as a part of one's last will and testament.[1] The Code in canons 1223–1227, where it is determined what qualifications are required on the part of the subject entitled to make the choice, which churches may be chosen, how the choice is to be made, and with what freedom, has repeated to a very great extent the law in existence prior to its promulgation. However, there are a number of instances in which the old law has been clarified with the result that several controversies found in the works of the pre-Code authors are eliminated. These instances will be pointed out in the commentary of canons 1223–1227 which follows immediately.

ARTICLE I. THE SUBJECT OF SELECTION

A. The Persons Capable of Choosing

Canon 1223, § 1: **Omnibus licet, nisi expresse iure prohibeantur, eligere ecclesiam sui funeris aut coemeterium sepulturae.**

§ 2: **Uxor et filii puberes in hac electione prorsus immunes sunt a maritali vel patria potestate.**

In the first paragraph of canon 1223 the Church grants to all the faithful the right to choose the church of the funeral or the cemetery of burial, unless they are expressly forbidden to do so

[1] Cf. *supra*, p. 11.

by the law. There is a double object of this choice. First, the funeral church or the church wherein the exequies are held may be selected. It will be remembered that the exequies are those acts which begin at the entrance to the church and are completed as the rite of the interment begins.[2] Secondly, the cemetery where the burial is to occur may be chosen. The two objects are obviously distinct. The use of the disjunctive correlative "*aut*" emphasizes the distinction. Canon 1231, § 1,[3] of course, does order the body to be buried, after the exequies have been completed in the church, in the cemetery of the funeral church, if a cemetery or tomb has not been chosen, or if there is not a family tomb. Yet, there is not such an intimate connection between the two that the choice of one inherently involves the choice of the other. Each choice may be made independently of the other. There is a double right, therefore, which the faithful may exercise. They have the right to select the funeral church, unless it is expressly forbidden to them, and also the right to select the cemetery of burial.

All the faithful, except those expressly forbidden by law, possess these rights. The right to choose for another is not granted by the law to any one except in one instance.[4] The introduction in canon 1223, § 1, of the word "*sui*" as modifying "*funeris*" gives clarity to the canon which cannot be denied. Each may choose only for himself. The relatives of the deceased cannot choose his funeral church unless he has authorized them to act in his stead.[5] In that event they must be able to prove that they have received a mandate from him. Although they may be good witnesses for the fact that a choice has been made and naturally would be the persons selected by the deceased as the bearers of his mandate, it does not follow that, if the deceased made no choice and did not authorize anyone else to make the choice for him,

---

[2] Cf. *supra*, p. 68.

[3] "Expletis in ecclesia exsequiis, cadaver tumulandum est ad normam librorum liturgicorum in coemeterio ecclesiae funeris, salvis praescriptis can. 1228, 1229."

[4] C. 1224, 1o; cf. *infra*, p. 106.

[5] C. 1226; cf. *infra*, p. 112.

the relatives or heirs may supply the omission and exercise the choice without showing any authority for it.[6]

The Code grants to every one, unless he is expressly prohibited, the right to choose either the funeral church or the cemetery of burial. In addition, in the second paragraph of canon 1223 it expresses succinctly the law in regard to the freedom of choice on the part of the wife, as found in the decretal of Pope Lucius III (1181–1185),[7] and on the part of those who have attained the age of puberty, as stated in the decretal of Pope Boniface VIII (1294–1303).[8] In the exercise of this choice, the wife is free from the domination of her husband, and the children who have attained the age of puberty[9] enjoy immunity from their father's authority.

If they have not selected a funeral church or a place for their burial, the wife and also the children who have attained the age of puberty, since they are completely free to make such a selection, are subject to the ordinary law contained in canons 1216–1218. Hence the husband cannot choose either the funeral church or the place of burial for the wife, nor can the father or guardian choose either the one or the other for his sons or male wards who have completed their fourteenth year of age or for the daughters or female wards who have completed their twelfth year. Of course, the husband or the father may transfer the bodies of the deceased wife and children respectively for mere burial to a family tomb,[10] but this is by no means an exercise of the right to make the selection for a wife or for such children on the part of the husband or the father.

B. The Persons Incapable of Choosing

Canon 1224: **Ecclesiam funeris aut sepulturae coemeterium eligere prohibentur:**

---

[6] S. C. C., *Dianen.*, 9 iul. 1921—*AAS,* XIII (1921), 535; reported in Bouscaren, *The Canon Law Digest,* I, 573.

[7] Cf. *supra,* p. 18.

[8] Cf. *supra,* p. 16.

[9] C. 88, § 2; "Minor, si masculus, censetur pubes a decimoquarto, si femina, a duodecimo anno completo."

[10] C. 1229, §§ 1, 2.

1. **Impuberes; verum pro filio aut filia impubere, etiam post eorum mortem, hanc electionem facere possunt parentes vel tutor;**
2. **Religiosi professi cuiuslibet gradus aut dignitatis, non tamen si sunt Episcopi.**

This canon indicates those to whom it is forbidden by law to choose the funeral church or the cemetery of burial. From the very beginning of the history of this institute, those who had not attained the age of puberty have been barred from choosing the place of burial. The choice, as previously noted, was founded on the capacity to make a last will. Since those under the age of puberty were never judged capable of this act, they were excluded also from making any choice in regard to the place of their ecclesiastical burial. The pre-Code law held that the father could make the selection for them, if custom approved such parental intervention; that the mother could also select the place of burial for them, if customary usage allowed her to do so. In this canon, the right to choose either the funeral church or the cemetery of burial for those under the age of puberty is granted unconditionally to the parents. Of old, also, the choice had to be made by the father while the child was alive. The dispute relative to the exercise of the right to choose after the death of the children which existed among pre-Code authors is ended by the present canon, since it concedes the right to the parents to make this choice for those under the age of puberty even when the latter have died.

The parents as well as the guardian can exercise this right. The father and mother obviously are directly intended as the recipients of this faculty. Coronata,[11] Wernz-Vidal,[12] Cappello,[13] and Beste[14] believe that the term *parentes* is to be extended to include the grandfather and the grandmother. Since in another matter in which the interests of the grandparents are the same as those of the parents the Code uses the term "*parentes*" to include the grandparents,[15] it seems that the opinion which would exclude

[11] *De Locis et Temporibus Sacris,* n. 191.

[12] *Ius Canonicum,* IV, Pars I, n. 594.

[13] *Summa,* II, n. 733.

[14] *Introductio in Codicem,* Commentary on c. 1224.

[15] C. 542, 2o: "Illicite, sed valide admittuntur: . . . Filii qui parentibus, idest

the grandparents from making the selection should be rejected.[16]

Besides those who have not attained the age of puberty, professed religious of any grade or dignity, except bishops, are forbidden by law from selecting the funeral church or the cemetery of burial. Not all religious are deprived of the right to make such a choice, but only those who have made profession either of solemn or of simple vows, or even of temporary vows. Novices[17] and postulants are not bound by this prohibition; nor are those who have obtained an indult of secularization, or have been expelled or dismissed from their institute.[18] On the contrary, those who have obtained the indult of exclaustration remain bound by this law,[19] as do the apostates and fugitives[20] even though they are still unabsolved from their incurred censure.[21]

Although by the prescriptions of the law in existence before 1918 it was forbidden to the regular clergy to choose their place of burial, "*cum velle et nolle non habeant,*" yet this right was granted to those religious who died at such a long distance from their religious houses that they could not be easily transferred to their monasteries for burial.[22] This right has been removed in the Code, since no such exception is granted in canon 1221, § 1. Furthermore, the law commands that the funerals of men religious if they die far away from home and if their bodies cannot be transferred easily to the church of their own religious house, or at least to a church of their institute, be celebrated in the church

---

patri vel matri, avo vel aviae, in gravi necessitate constitutis, opitulari debent, et parentes quorum opera sit ad liberos alendos vel educandos necessaria."

[16] Cf. Rossi, *Sepultura Ecclesiastica,* n. 58; Woywod, *A Practical Commentary on the Code of Canon Law,* II, p. 38.

[17] C. 1221, § 1: "Professi religiosi ac novitii, defuncti cum sint, transferendi sunt, funeris causa, ad ecclesiam vel oratorium suae domus vel saltem suae religionis, nisi novitii aliam ecclesiam ad suum funus elegerint."

[18] Coronata, *De Locis et Temporibus Sacris,* n. 191; Rossi, *Sepultura Ecclesiastica,* n. 58.

[19] Coronata, *De Locis et Temporibus Sacris,* n. 191; Rossi, *Sepultura Ecclesiastica,* n. 58.

[20] Cc. 644, 645.

[21] Rossi, *Sepultura Ecclesiastica,* n. 58; Coronata, *De Locis et Temporibus Sacris,* n. 191.

[22] C. 5, *de sepulturis,* III, 12, in VI°; cf. *supra,* p. 17 .

of the parish where they die, unless in the case of the novice the latter has selected another church for his funeral. For the funeral the superior can always have the body transfrered to a church of that particular institute, even though the transfer be budensome.[23]

Among ancient canonists, the right to select the place of burial was conceded to abbots and major superiors.[24] Because the Code uses simply the term "*Episcopi,*" the right to make the selection of the funeral church or of the place of burial must be understood to be granted to those religious who are titular bishops as well as to those who are residential bishops. Vicars apostolic and prefects apostolic,[25] and also abbots *nullius* and prelates *nullius,*[26] seem to be granted the same right.

There must be included among those who are forbidden to choose either the funeral church or the place of burial all individuals who are incapable of eliciting a human act and who are deprived by law of the right of receiving ecclesiastical burial.[27]

Among the authors it is disputed whether the word "*prohibentur*" of canon 1224 signifies that the choice made by those who have not attained the age of puberty or by religious is both illicit and invalid, or simply illicit. Coronata [28] believes that such a choice, if made by a religious of simple vows, is simply illicit, and that the solemnly professed can probably make the same choice with the permission of their superiors. However, if consideration be given to the history of this canon [29] as well as to other canons of the Code, it must be affirmed that the selection made by those

---

[23] C. 1221, § 2: "Si longe moriantur a domo, ita ut in ecclesiam suae domus vel saltem suae religionis nequeant commode asportari, funerandi sunt in ecclesia paroeciae ubi decedunt, nisi novitius aliam ecclesiam ad funus elegerit, et salvo Superioribus iure de quo in can. 1218, § 3."

[24] Panormitanus, *Commentaria,* ad c. 7, III, 28, n. 5.

[25] C. 294, § 1.

[26] Wernz-Vidal, *Ius Canonicum,* IV, Pars I, n. 594, nota 63.

[27] Coronata, *De Locis et Temporibus Sacris,* n. 191; Cocchi, *Commentarium,* V, n. 59; Wernz-Vidal, *Ius Canonicum,* IV, Pars I, n. 594, nota 65; Cappello, *Summa,* II, n. 733.

[28] Coronata, *De Locis et Temporibus Sacris,* n. 191.

[29] C. 10, X, *de sepulturis,* III, 28; c. 4, *de sepulturis,* III, 12 in VI°; Innocent X, const. "*Ex iniuncto,*" 22 febr. 1645, P. 6—*Fontes,* n. 230; S. C. C., *Ilcinen.,* 24 febr. 1872, 25 ian. 1873—*Fontes,* n. 4221, 4223.

prohibited by law is invalid. As Wernz-Vidal and Rossi state, the "*licet*" which is used in canon 1223 does not signify a simple permission, nor does it refer to the mere goodness of an act, but it denotes a juridical power or the right to place the act of choice for all those who are not forbidden by the law. Whoever is forbidden to choose the funeral church or the cemetery of burial simply does not have that right or juridical power.[80] In other words, they are juridically incapable of selecting the funeral church of the cemetery of burial.[81] If professed religious and those who are under the age of puberty make such a selection, they act invalidly. Moreover, it is very difficult to understand how solemnly professed religious, even with the permission of their superiors, could make a selection validly, since the superiors have no power to change the common law and the Superiors themselves could not select a place of burial for their subjects other than that permitted by the law.

ARTICLE II. THE FUNERAL CHURCHES WHICH MAY BE SELECTED

Canon 1225: **Ut electio ecclesiae funeris valeat, cadat necesse est vel in ecclesiam paroecialem, vel in ecclesiam regularium, non tamen monialium (nisi agatur de mulieribus quae famulatus, educationis, infirmitatis aut hospitii causa intra clausuram eiusdem monasterii non precario commorabantur), vel in ecclesiam iuris patronatus, si agatur de patrono, vel in aliam ecclesiam funerandi iure praeditam.**

The Code in canon 1225 deals only with the selection of the funeral church, that is, of the church in which the Requiem Mass and the Absolution over the deceased person are to be celebrated. There is no question, therefore, of the selection of a place of burial, of a cemetery, or of a particular grave.

To be a valid choice, the church selected must be either a parochial church, a church of the regular clergy, that is, of those who make solemn vows, or some other church endowed with the

[80] Wernz-Vidal, *Ius Canonicum,* IV, Pars I, n. 594; Rossi, *Sepultura Ecclesiastica,* n. 61.

[81] C. 11.

right to conduct the exequies. Further, the church of a monastery of nuns may be chosen by women who dwell within the enclosure of the monastery not merely in a transient or passing manner, but in view of service, education, illness or hospitality. The church over which he has the right of patronage may be chosen by the patron.

Any parish church may be chosen validly, whether it be conducted by the secular or by the religious clergy. It is of no importance whether it is a purely territorial parish or a national parish. Consequently, the person who makes the selection need not be of the same nationality as the members of the parish whose church he has chosen.[32] Thus a member of a purely territorial English-speaking parish may choose as his funeral church the church of a parish founded for those of any nationality.

The privilege of being chosen as a place of burial was granted in the old law to the churches of the regular clergy. Pope Clement IV (1265–1268) granted it to the Friars Minor; Pope Boniface VIII (1294–1303), to the Order of Preachers and the Hermits of St. Augustine.[33] Others obtained the privilege indirectly by way of participation in it with those to whom it had been conceded directly. In the present law, it is exclusively the churches of the regular clergy among the religious that may be chosen validly as funeral churches. Hence, the choice of a church belonging to even an exempt clerical congregation cannot be made validly according to the common law.

Other churches may acquire the right of conducting the exequies. This right may be obtained through apostolic privilege, through the concession of the bishop whether it be granted in or outside diocesan synod, through lawful custom, and also through legal prescription.[34] Not infrequently the right to conduct the exequies is given to various public or semi-public oratories, but at the same

---

[32] Schaaf, "*Right to Choose Church of Funeral,*" *AER,* XCIV (1936), 309.

[33] Cf. *supra,* p. 8.

[34] "Ad ius quod attinet: . . . Funerandi autem ius multipliciter acquiri potest, S. Sedis nempe aut Ordinarii concessione, legitima consuetudine et praescriptione."—S. C. C., *Gallipolitana,* 24 maii et 15 nov. 1930—*AAS,* XXV (1933), 157.

time it may be limited by certain restrictions, for example, requiring that it be exercised for only those who constantly dwell in a hospital or are students in a college. In these instances only those for whose benefit the right was conceded may choose the oratory as their funeral church.

The churches of nuns may not be chosen by men at any time, or even by women generally.[35] Four classes of women, namely, those who are servants of the nuns, those who receive their education in the monastery, those who because of ill health or of old age are nursed by the nuns, and those who live in the monastery as in a guest house, may select the church or the oratory of the convent as their funeral church. However, this selection may be made by those persons only on condition that they dwell within the cloister of the monastery in a permanent manner. One must be judged to dwell *non precario* in any place if one has lived there for some weeks, or at least for a number of days, with the intention of residing there a long time.[36] Since the law does not insist in this instance that they must have died within the monastery, such women can choose the church of the nuns as their funeral church even if they die outside the enclosure. On the other hand, if they do not exercise their right to select this church, their bodies must be brought to the church of their proper parish for the funeral.

---

[35] A definition of nuns is thus furnished in canon 488, 7°: ". . . *monialium,* religiosae votorum solemnium, aut, nisi ex rei natura vel ex contextu sermonis aliud constet, religiosae quarum vota ex instituto sunt solemnia, sed pro aliquibus locis ex Apostolicae Sedis praescripto sunt simplicia."

[36] Cappello, *Summa,* II, n. 732; "Non praecario commorabantur,—idest, non transeunter, sed saltem ab una alterave hebdomada diu noctuque ibi degebant."—Beste, *Introductio in Codicem,* Commentary on c. 1225; "Si iam ab aliquibus hebdomadibus commorabantur."—Cocchi, *Commentarium,* V, n. 59; "Etiam advertenda, pro mulieribus intra clausuram commorantibus, illa pericopes "non precario," qua datur intelligi, commorationem unius vel alterius diei, etiam diu noctuque, non sufficere ad eligendam ecclesiam monialium pro funere: sed requiri commoratio satis diuturna et quasi in perpetuum."—Fanfani, *De Iure Religiosorum ad Normam Codicis Iuris Canonici* (2 ed., Taurini-Romae: Marietti, 1925), n. 422 bis (hereafter this work is cited *De Iure Religiosorum*).

ARTICLE III. THE MODE OF SELECTING THE FUNERAL CHURCH; THE PROOF OF THE SELECTION

Canon 1226, § 1: **Ecclesiam funeris aut coemeterium sepulturae quis eligere potest per se vel per alium cui legitimum mandatum dederit; factamque electionem aut mandati concessionem quolibet legitimo modo probare licet.**

§ 2: **Si electio fiat per alium, hic suum mandatum explere potest etiam post mortem mandantis.**

The legislator, still intent on maintaining parochial rights, determines the manner in which the choice of the funeral church or the cemetery of burial may be made validly. The choice of the funeral church, which is to be made only by and for the individual, is a personal matter.[37] A person must make clear his own express will, or give to some one an explicit mandate to make the choice for him. Others, whether relatives, heirs or friends, acting either on the assumption that they know the mind of the deceased, or as if they had a presumed or interpretative mandate, will act invalidly in making the selection. If the relatives and others after the death of the deceased could without a mandate act validly in making the choice, there would be no case in which a choice could not be made, and thus there would be nullified the rights of pastors which the Code has wished to preserve.[38] In other words, since the choice of the funeral church outside one's proper parish limits the rights and the revenue of the pastors, it is evidently a matter of strict interpretation. Since, moreover, the established law has

---

[37] "*Ad ius quod attinet:* ". . . Ius eligendi ecclesiam funeris ex citato canone 1226, § 1, ad unum defunctum, non ad heredes pertinet, nisi legitimum mandatum acceperint. . . ."—S. C. C., *Gallipolitana,* 24 maii et 15 nov. 1930—*AAS,* XXV (1933), 157.

[38] "*Animadversiones:* ". . . non illud tamen sequitur, si defunctus de re nullam expresserit voluntatem, nullumque illis contulerit mandatum, consanguineorum esse talem defuncti omissionem supplere quasi praesumptum vel interpretativum mandatum habentium. Secus nullus esset casus in quo electio non intercederet, ac propterea actum esset de iuribus parochorum quae immo Codex sarta esse voluit."—S. C. C., *Dianen.,* 9 iul. 1921—*AAS,* XIII (1921), 535; reported in Bouscaren, *The Canon Law Digest,* I, 573.

attributed the faculty for selection in this instance to no other will than to that of the deceased, the arbitrary selection made by other persons cannot determine the place of burial, nor is any one permitted to select the place of burial for the deceased unless he has proved that he has a mandate to make the selection for the deceased.[39]

The choice must be a manifest expression of one's will, not of a mere desire, or preference or hint.[40] As has been mentioned, the act of selection in this instance is founded historically in the right to make a last will and testament. In one's last will, there is expected to appear a distinct disclosure of one's intention. On the other hand, there are not demanded all the solemnities which the law requires for the making of a valid last will.[41]

The choice may be made in writing, by word, or even by a nod, if the person cannot speak. A special form is not necessary; it is required only that it be sufficiently clear that the deceased has really elicited a choice or has in fact given a mandate.[42]

The choice may be made either explicitly or implicitly. An explicit choice occurs when one directly chooses the funeral church by himself or through another to whom he has given a mandate. One chooses implicitly when one, for example, gives his name to a confraternity whose church has the right to conduct the exequies, if by the very fact that he has joined a confraternity he is judged from the statutes of this group to have chosen the church of the confraternity as his funeral church. At the same time, however, it must be clear that it is customary for all the members of the confraternity to have their funerals in that church.[43] On the other

[39] *Loc. cit.*

[40] Coronata, *De Locis et Temporibus Sacris*, n. 195; Cocchi, *Commentarium*, V, n. 59.

[41] Cocchi, *Commentarium*, n. 59; Rossi, *Sepultura Ecclesiastica*, n. 57.

[42] S. R. Rota, *Sanctissimae Conceptionis de Chile*, 1 dec. 1930: "IN IURE: . . . Unde patet nullam esse solemnitatem electionis, i.e., formam eligendi sub nullitate praeceptam; quod est dicere validitatem electionis nullo pacto pendere ab eius probatione. . . ."—*Sacrae Romanae Rotae Decisiones seu Sententiae* (24 vols., Romae: Typis Polyglottis Vaticanis, 1912–1940), XXII (1930), 635.

[43] S. C. C., *Gallipolitana*, 24 maii et 15 nov. 1930—*AAS*, XXV (1933), 157; reported in Bouscaren, *The Canon Law Digest*, I, 576.

hand, the mere enrollment as a member of a confraternity does not imply a legitimate selection of the church of the confraternity as a funeral church, since the membership in a confraternity and the selection of the confraternity church as a funeral church are two very diverse matters not necessarily closely related to each other. Moreover, it is a fact that not all confraternities enjoy the right to conduct the exequies of their members in their churches.[44]

The selection of the funeral church or the commission of the mandate can be proved in any legitimate way. The selection of the funeral church and the concession of the mandate are facts, and as such they must not be presumed, but rather must be proved. Their proof may be established judicially[45] or extrajudicially.[46] They may be established through written public documents, or private writings,[47] such as personal letters,[48] and wills, even if these last are invalid,[49] through witnesses,[50] and even one witness and the confessor, if there are other presumptions and as long as no special reasons are present for considering their testimony as suspect.[51] The testimony of the pastor alone, as long as it does not favor himself, is sufficient.[52] The relatives of the deceased and the heirs are not to be excluded as witnesses; in fact, in this

---

[44] *Loc. cit.* Cf. also Cappello, "Annotationes," *Periodica,* XXII (1933), 149.

[45] S. C. C., *Dianen.,* 9 iul. 1921—*AAS,* XIII (1921), 535.

[46] Cocchi, *Commentarium,* V, n. 59; Blat, *Commentarium,* III, Pars II-VI, n. 84.

[47] Beste, *Introductio in Codicem,* Commentary on can. 1226.

[48] Wernz-Vidal, *Ius Canonicum,* IV, Pars I, n. 596: ". . . dummodo constet (scripturam) esse illius qui sepulturam elegit."—Coronata, *De Locis et Temporibus Sacris,* n. 195.

[49] Coronata, *De Locis et Temporibus Sacris,* n. 195.

[50] S. C. C., *Dianen.,* 9 iul, 1921: "*Animadversiones:* . . . Ast exinde hoc unum sequitur, credendum quidem sane, donec contrarium probetur, consanguineis vel heredibus testantibus de voluntate defuncti quoad electionem sepulturae, vel asserentibus se de hac re mandatum accepisse a defuncto: optimi enimvero testes voluntatis defuncti sunt consanguinei et heredes, et probatio per testes est quidem iuridica probatio (cfr. can. 1791, § 2);"—*AAS,* XIII (1921), 535.

[51] Wernz-Vidal, Ius Canonicum, IV, Pars I, n. 596.

[52] Beste, *Introductio in Codicem,* Commentary on can. 1226; Coronata, *De Locis et Temporibus Sacris,* n. 195.

matter, knowledge of which is so often exclusively within the province of the family, they should be considered the very best witnesses.[53]

Prior to the promulgation of the Code it was thought by some authors that the proxy had to carry out his commission before the death of the principal.[54] The second paragraph of canon 1226 ends the controversy that existed by declaring that the proxy can execute his mandate regarding the choice of the funeral church or of the cemetery of burial even after the death of the person who commissioned him.

ARTICLE IV. THE FREEDOM TO SELECT THE FUNERAL CHURCH

To insure the freedom of choice in regard to the funeral church and the cemetery of burial, the Code in canon 1227 repeats almost word for word the decretal of Pope Boniface VIII:

> **Religiosi et clerici saeculares districte vetantur ne quos ad vovendum, iurandum vel fide interposita seu aliter promittendum inducant ut apud ipsorum ecclesias funus aut apud ipsorum coemeterium sepulturam eligant, vel factam electionem non immutent; quod si contra factum fuerit, electio sit nulla.**[55]

The canon severely forbids religious and the secular clergy to induce any one to vow, swear, or to promise, either with an attendant obligation of fidelity [56] or otherwise, to select their church for the funeral, or their cemetery for the burial, or not to modify a choice once made. Should the clergy or the religious act contrary to this law, the choice is null and void.

The prohibition concerns the secular clergy, that is, those who have received at least the first tonsure, and all religious, hence even nuns and sisters.[57] Even the pastors of parishes, in which

---

[53] S. C. C., *Dianen.*, 9 iul. 1921—*AAS*, XIII (1921), 535.

[54] Pirhing, lib III, tit. 28, n. 28.

[55] C. 1, *de sepulturis*, III, 12, in VI°.

[56] ". . . fide interposita"—i.e.—" formali fidelitatis obligatione suscepta."—Blat, *Commentarium*, III, Pars II-VI, n. 85.

[57] Cappello, *Summa*, II, n. 735; Ayrinhac, *Administrative Legislation in the New Code of Canon Law*, n. 67.

the parishioners according to the law are to receive ecclesiastical burial, that is, if they have not chosen otherwise, are prohibited from exerting undue influence on them. Laymen, however, are not affected by this law.

Secular clerics and all religious are forbidden to induce any one to vow, to swear, or to promise in any way, to select their churches for the funeral, or their cemetery for the burial. The mere inducement of a person to make a choice of the funeral church or of the cemetery is not prohibited.[58] Suggestions, counsels, requests and persuasion are all permissible, provided that they do not lead a person to bind himself under vow or promise or oath to select a particular church of seculars or of religious as the funeral church, or their cemetery as the place of burial. Clerics and religious may, on the contrary, use their influence on persons with the result that they will bind themselves by oath, by vow, or by promise, to choose a certain church for the funeral or a certain cemetery for the burial, if the church chosen or the cemetery selected does not belong to those who exert this pressure.

The text of canon 1227 indicates that the prohibition is grave. Even though the penalties added to this law by Pope Clement V (1305–1314) and by Pope Sixtus IV (1471–1484) were removed long before the promulgation of the Code,[59] it is clear that the prohibition still remains grave in view of the very fact that the infringement of this law renders the selection of the funeral church or of the cemetery of burial invalid. This is also the common teaching of the authors.[60]

The only penalty, then, that remains in the present law is the nullity of the choice made under the influence of such inducement to vow, to swear, or to promise to choose the church or the cemetery of those who exert the undue influence. Since it is expressly determined that such inducement renders the selection null and

[58] Coronata, *De Locis et Temporibus Sacris,* n. 192; Rossi, *Sepultura Ecclesiastica,* n. 61.

[59] Cf. Many, *De Locis Sacris,* n. 165.

[60] Cocchi, *Commentarium,* V, n. 59; Blat, *Commentarium,* Pars II–VI, n. 85; Rossi, *Sepultura Ecclesiastica,* n. 61; Coronata, *De Locis et Temporibus Sacris,* n. 192.

void, this law must be numbered among the invalidating laws.[61] There can be no sanation of a choice which is null on account of such inducement, but for validation a new and distinct act of choice must be made, freely elicited by the person who was previously subjected to the inducement.[62]

ARTICLE V. THE NORMS REGULATING THE SELECTION OF A PLACE OF BURIAL

As has been mentioned, the cemetery of burial may be chosen by any and all of the faithful, except religious and those who have not attained the age of puberty. It has been seen also that it may be chosen by one personally or through another to whom a mandate has been given, that the fact of the choice and the concession of the mandate are amenable to proof in any legitimate manner, and that a grave prohibition binds the secular clergy and all religious not to induce any person to vow, to swear or to promise to choose their cemetery as the place of burial.

Any cemetery that is legitimately established may be chosen by the faithful in contemplation of burial.[63] Parish churches and houses of exempt religious according to law[64] have the right to have their own cemeteries. The bishop may allow other moral persons and even private families to have their own places of burial. Portions of civil cemeteries are also often reserved and blessed for deceased Catholics. Even the latter are subject to the choice of the faithful.

Canon 1228 enacts further practical norms to be followed in case the choice of burial has been made.

§ 1. Si electa fuerit sepultura in coemeterio diverso a coemeterio propriae defuncti paroeciae, cadaver in illo sepeliatur, dummodo nihil obstet ex parte eorum a quibus coemeterium pendet.

---

[61] C. 11.

[62] Cappello, *Summa,* II, n. 735.

[63] "[Potest eligere] *aut coemeterium sepulturae* inter diversa, quae ad normam can. 1208 existant prout de iure, vel, quantum ab Ecclesia pendet, inter plura coemeteria 'societatis civilis propria,' quae sint ad normam can. 1206, § 2, benedicta."—Blat, *Commentarium,* III, Pars II–VI, n. 81.

[64] C. 1208, §§ 1, 2.

§ 2. Electa sepultura in coemeterio religiosorum, ut cadaver in illo inibi sepeliri queat, requiritur et sufficit consensus Superioris religiosi, ad normam constitutionum cuiusque religionis.

If a person has chosen for his burial a cemetery distinct from that of his proper parish church, his body should be buried in it, provided that the authorities who have charge of the cemetery place no obstacles to his burial there. Should they reasonably object, the necessity of fulfilling the demand of the deceased no longer binds. In the case of refusal, it seems that the deceased should be buried in the cemetery of the church in which the funeral occurred,[65] or rather in the family plot, if one exists.

If a place of burial in a cemetery of religious is selected, the permission of the religious superior, without the consent of any other person, is indeed needed but it also suffices to permit the interment there. The religious superior who is capable of giving this consent will be determined according to the constitutions of each institute. If the constitutions do not determine the competent superior, the local superior will have the power to grant this consent, though he or the higher superiors are never bound to do so.[66]

Although the consent of the religious superior as well as that of the authorities mentioned in the preceding paragraph may not be necessary for a valid choice of the place of burial, yet it is obviously required if the choice is to attain its full juridical effect. If the superior of a house of exempt religious grants permission for the burial of a person who has chosen to be buried in the cemetery of the institute, the interment will properly occur there. However, it must be remembered that the right of the faithful to choose a church for the exequies or the funeral services, as opposed to the choice of the cemetery for burial, is determined by canon 1225. According to that canon, only the churches of the regular clergy can be chosen as funeral churches.[67]

---

[65] C. 1231, § 1: "Expletis in ecclesia exsequiis, cadaver tumulandum est ad normam librorum liturgicorum in coemeterio ecclesiae funeris, salvis praescriptis can. 1228, 1229."

[66] Augustine, *A Commentary on Canon Law,* VI, 132; Ayrinhac, *Administrative Legislation in the New Code of Canon Law,* n. 67.

[67] Cf. *supra,* p. 109.

Closely related in its effects to the choice of a cemetery of burial is the possession of a family tomb, plot or lot. If a person has not chosen a cemetery for his burial, but possesses a family tomb or lot in a certain cemetery, he is to be buried therein if the body can be transported there easily. Even if the transporting of the body cannot be done easily, still his family, heirs or those who are interested have the right to transport the body to this place of burial, provided that they pay the expenses.[68] If a wife has not chosen to be buried in some other cemetery, she should be buried in the family plot of her husband. If a wife has had several husbands, she should be buried in the family plot of her last husband.[69] If the family or the husband had several burial places, the family or heirs of the deceased should select the place of burial.[70] As a place for the interment of the body, such a family plot is to be preferred to the cemetery of the proper parish or to the cemetery of the funeral church,[71] but not to the cemetery which has been selected validly by the deceased.

ARTICLE VI. THE FUNERAL CHURCH IN SPECIFIC CASES OF SELECTION

It has been remarked that the Code allows a person to choose both the church where he wishes his exequies to be held and also the cemetery where he wishes to receive burial. It distinguishes the two very clearly in all of the canons dealing with this type of selection, that is, in the canons from canon 1223 to canon 1228 inclusive. Obviously, they are two very diverse objects of one's choice, separable one from the other and, as a matter of fact, often separated. The funeral church or the church where the exequies are held does not depend on the place selected for the interment of the body; the place of burial, on the other hand, is ordinarily to be the cemetery of the funeral church, provided that the deceased has not selected a different place of burial, or does not

68 C. 1229, § 1.
69 C. 1229, § 2.
70 C. 1229, § 3.
71 C. 1231, § 1.

possess an ancestral burying place in a cemetery other than that of the funeral church.[72]

A person may choose solely the funeral church, or solely the cemetery of burial, or also both of them. If he has validly chosen solely the funeral church, then his exequies are to be conducted in this church. His burial or interment will accordingly occur in the cemetery of the funeral church, unless he possesses a family plot.[73]

If he has chosen validly solely the place of his burial, or if he has a family plot, he is to be buried therein.[74] However, when there has been no valid choice of the funeral church, the latter must be determined according to the usual norms of the law, which are found in canons 1216 to 1222 inclusive.[75] If he dies after having made a separate and distinct valid choice both of the funeral church and of the cemetery for his burial, his exequies are to be conducted in the church he has chosen, and his interment is to occur in the cemetery which he has selected.

---

[72] C. 1231, § 1.

[73] C. 1231, § 1.

[74] Cc. 1228, §§ 1, 2; 1229, § 1.

[75] Beste, *Introductio in Codicem,* Commentary on c. 1223, § 1; Woywod, *A Practical Commentary on the Code of Canon Law,* II, 40; Ayrinhac, *Administrative Legislation in the New Code of Canon Law,* n. 68; Augustine, *A Commentary on Canon Law,* VI, 116.

CHAPTER VI

THE FUNERAL CHURCH IN SPECIAL CASES

The general rule of canon 1216, namely, that the body is to be transferred for the funeral to the church of the proper parish of the deceased, contains the notable exception, "*nisi defunctus aliam funeris ecclesiam legitime elegerit.*" The Code in canons 1219–1222 establishes further exceptions to the general rule by determining the funeral church for certain classes of persons, that is, for cardinals, residential bishops, abbots *nullius* and prelates *nullius*, residential beneficiaries, professed religious, novices, servants of religious and persons who live in a seminary. In canon 1222, also, there is to be found the law for those who have died in hospitals and in a religious house or college in which they dwelt as guests or for the purpose of education or health. As summarily as possible, the funeral church for each of these groups will be considered according to the regulations of the Code.

A. The Roman Pontiff

It seems fitting that mention should be made in this section of the funeral church of the popes. Among the laws of the Code itself, there cannot be found any reference to their funeral church. In the Constitution "*Vacante Sede Apostolica*" of Pius X (1903–1914), which document is appended to the Code, it is provided that the general preparatory congregations of cardinals should determine the day, the hour, and the manner, in which the body of the deceased pontiff is to be transferred.[1] It is also provided[2] that the Cardinals should take care that everything is prepared in

[1] "In memoratis Congregationibus generalibus haec precipue negotia expedienda sunt: . . . c) Constituendus est dies, hora ac modus, quo corpus defuncti Pontificis transferatur." Docum. I, Constitutio Pii PP. X "*Vacante Sede Apostolica,*" 25 Decembris 1904, n. 11.

[2] *Ibid.*, n. 11, d.

time, so that the exequies will be carried out on the established nine days.[3]

This Constitution rather presumes as still in force the provisions of the Instruction added to the Constitution "*Praedecessores Nostri*" of Leo XIII (1878–1903),[4] where it is determined that the body of the deceased pontiff is to be clothed with the pontifical vestments as quickly as possible, carried privately down the inner staircase to the Basilica of St. Peter to the chapel of the Blessed Sacrament, and there lie in state.[5] Further it is stated in this Instruction that the exequies shall be carried out publicly in the Basilica.[6] The Motu proprio of Pius XI (1922–1939), entitled "*Cum proxime,*"[7] does not change this regulation of the Instruction, but adds that the Cardinals in their first general preparatory meeting should fix the first six days as those on which the exequies of the deceased pontiff are to be celebrated.

B. Cardinals

Canon 1219, § 1: **Si S. R. E. Cardinalis in Urbe decesserit, corpus transferendum est, funeris causa, in ecclesiam quam Romanus Pontifex designaverit; si extra Urbem, in ecclesiam insigniorem civitatis seu loci ubi mors accidit, nisi Cardinalis aliam elegerit.**

The Code in the first paragraph of canon 1219 enacts the rule that the body of a cardinal who has died in Rome is to be transferred for the funeral to the church which the Roman Pontiff has designated; that, however, if he has died outside Rome, the body is to be transferred to the most prominent church of the city or place of his death, unless the cardinal has chosen a particular church for his exequies.

The canon refers obviously to cardinals who are not residential

---

[3] *Ibid.*, n. 26.

[4] Docum. III, const. Leonis XIII "*Praedecessores Nostri,*" cum adiecta Instructione, 24 maii 1882.

[5] *Ibid.*, n. 24.

[6] "Praeter exsequias, quae publice in Basilica S. Petri peragentur, alias privatim Cardinales persolvent in Syxtino Sacello, . . ."—*Ibid.*, n. 26.

[7] Docum. IX, motu propr. Pii XI "*Cum proxime,*" 1 mart. 1922.

bishops, since direct reference is made to these in the second paragraph of the canon. However, the funerals of cardinals who are bishops of the suburbicarian sees[8] are regulated by the law of this first paragraph.

In opposition to Cappello,[9] such authors as Ayrinhac,[10] Cocchi,[11] Coronata,[12] and Beste[13] vindicate the right of a cardinal to choose his funeral church in every instance, even though the last clause of paragraph one in canon 1219, i.e., "*nisi Cardinalis aliam* [*ecclesiam*] *elegerit*," seems to refer only to the case in which he dies outside the city of Rome. In practice, according to Wernz-Vidal, their funerals are customarily held in the parochial church of their domicile, or in a church designated by the Roman Pontiff.[14]

It is difficult to determine clearly the order of precedence among the churches to which the body of the deceased cardinal is to be transferred when death occurs outside the city of Rome. Coronata supplies the following order:

(1) Major Basilica
(2) Cathedral Church
(3) Collegiate Church
(4) Parish Church of the Deanery
(5) Simple Parish Church
(6) Church of the Regular Clergy[15]

C. Bishops

Canon 1219, § 2: **Defuncto Episcopo residentiali, etiam cardinalitia dignitate aucto, aut Abbate vel Praelato nullius, corpus, funeris causa, transferri debet in ecclesiam cathedralem, abbatialem vel praelatitiam, si id commode fieri possit; secus, in ecclesiam insigniorem**

---

[8] Cc. 238, §§ 1, 2; 240, § 1.

[9] *Summa*, II, n. 725.

[10] *Administrative Legislation in the New Code of Canon Law*, n. 62.

[11] *Commentarium*, V, n. 58.

[12] *De Locis et Temporibus Sacris*, n. 173.

[13] *Introductio in Codicem*, Commentary on c. 1219, § 1.

[14] *Ius Canonicum*, IV, Pars I, 580.

[15] *De Locis et Temporibus Sacris*, n. 12, note 1; n. 174. Cf. also Cappello, II, *Summa*, n. 726.

civitatis seu loci, nisi in utroque casu defunctus aliam ecclesiam elegerit.

The Code declares that the body of a deceased residential bishop, even though he had been raised to the dignity of the cardinalship, or of an abbot *nullius* or of a prelate *nullius*, should be transferred for the exequies to the cathedral, abbatial or prelatic church respectively, if it can be done easily; that, if it cannot be done conveniently, the body of each of these individuals is to be transported to the more distinguished church of the city or of the place where death occurred, unless in both instances the deceased has chosen a particular church for his funeral.

The funeral church for deceased vicars apostolic and prefects apostolic seems to be determined by the same law.[16] Since the Code makes no provision for the funeral church of titular bishops, they must conform to the ordinary law, unless they have chosen a particular church for their funeral, or are exempted from its obligations for some other reason.[17]

Obviously, the church which is chosen for the funeral by any member of the groups under discussion is to be preferred to the churches mentioned. The convenience of the transfer of the body in these instances is not determined by the fact that the funeral procession can be made on foot.[18] In these cases, too, the more distinguished church of the city where the death occurred, to which church the bodies of the bishop, of the abbot *nullius* and of the prelate *nullius* are to be conveyed when the transfer to their own churches is not convenient, may be determined according to the same order as given above in the case of deceased cardinals.[19]

---

[16] C. 294, § 1.

[17] Cocchi, *Commentarium,* V, n. 58; Beste, *Introductio in Codicem,* Commentary on c. 1219, § 2; Coronata, *De Locis et Temporibus Sacris,* n. 174; "I Vescovi titolari nel nuovo diritto rimane che siano funerati non nella Cattedrale, ma nella parrochia dove hanno domicilio ecc. secondo i canoni 1216, 1218, salvo se siano beneficiati residenziali o abbiano altro titolo di far eccezione alla regola commune, ovvero abbiano eletto altra Chiesa."—Rossi, *Sepultura Ecclesiastica,* n. 55, in nota.

[18] Cocchi, *Commentarium,* V, n. 58; Blat, *Commentarium,* III, Pars II–VI, n. 77.

[19] Cf. *supra,* p. 123.

D. Residential Beneficiaries; Priests

Canon 1220: **Beneficiarii residentiales ad ecclesiasm sui beneficii transferendi sunt, nisi aliam sibi elegerint ecclesiam funeris.**

Canon 1220 rules that an ecclesiastic who possesses a residential benefice is to be transferred for his funeral to the church of his benefice, unless he has chosen another church for his funeral. The Code defines a benefice as a juridical entity, permanently constituted or erected by the competent ecclesiastical authority, consisting of a sacred office together with the attached right to receive the revenues accruing to that office from an endowment,[20] which consists either of goods owned by the benefice itself, or of definite obligatory payments of some family or moral person, or of definite voluntary offerings of the faithful, which belong to the rector of the benefice, or of socalled stole fees received within the limits of the diocesan taxation or legitimate custom, or of choir distributions.[21] A residential benefice is described in the Code as an ecclesiastical office which, in addition to the beneficial office, has annexed to it the obligation of residence.[22] Residence signifies an almost continuous stay in the place where the benefice exists for the purpose of fulfilling personally the duties of the office.

Canons of the chapters of cathedral and collegiate churches, since they possess residential benefices,[23] are to be transferred to their proper cathedral or collegiate church for their funerals.

[20] C. 1409.

[21] C. 1410.

[22] "Beneficia ecclesiastica dicuntur: . . . *Duplicia* seu *residentialia* . . . prout, praeter officium beneficiale, adnexam habent . . . obligationem residendi"—c. 1411, 3o.

[23] Cappello, *Summa,* II, n. 727; Coronata, *De Locis et Temporibus Sacris,* n. 174; Cocchi, *Commentarium,* V, n. 58; "Honorary Canons, of course, are Canons practically only in name, and participate in only a few of the honors and privileges connected with the position. Supernumerary Canons, or those who are constituted without the right to receive revenues, are the exception, and can be created only with the special permission of the Holy See. . . . Consequently, the office of a Canon Capitular is, in most instances, a residential benefice."—McBride, *Incardination and Excardination of Seculars,* The Catholic University of America Canon Law Studies, n. 145 (Washington, D. C.: The Catholic University of America Press, 1941), p. 472.

The *mansionarii*, or those who possess inferior benefices in a cathedral or collegiate church, if their benefices are residential, must also be buried from the church of their benefice.[24] Therefore, according to the common law the parochial church of their domicile or quasi-domicile cannot be considered the funeral church for canons and for those who possess inferior residential benefices. On the other hand, the proper church for the funeral of honorary canons is normally the parish church of their domicile.[25]

Pastors also possess true benefices,[26] which are residential.[27] This must be affirmed of the pastors of territorial, of personal and of mixed parishes.[28] Hence, the body of the pastor is to be transferred for the funeral to the church of which he was the pastor.

McBride in his able discussion of the nature of a residential benefice, and of those who may possess an ecclesiastical benefice of this kind,[29] numbers among the incumbents of such benefices the rector of the seminary, the secular priest who is a parochial vicar of a moral person, and the secular priest who is appointed to a parish which has been united by the Holy See to a religious house *ad temporalia tantum*. He remarks that the offices of the official and of the synodal or prosynodal judge could be erected into benefices, and become residential benefices also if the obligation of residence was attached to them in one of three ways, namely by the canonically approved will of the founder as expressed in the law of foundation, by provincial statute, or by cus-

---

[24] Rossi, *Sepultura Ecclesiastica*, n. 55; Cocchi, *Commentarium*, V, n. 58.

[25] S. C. C., *Dioecesis C., Iuris funerandi canonicos honorarios*, 9 et 16 dec. 1939—*AAS*, XXXII (1940), 75; reported in Bouscaren, *The Canon Law Digest*, II, 352.

[26] " Ex his responsionibus officialibus patet, omnes paroecias in Statibus his Unitis, quibus sunt tres requisitae notae, scil. pastor residentialis, dos (proventus vel reditus) iuxta dispositiones can. 1410 vel 1415, § 3, et limites, esse non tantum paroecias sensu stricto canonicas sed etiam beneficia ecclesiastica."—Letter of His Excellency, John Bonzano, Apostolic Delegate to the United States, to the Most Reverend Ordinaries of the United States, Nov. 10, 1922, as cited in Beste, *Introductio in Codicem*, Commentary on c. 216, § 1.

[27] C. 465, § 1.

[28] Cf. *supra*, p. 83.

[29] *Incardination and Excardination of Seculars*, pp. 461–509.

tom, affecting all the officials or judges respectively of a province. The learned author also states that the office of a vicar forane could be made a benefice, which would then be residential, since this office has the obligation of residence annexed to it by the common law. In regard to various kinds of chaplains, he asserts that their offices can be erected into benefices in particular cases, and that a chaplaincy so erected would be a residential benefice indirectly if it involved the care of souls, and directly if the obligation of residence were attached to it.

The same author excludes from his list of residential benefices the following offices: those of the vicar general, the chancellor, the vice chancellor, the notary, the synodal examiner, the parish priest consultor, the vice official, the promoter of justice, the defender of the bond, the auditor, the court beadles, the diocesan consultor, the vicar capitular, the parochial administrator, the substitute pastor, the parochial adjutant, the assistant pastor,[30] the rector of a church, and the offices in a seminary other than that of the rector. It is proper to note that the incumbents of all these offices and of the others which, as a matter of fact, have not been erected into residential benefices are held to the observance of the ordinary law in regard to funerals, that is, their funerals are to be conducted at the parish church of their domicile or quasi-domicile.[31]

Residential beneficiaries may freely select their funeral church. In fact, the funeral church chosen is to be preferred as their funeral church to the church of the benefice. The right to select their funeral church may be exercised by all priests who are not members of religious institutes.[32] All of those clerics to whom reference has been made in this section, therefore, may select their funeral church, provided that they are not members of religious institutes.

Cappello,[33] Coronata,[34] and Ayrinhac[35] maintain that the transfer of deceased residential beneficiaries is to be made to the church

[30] Cf., however, *Incardination and Excardination of Seculars,* pp. 488–503.
[31] Cc. 1216–1218.
[32] Cc. 1223–1224.
[33] *Summa,* II, n. 727.
[34] *De Locis et Temporibus Sacris,* n. 175.
[35] *Administrative Legislation in the New Code of Canon Law,* n. 62.

of the benefice only if the corpse can be transported easily in procession to the church of the benefice, or if those who are interested undertake the transfer and shoulder its expenses;[36] that if the corpse cannot be transferred easily, or if those interested do not care to transfer the body, the funeral church will be the church of the parish in which the deceased had a domicile or quasi-domicile; and that the funeral church will be the church of the parish in which death occurred, if the deceased did not possess a proper parish.

The general principles of canons 1216–1218 are, of course, applicable to the funerals of clerics who do not possess residential benefices,[37] unless the Code provides otherwise, as it does, e.g., for seminarians and religious.

E. Men Religious

Canon 1221, § 1: **Professi religiosi ac novitii, defuncti cum sint, transferendi sunt, funeris causa, ad ecclesiam vel oratorium suae domus vel saltem suae religionis, nisi novitii aliam ecclesiam ad suum funus elegerint; ius autem levandi cadaver et illud deducendi ad ecclesiam funerantem pertinet semper ad Superiorem religiosum.**

§ 2: **Si longe moriantur a domo, ita ut in ecclesiam suae domus vel saltem suae religionis nequeant commode asportari, funerandi sunt in ecclesia paroeciae ubi decedunt, nisi novitius aliam ecclesiam ad funus elegerit, et salvo Superioribus iure de quo in can. 1218, § 3.**

The first paragraph of canon 1221 rules that at death professed men religious and novices are to be brought for the funeral to the church or oratory of their house, or at least to a church or oratory of their religious institute, unless the novices have chosen another church for their own funerals; that the religious superior always has the right to receive the body in liturgical procession, and to

[36] C. 1218.

[37] Cf. *supra*, pp. 76–102.

conduct it to the funeral church. Since this last provision of the first paragraph pertains to the minister of ecclesiastical burial, it will be treated in a subsequent chapter.[38] The present discussion will be restricted to a determination simply of the funeral church of men religious, or, in other words, to the church in which their exequies are to be held.

According to the second paragraph, if professed religious and novices die so far from home that they cannot be brought easily to the church of their house or to a church of their institute, their exequies are to be carried out in the church of the parish in which they died. Two exceptions to this rule must be noted. First, deceased novices are to be brought to the church they have selected for their funeral rather than to the local parish church. Secondly, in the event the religious or the novice dies so far from home that the transfer is inconvenient, the religious superior, provided that he assumes the responsibility for the expenses, always has the right to bring the body to the funeral church or to the place of interment belonging to the religious institute.[39]

Professed religious are those who have made a valid profession of temporary or of perpetual, of simple or of solemn, vows, in any order or congregation.[40] The institute in which the profession is made may be a clerical or a lay institute, exempt or non-exempt, of diocesan or of papal approval. Canon 1221 in its determination of the funeral church for professed religious men does not contain diverse law for orders and for congregations, nor for institutes of papal and for institutes of diocesan approval. In his simple use of the words "*professi religiosi,*" the legislator extends to all institutes of men the right, established by the law in existence prior to the promulgation of the Code in favor of the regular clergy and conceded frequently by indult or privilege to institutes of simple vows,[41] namely to bring the body of a de-

---

[38] Cf. *infra,* p. 181.

[39] C. 1218, § 3: "Licet translatio ad ecclesiam funeris aut ad locus sepulturae incommoda sit, semper tamen integrum est familiae, heredibus, aliisque quorum interest, cadaver illuc deferre, susceptis translationis expensis."

[40] Cc. 487, 488. Cf. c. 673.

[41] Wernz-Vidal, *Ius Canonicum,* IV, Pars I, n. 582; Many, *De Locis Sacris,* n. 187.

ceased religious to the religious house of which he was a member, or to a house of the institute. The funeral church of every deceased religious is the oratory or the church of his religious house, or at least the oratory or the church of one of the houses of his institute. The text of the canon is so clear that any doubts which might be entertained concerning the application of the canon to diocesan congregations or to lay institutes must be promptly laid aside.[42]

The professed religious are not only given the right to have their funerals in a church of their own institute instead of the local parish church, but the religious superior especially as well as the religious in general have the duty to bring the body of a deceased religious to an oratory or church of the institute. This obligation seems to the writer to be of the same gravity as that imposed on the faithful in canon 1215. This fundamental canon, which is an expression of the public ecclesiastical law, recognizes only a grave cause as sufficient to excuse from the obligation of the next of kin to bring the bodies of the faithful to the funeral church.[43]

If the religious dies in the religious house, his body must be brought for the funeral to the oratory or church of that religious house, or at least to an oratory or church of his institute. According to the wording of the law, there does not seem to be an obligation to bring the body for the funeral to the oratory of the particular house of which the deceased was a member at the time of his death. Hence, the superior is free to transfer the body to any church of the institute for the funeral. If the religious dies far from the religious house of which he was a member, but near enough to a house of the institute that the body can be brought

---

[42] Fanfani, *De Iure Religiosorum,* n. 421; Schaefer, *De Religiosis ad Normam Codicis Iuris Canonici* (3. ed., Romae: S. A. L. E. R., 1940), nn. 471–473 (hereafter this work is cited as *De Religiosis*); Creusen-Garesché-Ellis, *Religious Men and Women in the Code* (4. English ed., Milwaukee: The Bruce Publishing Co., 1942), n. 153; Augustine, *A Commentary on Canon Law,* VI, 123; Wernz-Vidal, *Ius Canonicum,* IV, Pars I, n. 582; Larraona, "Commentarium Codicis," *Commentarium pro Religiosis* (Romae: 1920–), IX (1928), 205 (hereafter this periodical is cited *CpR*).

[43] Cf. *supra,* p. 47.

to its church or oratory, the superior has the obligation to bring the body to this church or oratory.[44]

As was noted above,[45] according to the pre-Code law the regular clergy, if they died so far from their monastery that their bodies could not be brought to it easily, could choose their place of burial. This right, granted also through privilege to some other religious institutes before the year 1918, has been withdrawn in the Code.[46] Although the privilege of selecting the church for the funeral, or the cemetery for burial, is denied to all professed religious[47] under any conditions, there is granted to religious superiors the unlimited right to transfer the body of the deceased religious to any church or oratory of the religious institute.

Under the pre-Code law it was also prescribed that, if the professed member of the regular clergy who died far from home had not selected a place for his burial, his body was to be buried in the parish church of the place of his death.[48] Except for its omission of any reference to the privilege of selecting the church for the funeral, or the cemetery for the burial, the second paragraph of canon 1221 is an expression of the old law which governed the funerals of the members of the regular clergy. Of course, the law of the Code now refers to all institutes of men religious.

Canon 1221, § 2, provides that, if professed religious die far away from their own religious house, with the result that they cannot be easily brought to the church of their own house or to a church of their institute, their funerals must take place in the church of the parish in which they died. However, the superior always has the right to bring the body to any church of the institute for the funeral, or to its own place of burial, as long as he pays the expenses of the transfer.

The canon uses the word "*commode,*" which is found also in canon 1218, § 1. The same conclusions which were reached above

---

[44] Larraona, "Commentarium Codicis,"—*CpR,* IX (1928), 206.

[45] Cf. *supra,* p. 17.

[46] C. 1224.

[47] ". . . non tamen si sint Episcopi"—C. 1224, 2°.

[48] Cf. *supra,* p. 17.

in the discussion of the word are applicable in this instance as well.[49] Likewise, the evaluation made in the discussion of canon 1218 § 2, of the circumstances which render the transfer inconvenient is apropos. However, in this instance it will be incumbent on the superior to consider the circumstances and to judge whether the transfer can be made easily.

The funerals of religious who have obtained an indult of secularization,[50] or who have been dismissed[51] from their institute, are to be conducted according to the ordinary law which governs the funerals of the faithful.[52] Those who have received an indult of exclaustration[53] are still subject[54] to the law of canon 1221, as are the apostates and fugitives,[55] though in regard to the last two groups mentioned, as Cappello states, it may be practically impossible for the special law for religious to be applied.[56]

Novices enjoy the same rights as the professed religious. Moreover, the Code grants to them as it does to all the faithful, except to professed religious and to those who have not attained the age of puberty, the right to choose legitimately the church for their funeral or the cemetery for their burial.[57] Like the professed religious, they are to be brought for the funeral to the church of the religious house, or to a church of the institute, but only on the condition that they have not selected another church for their funeral. If they have chosen a particular church, they are to be brought at death to the church selected, whether they have died in the novitiate or far away from it.

---

[49] Cf. *supra*, p. 124.

[50] C. 640.

[51] "Quando vota cessant nulla difficultas, sicut saecularizati ipsi non sunt amplius Religiosi. . . . Etsi vota non cessent, dum dimissio perdurat tractatur ut a Religione separatus. Cfr. c. 671."—Larraona, "Commentarium Codicis," *CpR*, IX (1928), p. 208, nota 595.

[52] Larraona, *loc. cit.*; Coronata, *De Locis et Temporibus Sacris*, n. 176; Cappello, *Summa*, II, n. 728.

[53] C. 638.

[54] Schaefer, *De Religiosis*, n. 472; Blat, *Commentarium*, III, Pars II–VI, n. 79.

[55] C. 645, § 1.

[56] Cappello, II, *Summa*, n. 728; Coronata, *De Locis et Temporibus Sacris*, n. 176; Larraona, *loc. cit.*

[57] Cc. 1223–1224; 1221, §§ 1, 2.

Before the publication of the response of the Pontifical Commission for the Authentic Interpretation of the Code it was the common opinion [58] among canonists that postulants and the students of apostolic schools are governed in regard to the determination of the funeral church by the same law as are the novices.[59] Some of the authors felt that the postulants could be considered as religious in those matters which favor religious; [60] others were of the opinion that postulants could at least be numbered among the members of a religious family, and would therefore at least be equal in their rights to the servants who are actually employed and dwell in the religious house,[61] whose funeral church, provided that they died in the religious house, is the same as that of the novices.[62]

To the question: " May the prescription of canon 1221 be extended also to postulants and to students of apostolic schools in religious institutes? " the Pontifical Commission replied on July 20, 1929: " In the negative." [63] Hence the funeral church of postulants and of students in apostolic schools is determined by the ordinary law of canons 1216–1218. It seems quite unnecessary to remark that, if they have completed fourteen years of age, they can select their funeral church in accordance with the provisions of canons 1223–1226.

F. Servants in Houses of Men Religious

Canon 1221, § 3: **Quae de novitiis dicta sunt §§ 1, 2, valent quoque de famulis actu servientibus et**

[58] Cf. Schaefer, *De Religiosis*, n. 472.

[59] Apostolic schools are schools or seminaries in which, at the expense of the religious institute, selected young men and boys are instructed in the subjects usually taught in our elementary and high schools, and are trained to the religious life of the institute, which, it is hoped, many of them will embrace.

[60] Fanfani, *De Iure Religiosorum*, n. 421.

[61] C. 1221, § 3.

[62] Cf. Maroto, " Annotationes ad Responsum Quartum "—*CpR*, X (1929), 334–341.

[63] " D. An praescriptum canonis 1221 extendatur etiam ad postulantes et ad alumnos scholarum apostolicarum in religionibus . . . R. Negative."—*AAS*, XXI (1929), 573; reported in Bouscaren, *The Canon Law Digest*, I, 572.

intra domus septa stabiliter commoranti-bus, qui tamen, si extra religiosam domum decesserint, funerandi sunt ad normam can. 1216-1218.

In the Council of Trent (1545–1563) it was decreed that servants of the regular clergy, provided that they actually labored in the monasteries, dwelt within its grounds and houses, and lived subject to the authority of the religious,[64] so that they really belonged to the family of the monastery,[65] could receive burial in their churches. The present law is more extensive in its application, for the servants in all houses or institutes of men enjoy the right formerly possessed only by those residing in the houses of the regular clergy.

The Code provides that the law which governs the determination of the funeral church for the novices is applicable also to the servants of men religious under certain conditions not greatly unlike those mentioned by the Council of Trent. The servants must be truly servants and actually in service at the religious house; they must dwell constantly within the limits of the property of the religious house;[66] and they must have died within these limits. If one of these conditions is lacking, their funerals must be conducted in accordance with the provisions of the ordinary law contained in canons 1216–1218.

Like the novices, servants who died in the religious house must be brought for their exequies to the church or the oratory of the religious house, and not to the church of their proper parish or to the church of the parish in which the convent is located. Like the novices also, they may select the church for their funeral.

---

[64] "Qui praedictis locis (monasteriis) actu serviunt, et infra eorum septa ac domos resident, subque eorum obedientia vivunt . . ."—Conc. Trident., sess. XXIV, *de ref.*, c. 11.

[65] Conc. Trident., sess. XXV, *de regularibus*, c. 11.

[66] "Nomine religiosae domus intelligi debent omnia aedificia quae intra septa seu muros continentur, religiosorum habitationem delimitantia. Nihil refert de charactere horum aedificiorum an sunt hospitia vel scholae, vel collegia, vel aedes ad operarios seu domesticos destinatae, etc."—Larraona, "Commentarium Codicis," *CpR*, IX (1928), 104; Schaefer, *De Religiosis*, n. 42.

Especially worthy of note is the great difference between the law which governs the determination of the funeral church for the novices and that established for the servants actually employed and constantly residing at the religious house. On the one hand, if a novice died outside the religious house, his body is to be brought, if it can be done easily, at least to one of the churches or oratories of his institute. On the other hand, if a servant died outside the religious house, his body is to be brought to the parish church of his domicile or quasi-domicile, whichever church is the closer. If it cannot be transferred easily to his proper parish church, his funeral will occur in the church of the parish in which he died, unless his friends or relatives are prepared to pay the expenses of the transfer of his body to his proper parish church. In the event that he died outside the religious house, the church of the religious house where he was employed can never be his funeral church, unless he had legitimately selected it for his exequies.[67]

The word "*famulus*" is not defined in the Code. It seems to the writer that it cannot be identified with the word "*familiaris*," which is found in canon 509. According to Barbosa (1589–1649) the "*familiares*" were domestic servants who were in the service of the master of the house and who continually lived with him at his expense and boarded at his table.[68] Creusen, however, remarks that some good authors before 1918 were of the opinion that the jurisdiction of the Holy See permitted the extension of its meaning a little, and that the two elements sufficient to consitute a domestic were a real dependence on the head of the house and the fact that these persons were boarded in the household.[69] In the course of time, all those who lived "*diu noctuque*" in the religious house to be cared for while they were ill, to be engaged

[67] Cc. 1223, 1225.

[68] "Familiares—duo debent concurrere copulative, quod scilicet inserviant actu, et vivant expensis domini. . . . Familiarium appellatione, vere illi comprehenduntur, qui expensis illius, cuius dicuntur familiares, continuo vivunt, et morantur cum eo, indeque continui commensales dicuntur."—*Tractatus Varii, De appellativa verborum utriusque Iuris significatione* (Lugdini: 1660), ad v. *Familiares.*

[69] *Religious Men and Women in the Code,* p. 63.

in service, to be retained as guests, or to be given an education, were included in the term "*familiares.*"[70]

The word "*famulus*" seems to the writer to signify simply a "servant" or "a person in the employ of another." Employment may be of different kinds. One form may require the continual presence of a person in the house or within the grounds; another may require his presence through only the day or the night. If his employment is of such a nature that he may live far from the environs of the house, he will be a "*famulus*" of the religious house, but not a "*familiaris.*"

A person may be in the employ of a religious house in any one of several capacities. He may be employed as a cook, a baker, a carpenter, a teacher, a stenographer. In fact, the number of positions in which a layman may be employed in a large institution, e.g., a college or hospital, is very great. Since the term is so general, it seems that it may be applied to any layman who is employed in any capacity in the religious house, whether the work in which he is engaged is of an intellectual or a physical nature. It should not be so restricted in its meaning that it indicates only those persons who are engaged in work that exclusively entails manual labor.[71]

The Code does not extend the rights of the novices to all who are employed in the religious house. Only those employees who actually work for the religious and at the same time live continually within the limits of the property pertaining to the religious house can enjoy them. The Code uses the words, "*et intra domus septa stabiliter commorantibus.*" The phrase, "*stabiliter commorantibus,*" reminds one of the phrasing of canon 1225, "*non precario commorantes.*" It seems that they are not unlike in meaning.[72]

---

[70] "*Familiares* sunt qui *in religiosa domo diu noctuque* degunt causa *famulatus* aut *educationis* aut *hospitii* aut infirmae *valetudinis,* ut postulantes, famuli, alumni convictores exceptis feriis, hospites vel infirmi saltem per aliquot dies in ipsa religiosa domo, quamvis extra clausuram, diu noctuque degentes."—Genicot-Salsmans, *Institutiones Theologiae Moralis* (10 ed., 2 vols., Bruxellis, 1922), II, n. 338.

[71] "Famuli . . . sunt qui aliquod opus materiale, vel etiam spirituale susceperunt, licet stipendio ducti; ita e.g. hortulani, coqui, sacristae, magistri."—Coronata, *De Locis et Temporibus Sacris,* n. 179 e.

[72] Cf. *supra,* p. 111.

Coronata [73] remarks that, in order to be said to be living continually in the religious house, it does not seem necessary that one should really live in a monastery for a determined length of time, e.g., for a month or several weeks, but that it is sufficient if a person fulfills the conditions required for the establishment of a domicile or quasi-domicile in any place, that is, if he has the intention of living "*intra domus septa*" and actually begins to dwell there. Workmen who live at a religious house only temporarily in order to do some particular piece of work, e.g., to paint the buildings or to repair the plaster, cannot be said to dwell there "*stabiliter.*" [74]

G. Women Religious

Canon 1230, § 5: **Religiosas et novitias, in religiosa domo defunctas, ad clausurae limen deferant aliae religiosae; indeque, si de religiosis agatur iurisdictioni parochi non obnoxiis, ad propriam religiosae domus ecclesiam vel oratorium deducit et exsequias peragit cappellanus; si de aliis religiosis, valet praescriptum § 1; quod vero ad religiosas attinet extra domum defunctas, serventur generalia canonum praescripta.**

Canon 1230, § 5, prescribes that the women religious of the particular convent should carry the bodies of their deceased sisters and novices who have died in the convent to the limit of the enclosure; that thence, if the deceased belonged to a body of religious who are not subject to the jurisdiction of the pastor, the chaplain of the convent escorts the body to the proper church or the oratory of the convent, and there conducts the exequies; that if, however, the religious community of which she was a member is subject to the jurisdiction of the local pastor, he escorts the body to his parish church and conducts the exequies there.[75] In regard

[73] *De Locis et Temporibus Sacris*, n. 179.

[74] Beste, *Introductio in Codicem*, Commentary on c. 1221.

[75] C. 1230, § 1: "Proprius defuncti parochus non solum ius sed etiam officium habet, excepto gravi necessitatis casu, levandi per se vel per alium cadaver, illud comitandi ad suam ecclesiam paroecialem, ibique exsequias persolvendi, firmo praescripto can. 1216, § 2."

to women religious who die outside their convent, the Code provides that the general rules of the canons should be observed.

Since the legislator first considers the circumstance of the death of the woman religious within the religious house, and secondly its occurrence outside the convent, the commentary will follow his division of the subject matter.

1. The Death of a Woman Religious in Her Convent

Women religious are exempted from the jurisdiction of the local pastor in virtue either of the common law or of a concession granted to them by the local Ordinary. In virtue of the common law, nuns subject to the regular clergy are exempt from the jurisdiction of the local Ordinary,[76] and *a fortiori* from that of the local pastor.[77] The superior of the regular clergy appoints their chaplains,[78] who have then by reason of the ruling of canon 1230, § 5, the right to conduct the funerals of these nuns in the oratory or church of the convent.

The local Ordinary has the right to appoint the chaplain to convents of nuns who are not exempt from his jurisdiction,[79] and to convents of nuns who are subject to the Supreme Pontiff.[80]

It could seem that, if a chaplain were appointed to a convent of nuns not exempt from the jurisdiction of the local Ordinary and did not have committed to him also the right to conduct the funerals of the nuns, which arrangement is conceivable according to the regulation of canon 464, § 2, the pastor would still have the right to conduct the funerals of these nuns. In opposition to such a conclusion is the response of the Pontifical Commission for the Authentic Interpretation of the Code. In answer to the

[76] " Regulares, novitiis non exclusis, sive viri sive mulieres, cum eorum domibus et ecclesiis, exceptis iis monialibus quae Superioribus regularibus non subsunt, ab Ordinarii loci iurisdictione exempti sunt, praeterquam in casibus a iure expressis."—C. 615.

[77] Fanfani, *De Iure Religiosorum*, n. 351.

[78] " Si agatur de religionibus laicalibus non exemptis, Ordinarii loci est sacerdotem a sacris designare et a concionibus probare; si de exemptis, Superior regularis eosdem sacerdotes designat eiusque negligentiam supplet Ordinarius "—c. 529.

[79] C. 529.

[80] Schaefer, *De Religiosis*, n. 182.

question: "Does the pastor or the chaplain, according to the rule of canon 1230, § 5, possess the right to conduct the funerals of the nuns who according to canon 615 are not exempt from the jurisdiction of the local Ordinary?", the Pontifical Commission replied that the chaplain possessed this right.[81] Hence it must be admitted that nuns who are not exempt from the jurisdiction of the local Ordinary are exempt from the jurisdiction of the local pastor in regard to their funerals as soon as a chaplain has been appointed. When these nuns die in the convent, their funeral church is then the oratory or the church of the convent where they live.

Women religious of simple vows do not enjoy exemption from the local Ordinary,[82] and are subject likewise to the jurisdiction of the local pastor. However, canon 464, § 2, states that the bishop for a just and grave cause can withdraw from the care of the pastor not only religious communities but also pious houses which are within the territory of the parish and are not exempt by law.[83]

This withdrawal of a religious community by the bishop is in the nature of an exemption. It moreover implies the appointment of a chaplain. This withdrawal for a just and grave cause may be total or, for a lesser cause, partial, so that only some of the pastor's rights are transferred to the chaplain,[84] while the pastor retains those which have not been committed to the chaplain. The Code provides that the chaplain of a religious community which is exempt from the jurisdiction of the pastor has the right to escort the body of a member who has died in the

---

[81] "D. Utrum parocho an cappellano, ad normam canonis 1230, § 5, competat ius funerandi moniales ab Ordinarii loci iurisdictione non exemptas iuxta canonem 615. . . . R. Negative ad primam partem, affirmative ad secundam."—*ASS,* XXXIV (1942), 50; reported in Bouscaren, *The Canon Law Digest,* II, 353.

[82] "Religiones votorum simplicium exemptionis privilegio non gaudent, nisi specialiter eisdem fuerit concessum."—c. 618, § 1.

[83] "Potest Episcopus iusta et gravi de causa religiosas familias et pias domus, quae in paroeciae territorio sint et a iure non exemptae, a parochi cura subducere."

[84] Larraona, "Commentarium Codicis"—*CpR,* IX (1928), 109.

convent to the oratory or church of the convent and to conduct the exequies there.

His mere appointment as chaplain to a religious community does not give to a priest the right to conduct the exequies of deceased sisters. Unless the Ordinary formally exempts a religious community of sisters and commits to the chaplain the right to conduct their funerals, the pastor's right to conduct the funerals of sisters who are not exempt from his jurisdiction must be sustained. It is of no importance whether the sisters belong to a congregation of pontifical or of diocesan approval.

The funeral church for women religious who are subject to the jurisdiction of the pastor is determined explicitly in canon 1230, § 5. It provides that the rule of paragraph one of the same canon is to be observed, that is, the proper pastor should escort the body to his parish church and there conduct the exequies.

2. The Death of a Woman Religious Outside Her Convent

When a woman religious dies outside of the convent, her funeral, according to canon 1230, § 5, is governed by the general prescriptions of the canons. Fanfani,[85] Augustine,[86] Schaefer,[87] and Cocchi [88] believe that the words of the canon, namely, "*serventur generalia canonum praescripta,*" refer to the law which governs the funerals of the faithful. Geser,[89] on the contrary, seems at least in one instance to apply the law of the Code established for the funerals of men religious to the funerals of women religious.

Coronata [90] has recourse to two arguments in order to demonstrate that nuns are to be brought for their funerals to the church or oratory of their house or of their institute, provided that the transfer can be made easily, or that those who have an interest take pains to bring the body to the church or oratory. First, like Geser, he believes that in canon 1221, § 2, there is enunciated a

---

[85] *De Iure Religiosorum,* n. 151.

[86] *A Commentary on Canon Law,* VI, 138.

[87] *De Religiosis,* n. 475.

[88] *Commentarium,* V, n. 62.

[89] *The Canon Law Governing Communities of Sisters* (St. Louis, Mo.: B. Herder Book Co., 1939), n. 382.

[90] *De Locis et Temporibus Sacris,* n. 177.

general rule for all men and women religious, though it provides that men religious who die so far away from their religious house that their bodies cannot be brought easily at least to a church of their institute are to have their exequies in the church of the parish in which they die, unless the superior uses his right to bring the bodies at the institute's expense to any church of the institute. He contends that canon 490, which states that the laws of the Code for religious when expressed in the masculine gender apply in the same manner to women religious, is applicable at least in this instance.[91] Moreover, he is of the opinion that the words of canon 1230, § 5, namely, "*serventur generalia canonum praescripta,*" need not refer necessarily to the ordinary law which governs the faithful,[92] but only to the law which governs the funerals of men religious, which he says can be called general law, and thus be in accord with the words of the canon, "*generalia praescripta canonum.*"

Larraona[93] rejects the application of the law which determines the funeral church of men religious to the funeral church of women religious, and rightfully so in the opinion of the writer. A comparison made between the two canons, 1221 and 1230, § 5, shows clearly that there is a great diversity between the two laws.

The funeral church of women religious who are subject to the pastor is the local parish church, while on the contrary the funeral church for men religious is always an oratory or church of their institute. The first paragraph of canon 1221 grants the right to superiors of men religious to remove and escort the body of the deceased religious to any church or oratory of the institute, a concession which cannot be said to be granted to women religious. The second paragraph of canon 1221 grants to superiors of men religious the right to transfer for the funeral the body of a deceased religious who has died far away from home to an oratory

---

[91] "Quae de religiosis statuuntur, etsi masculino vocabulo expressa, valent etiam pari iure de mulieribus, nisi ex contextu sermonis vel ex natura rei aliud constet."

[92] Cc. 1216–1218.

[93] "Ipse c. 490 obstat quia *contextus* et *rei natura* clare indicant sermonem in c. 1221 ad viros esse contrahendum."—"Commentarium Codicis"—*CpR,* IX (1928), 204, nota 578.

of the institute. If this provision would be applicable also to institutes of women religious, there would be granted to the superioress of sisters who are not exempt from the jurisdiction of the pastor a greater right on the occasion of their death outside the convent than is granted by canon 1230, § 5, to the superioress on the occasion of the death of women religious in the convent. The third paragraph of canon 1221 provides that male employees who die "*intra septa*" of the religious house enjoy the same rights as novices. This provision of the canon is obviously inapplicable to institutes of women religious.

It seems to the writer therefore that any attempt to apply the norms of canon 1221 to the determination of the funeral church for women religious must end in failure. The law of canon 1230, § 5, namely, "*serventur generalia canonum praescripta,*" must refer then to canons other than canon 1221.

The second argument of Coronata is of greater weight. He maintains that the local pastor can never assert that his parish church is the proper parish church of exempt women religious, but that the proper parish church of exempt nuns is the church or oratory of their religious house. With this judgment the writer is in agreement. Moreover, canon 1230, § 5, indicates clearly that the chaplain of exempt women religious is constituted their pastor in regard to the right to conduct their funerals. At the same time, the canon seems to specify the funeral church for women religious. For those who are exempt from the jurisdiction of the pastor, the oratory or church of their convent is so designated; for those who are not exempt from the jurisdiction of the pastor, the funeral church is the local parish church.

If these principles are assumed, it seems that the use of canons 1216–1218 will afford a very probable solution to the problem of the funeral church of a woman religious who has died outside her convent. The body of an exempt woman religious, whether she is a nun subject to the regular clergy or subject to the local Ordinary or to the Roman Pontiff, or a sister who is a member of a community which has been withdrawn from the jurisdiction of the local pastor according to canon 464, § 2, ought to be brought to her funeral church, that is, to the oratory or church of her convent, if the transfer can be made easily.[94] If it is inconvenient to make the transfer, her funeral ought to take place in the church of the parish in which she died.[95] Those persons who have an interest, especially her superioress, always have the right to bring the body to the proper funeral church, that is, to the oratory or church of her convent.[96]

The bodies of sisters who are subject to the jurisdiction of the pastor are to be brought at death to the church of the parish within whose limits is located the religious house to which they were assigned, if it can be done easily.[97] If the transfer to the parish church cannot be made conveniently, their funeral church is the parish church of the place in which they died.[98] However, the religious community has the right to have the body brought to the proper funeral church, that is, to the parish church of the convent in which the sister was stationed prior to her death.

3. Novices: Postulants

Novices are subject generally to the same laws as women religious in funeral matters. However, according to canon 1223, § 1, and canon 1224, they are not forbidden to choose their funeral church.

Postulants or aspirants, since they are neither religious nor novices, are governed by the usual norms which regulate the funerals of the faithful.[99]

4. Servants in Houses of Women Religious

Although Larraona [100] and Beste [101] admit that canon 1221, § 3, which provides that male employees, if actually in the service of the men religious, and if dwelling constantly within the precincts of a religious house, who die within its limits enjoy the same rights

---

[94] C. 1216, § 1.
[95] C. 1218, § 1.
[96] C. 1218, § 3.
[97] C. 1216, § 1.
[98] C. 1218, § 1.
[99] Cc. 1216–1218.
[100] " Commentarium Codicis "—*CpR,* IX (1928), 313.
[101] *Introductio in Codicem,* Commentary on c. 1221.

as the novices in regard to their funerals, is not applicable to the women employees in communities of women religious, they believe that the right conceded to the male employees in that canon should be extended to women employees of communities of women religious because of the evident equality and juridical resemblance of their positions. The Code, however, grants to the women who live within the enclosure as employees, students, guests or as nursing cases, the right to select the oratory of the nuns as a funeral church.[102] From its classification in canon 1225 of women employees with the others, e.g., guests, to whom there is denied the right to have their funerals in the oratory of the nuns,[103] unless they choose the oratory as their funeral church, it seems that the legislator supposes that the funerals of women employees cannot occur there unless they have chosen the oratory of the nuns as their funeral church.

It appears to the writer that the opinion of Larraona and Beste, to which Coronata [104] and Cappello [105] are opposed, cannot be maintained, especially in view of the fact that there is a presumption that such employees are subject to the pastor.[106] It must be remembered of course that the only women employees who could possibly be conceived as being exempt from the jurisdiction of the pastor are those employed in the convents of nuns or in a community which has been withdrawn from the jurisdiction of the pastor. In other communities of sisters, the sisters themselves are subject to the jurisdiction of the pastor.

H. Guests, Students, the Sick, in Religious Houses, Colleges, Hospitals

It has been noted above [107] that in the monasteries of the regular clergy the only persons considered exempt from the jurisdiction of the local Ordinary by the Council of Trent were the actual

---

[102] C. 1225.
[103] C. 1222.
[104] *De Locis et Temporibus Sacris*, n. 179.
[105] *Summa*, II, n. 729.
[106] C. 1217.
[107] Cf. *supra*, p. 134.

servants of the regular clergy who lived *intra septa monasterii.* The Council decreed that all other persons residing in the monasteries, colleges, and hospitals, such as guests, students or the infirm, were subjects of the local Ordinary and consequently of the pastor. However, after the Council of Trent colleges [108] and hospitals for externs [109] frequently obtained exemption from the jurisdiction of the local Ordinary and from that of the local pastor, especially in virtue of the privilege of exemption accorded them by the Holy See. Occasionally these institutions became exempt from the pastor's jurisdiction by virtue of the immemorial custom of entrusting the spiritual care of the persons resident in them to a chaplain.[110] Shortly after the middle of the nineteenth century it became more and more clear from the constant practice of the Roman Curia that the local Ordinary also could exempt pious houses from the jurisdiction of the local pastor.[111]

Canon 1222 is substantially a repetition of the pre-Code legislation. This canon rules that the funerals of those persons who were accustomed to stay in a religious house, even in a monastery of any order, or in a college, either as guests, or as students, or as persons there confined through physical infirmities, as well as the funerals of those persons who died in a hospital, are regulated by the ordinary law of canons 1216–1218, which governs the conduct of the funerals of the faithful, unless it is clear that a particular law or a granted privilege provides otherwise.

An exception is made in this canon to the general import of canon 6, which states that all laws, both universal and particular, if they be opposed to the provisions of the Code, are abolished.[112] In the matter of funeral rights of the persons mentioned in canon 1222, the particular law and granted privileges are given prefer-

[108] Many, *De Locis Sacris,* n. 184.

[109] Bouix, *Tractatus de Parocho* (3. ed., Parisiis, 1880), p. 653.

[110] *Loc. cit.*

[111] "Per Ordinarii decretum, dummodo graves adsint rationes, etiam conservatoria a iurisdictione parochiali eximi posse."—S. C. C., 3 ian. 1873—*ASS,* VIII (1874), 546; S. R. Rota, *in Vincentina,* 25 mart. 1915—*AAS,* VII (1915), 332; S. C. C., *Lisbonen.,* 21 apr. 1917—*AAS,* X (1918), 141.

[112] C. 6, 1°: "Leges quaelibet, sive universales sive particulares, praescriptis huius Codicis oppositae, abrogantur, nisi de particularibus legibus aliud expresse caveatur."

ence over the common law of canons 1216–1218. Legitimate custom, legal prescription, the diocesan statutes, the decrees of a provincial or of a plenary council, and the law established for the government of any pious house at the time of its foundation, may be understood as forms of particular law.[113] The privilege to conduct the funerals of all the inmates therein may be granted to institutions by the Apostolic See or by the bishop.[114] This privilege may be acquired by legitimate custom and by legal prescription.[115] The possession of the privilege for one hundred years or from time immemorial begets the presumption that a privilege has been granted.[116] The particular law or privilege will at least implicitly indicate the priest who has the right to conduct the funerals in the privileged institutions. Normally it is the chaplain of the institution, or the priest to whom the care of the church in which the ceremonies occur is committed.

Worthy of special attention is the rule of canon 464, § 2, which states that the bishop for a just and grave cause can withdraw from the care of the pastor religious communities and pious houses which are in the parochial territory and are not exempt by law. A pious house is to be understood as any institution dedicated to religion or charity, provided that its spiritual care is subject to ecclesiastical authority. The kinds of pious houses in the Church are too numerous to record. By way of example there may be named some institutions for the relief of the destitute and the afflicted, such as orphanages, homes for the aged, sanitariums, asylums and hospitals, and some others established for purposes of education, such as academies, preparatory schools, colleges and

---

[113] Cappello, *Summa*, II, n. 730.

[114] "In iure—Privilegium hoc, nedum ab Apostolica Sede, sed etiam ab Episcopo concedi potest; maxime in Synodo Dioecesana. Immo potest esse quoque objectum conventionis inter parochos, et acquiri vi legitimae consuetudinis. Neque dicatur exemptionis privilegium, utpote iuri communi contrarium, non posse constituere objectum legis dioecesanae, et tanto minus episcopalis decreti; privilegium enim hoc, quo hospitalia gaudent, iuris favorem habet; . . . Iuris intentioni plene respondet; et ideo si quae hac super re lex dioecesana sit lata, optime sustinetur, et iuri communi derogat." —S. R. R. Decisio, *Iuris Funerandi, Bergomen.,—AAS,* XII (1919), 129.

[115] *Loc. cit.*

[116] C. 63, § 2.

universities.[117] If pious houses are withdrawn from the jurisdiction of the pastor, his funeral rights are then committed by the bishop to the chaplain who is appointed to supply for the pastor in funeral matters.

Since the Code designates "pious houses" as the institutions which the bishop can withdraw from the pastor's jurisdiction, it is not clear that his power can extend also to merely profane, philanthropic and public institutions in which there is no regard for his authority, e.g., reform schools, insane asylums, prisons, sanitariums for tubercular patients and homes for cripples, blind or feeble-minded persons. Ordinarily the funeral church of the inmates of these institutions is determined according to the rules of canons 1216–1218. Occasionally, and especially if the institutions are large, a priest is designated as a chaplain to one or the other of them. It seems that this special chaplain could acquire the right to conduct the funerals of the inmates in virtue either of an agreement entered into by the pastors of the particular locality,[118] or of an agreement with the local pastor who, because he is unable to take care both of the persons in these institutions and also of his parishioners at the same time, requests the appointment of a chaplain. Practically the church in which the funerals would be conducted could also be determined by agreement if the institution does not have its own oratory or church.

Unless religious houses, colleges and hospitals have a special privilege or are governed by particular law, canon 1222 prescribes that the ordinary law of canons 1216–1218 must be followed in regard to the funerals of the guests, of the students and of the sick in any religious house, college or hospital.[119] The guest, student or sick person who has died in a religious house, college or

---

[117] Beste, *Introductio in Codicem,* Commentary on c. 464, § 2.

[118] S. R. R. Decisio, *Iuris Funerandi, Bergomen.,—AAS,* XII (1919), 129 ff.

[119] "Hospitals operated and used exclusively by clerics regular have naturally the same complete exemption which the exempt community itself enjoys. . . . Similarly hospitals or infirmaries established exclusively for clerical religious who are not exempt and even for clerical religious of merely diocesan approval are exempt from parochial jurisdiction."—Drumm, *Hospital Chaplains,* The Catholic University Canon Law Studies, n. 178 (Washington, D. C.: The Catholic University of America Press, 1943), 80.

hospital is to be transferred for his funeral to his proper parish church unless he has chosen another church for his funeral. If he has several proper parishes, the church for his funeral is the church of the parish in which he died. Although he died outside his proper parish, his body is to be brought for his funeral to his proper parish church which is nearest to his place of death, if the transfer can be made easily; if it cannot, the body must be brought not to the church or oratory of the institution, but to the church of the parish within whose territory he died. Those who have an interest may always transport his body to the proper funeral church, provided that they pay the expenses involved.

The guests may be either merely casual visitors simply enjoying the hospitality of one of these institutions during some days, or lodging and boarding in them as in an inn. If they happen to die while they are present in or staying at these institutions, their funerals are determined by the law of canons 1216–1218. Of course they can choose the church of the religious house, of the college or of the hospital, if it is one that can be chosen legitimately. In this connection it may be noted that guests of nuns who live constantly within the enclosure of the convent may choose the oratory of the nuns for their funerals.[120]

Students who live in a religious house or in a college in order to obtain an education are bound also by the common law in funeral matters. If they have reached the age of puberty, they may exercise their right of selecting their funeral church. This funeral church may be the church of the institution, if it can otherwise be legitimately selected.[121] Thus, students who live continually within the enclosure of a convent of nuns may select the oratory of the convent as their funeral church.

It must be noted that students in boarding schools may establish very easily a quasi-domicile in the parish in which their schools are located, since a quasi-domicile is acquired by a person who lives in a parish with the intention of remaining there at least for the greater part of a year, or whose stay in the parish is protracted beyond six months. In regard to funerals the parish

---

120 C. 1225.

121 C. 1225.

church of one's quasi-domicile is a proper parish church within the meaning of canon 1216. Hence, in the event that a student dies in the school after having acquired a quasi-domicile in the territory of the parish in which the school is located, his body must be brought for the funeral to the church of the parish in which the school is situated, and not to the parish church of his domicile.[122]

The funeral church of persons who because of sickness or of various kinds of physical infirmities reside in a religious house, or in hospitals, infirmaries, rest homes, sanitariums or convalescent homes, is determined also by the ordinary law of canons 1216–1218. The inmates of these institutions can, of course, select a particular church for their funerals. It is permitted to women who because of physical disabilities dwell continually within the enclosure of a convent of nuns to choose the oratory of the convent as their own funeral church. At least a quasi-domicile, if not a domicile, in the parish in which the institution is situated can also be acquired very easily by the persons who dwell in such institutions. The same conclusion therefore must be drawn in regard to their funerals as was indicated in the preceding paragraph concerning the funerals of students in boarding schools. It may be noted also that the funeral church of students in schools of nursing, and of women nurses who reside in hospitals, is also determined by the regulations of canons 1216–1218.

I. Persons Who Die in a Seminary

Canon 1222: . . . **quod vero ad illos attinet qui in Seminario moriuntur, servetur praescriptum can. 1368.**

The regulation in regard to those who die in the seminary is new legislation. It is a consequence of the law of canon 1368,[123] which rules that the seminary shall be exempt from parochial

[122] "Si defunctus plures habuerit paroecias proprias, ecclesia funeris est ecclesia paroeciae in cuius territorio decessit."—c. 1216, § 2.

[123] "Exemptum a iurisdictione paroeciali Seminarium esto; et pro omnibus qui in Seminario sunt, parochi officium, excepta materia matrimoniali, et firmo praescripto can. 891, obeat Seminarii rector eiusve delegatus, nisi in quibusdam Seminariis fuerit aliter a Sede Apostolica constitutum."

jurisdiction, and that the rector of the seminary or his delegate shall discharge the office of a pastor for all the persons in the seminary, except in matters pertaining to marriage, and with due observance of the precept of canon 891, namely, that the rector abstain from hearing the confessions of the seminarians, unless in particular cases they freely approach him for some serious and urgent reason.

The rector of the seminary has parochial jurisdiction over all persons who are in the seminary, whether it be a major or a minor seminary, diocesan, provincial, or national in character. Not only the seminarians, but also the officials of the seminary, in positions subordinate to that of the rector, namely, the teachers, the employees, the sisters and others who live in the seminary or within its grounds, must look to him as their proper pastor. Even guests, such as priests who, although they may be students at a neighboring college or university, reside permanently in the seminary, seem likewise to be numbered among his subjects.

In view of the fact that canon 1368 uses such general terms, namely, "*qui in Seminario sunt,*" Beste [124] thinks that even visitors who habitually live elsewhere are subject to his jurisdiction as long as they stay in the seminary. Coronata's doctrine [125] agrees in the main with Beste's interpretation, but he excludes from subjection to the rector those visitors who have a domicile near the seminary. It seems to the writer that more worthy of merit is the opinion of Cocchi,[126] who insists on an abiding and fixed residence in the seminary as a prerequisite for the qualification of any person as a subject of the rector.

In regard to all persons in the seminary, the rector acts as the proper pastor. According to canon 1222, he is empowered to conduct their funerals only if they die in the seminary.

It must be recalled also that students and teachers, in fact all who are not religious and have attained the age of puberty, may choose their funeral church. Moreover, it is the common opinion of the commentators on the Code that the funeral church of men

---

[124] *Introductio in Codicem,* Commentary on c. 1368.

[125] *De Locis et Temporibus Sacris,* n. 185.

[126] *Commentarium,* V, n. 58.

religious who live in the seminary, and to whom perhaps the conduct of the seminary or its educational work is entrusted, is determined not by canon 1368 but by the law for men religious.[127]

Naturally, the funerals of those who die in the seminary will be conducted by the rector or his delegate in the church or oratory of the seminary. The funeral of the rector should be conducted there also. If a person who died in the seminary had legitimately chosen a church for his funeral, the body must be brought to the church selected for the services. If a lay person subject to the rector dies outside the seminary, the funeral church will be determined by the ordinary law of canons 1216–1218. If a woman religious dies outside her convent, which is within the jurisdiction of the rector, the law determining the funeral church for women religious will be obligatory.

[127] Cocchi, *Commentarium,* V, n. 58; Cappello, *Summa,* II, n. 730; Coronata, *De Locis et Temporibus Sacris,* n. 185; Beste, *Introductio in Codicem,* Commentary on c. 1222.

CHAPTER VII

THE MINISTER OF THE FUNERAL

The preceding chapters of this canonical commentary have presented a study of the necessity of conducting the funerals of deceased Catholics in a church, furnished a definition of the funeral church, and indicated the determination in specific instances of the proper church in which the exequies are held. It will be recalled that the Code of Canon Law designates the church in which the exequies are ordinarily held; that it permits the legitimate selection of a church for one's exequies; and that it determines a particular church for the funerals of certain classes of persons. At this point consideration must be given to the determination of the proper minister who according to law officiates as the corpse receives Christian burial.

It must be recalled that Christian burial consists of three elements, the transfer of the body to the church, the exequies celebrated over the body in the church, and the interment of the body in a place legitimately set aside for the burial of the bodies of the faithful departed. In conferring ecclesiastical burial, the minister uses the rites and performs the ceremonies prescribed by the Roman Ritual.

At the time set for the transfer of the body to the church, the clergy and the other persons who are to be present at the funeral come together in the parish church according to their rank. The pastor, vested in a surplice and black stole or also a black cope, proceeds with the others to the home of the deceased. In this procession, one cleric carries the holy water, another bears the cross.[1]

Before the body is carried from the house, the pastor blesses it with holy water. Then he says the antiphon, "*Si iniquitates,*"

---

[1] Rituale Rom., tit. VI, c. 3, *Exsequiarum ordo,* n. 1.

the psalm, "*De profundis,*" and the entire antiphon, "*Si iniquitates observaveris, Domine: Domine, quis sustinebit?*" The performance of these acts by the minister constitutes the "*levatio.*" "*Levare corpus*" means literally to raise or to take up the body. For centuries the phrase has been used to designate the first acts performed by the priest who conducts a body to burial. It seems to the writer that the phrase "reception of the body" retains the meaning of the Latin phrase, and at the same time indicates clearly the act that is performed. Hence the phrases "*levare corpus*" and "*ius levandi corpus*" will be rendered henceforward by the English phrases "the reception of the body" and "the right to receive the body," respectively.

While the priest is receiving the body, another procession is formed. At its head are the lay confraternities, followed in order by the cross-bearer, and the regular clergy and the secular clergy according to their rank. As he comes out of the house, the priest intones the antiphon, "*Exsultabunt Domino.*" Simultaneously the casket is carried from the house by the pallbearers. The priest follows the procession of the clergy just ahead of the casket. The casket, carried by the pallbearers or in a hearse, is immediately behind him. The mourners take their place after the hearse. During this procession to the funeral church the persons accompanying the body chant the prescribed psalms.[2]

The position before the casket is the highest place of honor in the funeral procession. The priest in this position as the procession moves toward the funeral church is said to accompany the body or to be exercising the right to escort the body (*ius comitandi, ius deducendi in ecclesiam*) to the church.

At the entrance to the church the antiphon "*Exsultabunt*" is chanted again. The psalm "*Subvenite*" is sung as the coffin is moved into the position it will occupy during the exequies.[3] The office of the dead is said,[4] followed by the offering of the exequial Mass.[5] The prayers, chant and rites of the Absolution over the dead body are then performed. After the prayer which begins

---

[2] Rituale Rom., tit. VI, c. 3, *Exsequiarum ordo,* n. 2.

[3] Rituale Rom., tit. VI, c. 3, *Exsequiarum ordo,* nn. 2, 3.

[4] Rituale Rom., tit. VI, c. 3, *Exsequiarum ordo,* n. 4.

[5] Rituale Rom., tit. VI, c. 3, *Exsequiarum ordo,* n. 6.

"*Deus, cui proprium est misereri et parcere*" has been said, the body is carried from the church to its place of burial. The various acts that occur in the church are called the exequies. The priest who has the right to officiate during their performance is said to have the right to conduct the exequies (*ius exsequias peragendi*) or the funeral proper.

To determine as clearly as possible which priest is competent to exercise these rights, namely to receive the body, to escort it to the church and to conduct the exequies over it, is the immediate purpose of this chapter.

ARTICLE I. THE MINISTER IN FUNERALS CONDUCTED ACCORDING TO THE ORDINARY LAW

A. Of Parishioners Who Die in Their Proper Parish

Canon 1230, § 1: **Proprius defuncti parochus non solum ius sed etiam officium habet, excepto gravi necessitatis casu, levandi per se vel per alium cadaver, illud comitandi ad suam ecclesiam paroecialem ibique exsequias persolvendi, firmo praescripto can. 1216, § 2.**

The Code in canon 1230, § 1, states that the proper pastor of the deceased is entitled and obliged, unless excused by grave necessity, to go himself or to send a delegate to the house to receive the body, to accompany it to his parish church and there to hold the exequies; that in the event the deceased had several proper parishes the proper pastor is the pastor of the parish in which the person died. In paragraph one of canon 1230 the legislator considers the case in which the parishioner dies in his proper parish.

It has been noted in the discussion of canon 1216 that, if the parishioner does not choose a church for his funeral, the church to which his body is to be brought is his local parish church.[6] Canon 462, 5°, numbers among the functions reserved to the pastor the conduct of the proper ceremonies in funerals as regulated by canon 1216.[7] Canon 1230, § 1, now indicates that the proper pas-

[6] Cf. *supra*, p. 76.

[7] "Functiones parocho reservatae sunt, nisi aliud iure caveatur: 5°. Iusta funebria persolvere ad normam can. 1216."

tor of the person who has died in his own parish without having selected previously a particular church for his funeral has the right and the duty to receive the body, to escort it to his parish church, and to conduct the funeral there.

It is necessary to recall the provisions of the Code regarding the determination of the proper parish [8] and the proper pastor. The term " pastor " in the strict sense signifies an individual priest or a moral person to whom a parish has been conferred in title with the care of souls to be exercised under the authority of the local Ordinary.[9] In those instances in which the parish is handed over to a moral person, e.g., a religious community, the moral person cannot be the actual pastor, but only the pastor in title. The moral person must then entrust the entire actual care of souls to an individual priest who acts in the capacity of a parochial vicar and possesses all the rights and obligations of pastors as defined by the common law and as established by diocesan statutes or by laudable customs.[10]

The Code [11] extends the term " pastor " to include those priests who enjoy all parochial rights and are subject to all parochial obligations:

I. *Quasi-pastors:* those priests who are entrusted with the full parochial care of souls in quasi-parishes, which are separate territorial divisions of a vicariate or of a prefecture apostolic.[12]

II. *Parochial vicars:* those priests who take the place of the pastor in the performance of the parochial duties in the care of souls.[13] The Code distinguishes various classes of parochial vicars with distinct rights and duties.

A. *Actual vicars:* the priests who exercise the actual care of souls in a parish held in title by a moral person.[14]

B. *Administrators:* the priests placed in charge of a vacant parish.[15]

---

[8] Cf. *supra*, pp. 77 ff.
[9] C. 451, § 1.
[10] Cc. 452; 471, §§ 1, 4.
[11] C. 451, § 2.
[12] C. 216, § 3.
[13] Beste, *Introductio in Codicem*, Commentary on c. 471.
[14] Cc. 471; 1425.
[15] Cc. 472, § 1; 473.

C. *Substitutes.* Of this class the Code lists three kinds, namely:

1. The priest who with the approval of the local Ordinary has charge of the parish when the pastor is lawfully absent from his parish for more than a week;[16]

2. The priest who is designated by the local Ordinary to take the place of the pastor who has appealed to the Holy See after having been removed from his benefice by judicial sentence;[17]

3. The priest who has been selected by the pastor to serve as his substitute when the pastor was constrained for a serious reason to leave his parish quickly and to be absent from it for more than a week.[18]

D. *Parochial adjutants:* the priests who are deputed by the local Ordinary to assume the duties of a pastor who is permanently incapacitated.[19] If a parochial adjutant is appointed to supply for the pastor in all parochial affairs, he has all the rights and duties of a pastor with the exception of the application of the Mass in behalf of the congregation (*Missa pro populo*). If, however, he has only a part of the pastoral duties to attend to, his rights and obligations must be learned from his letter of appointment.[20]

E. *Assistants:* the priests who are assigned by the local Ordinary to assist the pastor, who by himself cannot take proper care of the parish either because of its size or for other similar objective reasons. However, according to the law of the Code an assistant can be treated as on an equal juridical basis with a " pastor " only if full parochial power is granted to him either by the diocesan statutes, through the Ordinary's letter of appointment, or in consequence of the commission of the pastor himself.[21] The Code states that, unless it is otherwise expressly provided, the assistant pastor by virtue of his office is obliged to take the place of the pastor and to help him in the whole parochial minis-

[16] Cc. 465, § 4; 474.
[17] Cc. 474; 1923, § 2.
[18] Cc. 465, § 5; 474.
[19] C. 475, § 1.
[20] C. 475, § 2.
[21] Cc. 451, § 2, 2o; 476, § 6.

try, the application of the Mass in behalf of the congregation (*Missa pro populo*) alone being excepted.[22]

III. *Military chaplains.* If full parochial jurisdiction is given to them by the particular regulations of the Holy See, they will have the status of personal pastors.[23] The norms enacted by the Sacred Consistorial Congregation for the Military Ordinariate of the United States of America indicate expressly that the jurisdiction of military chaplains is strictly personal, and can be exercised by them over their proper subjects any place on earth; that this jurisdiction embraces parochial power in regard to their own subjects.[24]

IV. The rector of the seminary has the office of a pastor in funeral matters in regard to all persons who as abiding residents die in the seminary.[25]

V. In clerical religious organizations, the superior to whose church the body of the professed religious or of the novice is brought for the funeral is authorized to exercise all the rights of the proper pastor.[26]

VI. The chaplains of nuns and of religious communities which have been withdrawn from the jurisdiction of the local pastor in funeral matters have the status of a pastor in the conduct of the funerals of the nuns and of the members of the communities which have been withdrawn from parochial jurisdiction.[27]

VII. Other chaplains according to the Code ordinarily do not possess the pastoral right to conduct funerals. However, in virtue either of a privilege, or of a particular law, or by reason of the withdrawal of a pious house from the jurisdiction of the pastor [28] and the subsequent delegation of the pastor's rights by the local Ordinary, the chaplain may receive the right to conduct the com-

[22] C. 476, § 6.

[23] C. 451, § 3.

[24] *Litt. ad Excmum. ac Revmum. Delegatum Apostolicum, Amer-Sept., die 1 Julii, 1940—Prot. num. 186/39; Decretum—Neo-Eboracensis—die 9 Aprilis 1941, Prot. num. 186/39;*—Bouscaren, *The Canon Law Digest,* II, 587.

[25] Cc. 1222; 1368. Cf. *supra,* p. 149.

[26] Cf. *infra,* p. 181.

[27] Cf. *infra,* p. 184.

[28] C. 464, § 2.

plete funeral of all or of certain classes of persons who died in the institution.[29]

Canon 1230, § 1, concedes to the proper pastor the right to receive the body of a parishioner who has died in the parish, to escort it in liturgical procession to his church, and to conduct the exequies there. If the pastor is hindered from exercising his rights, he can depute another priest to perform all these acts. Moreover, for a just cause a deacon can be granted permission to perform the acts by either the Ordinary or the pastor. If the deacon has the express permission of the Ordinary or of the pastor, a permission which in a case of necessity is legitimately presumed to be present, he must observe all the rites prescribed by the Ritual.[30]

It has been remarked above that a person may have one or several proper parishes.[31] If a person has one proper parish and dies in it, his funeral church is the parochial church of his one proper parish. The pastor who has the rights to receive the body, to escort it to his own church, and to conduct in it the exequies of the deceased member of the parish, is the pastor of the deceased's one proper parish.

If a person has several proper parishes and dies in one of them, the funeral church is the church of his proper parish within whose limits he died, whether this be the parish church of his domicile or of his quasi-domicile. The pastor of the parish in which the person died has the rights to receive the body, to escort it to his own church, and to conduct the exequies there.

Regarding the parishioner who dies in his own parish, the proper pastor is also obliged to receive the body, to escort it to his parish church, and to conduct the exequies over the body in the church. The Code here imposes a grave obligation on the pastor, since only in a case of grave necessity is he excused from its fulfillment.

A case of grave necessity is not to be found in the fact that the parishioners are poor. The Code[32] and the Roman Ritual[33]

---

[29] Cf. *supra*, p. 146.

[30] S. R. C., *Tonkini Occidentalis*, 14 aug. 1858; Rituale Rom., tit. VI, c. 3, *Exsequiarum ordo*, n. 19.

[31] Cf. *supra*, pp. 77–81.

[32] C. 1235, § 2: "Pauperes gratis omnino ac decenter funerentur et

prescribe that the funeral and the burial of the poor are to be conducted in a becoming fashion and wholly free of expense to the poor. The Ritual moreover rules that the priests upon whom the care of the deceased belongs should provide the customary candles at their own expense, if necessary.

The case of grave necessity which excuses the proper pastor from his obligation is to be judged from similar cases. In the commentary on canon 1215 [34] there have been noted a number of grave causes, e.g., an epidemic, a state of war, the prohibition of the civil law, each of which would constitute a case of grave necessity excusing the pastor from his duty to receive the body and to conduct it to his church for the funeral. However, it is certainly the mind of the Church that, if the body cannot be brought to the church for the funeral, the exequial Mass and the ceremony of the Absolution should always be celebrated even though the remains are present only in a moral sense.[35]

The obligation for the pastor is not of the same gravity in regard to the performance of all the prescriptions of the Ritual.[36] It may be recalled, too, that in the United States of America there is a prevailing custom to the effect that the pastor does not go in procession to the house of the deceased, but simply receives the body at the door of the church.

B. Of Parishioners Who Die Outside Their Proper Parish

Canon 1230, § 2: **Quod si mors acciderit in loco alienae paroeciae, et cadaver ad ecclesiam propriae paroeciae commode asportari possit, parochi proprii est, praemonito parocho loci, illud levare, comitari ad suam ecclesiam ibique exsequias peragere.**

The Code in paragraph two of canon 1230 declares that, if a person has died in a strange parish and the body can be brought

---

sepeliantur, cum exsequiis, secundum liturgicas leges et dioecesana statuta, praescriptis."

[33] Tit. VI, c. 1, *De exsequiis,* n. 11.

[34] Cf. *supra,* pp. 48–50.

[35] Cf. *supra,* p. 49.

[36] Cf. *supra,* pp. 51–53.

conveniently to his own parish church, the proper pastor has the right and duty to receive the body, to accompany it to his own church, and to have the funeral there, after previously informing the pastor of the strange parish that he is coming in procession for the body.

It was noted above [37] that for the person who has only one proper parish and dies outside its limits the proper funeral church is the parochial church of his one proper parish, if his body can be brought easily to that church. The proper pastor of his parish has the right and the duty to enter the other parish to receive his body, to escort it to his own parish church, and to conduct the exequies there.

In every instance, however, in which the pastor enters another parish in order to perform the first liturgical act, he should inform the pastor of the strange parish beforehand that he is coming in the usual procession to receive the body of his deceased parishioner. This previous information communicated by the pastor of the deceased to the pastor of the place of the death of the parishioner is not to be understood as a request for permission to enter his parish in order to receive the body. Moreover, as he escorts the body to the funeral church, the proper pastor can pass freely through the territory of another parish or diocese without the permission of the pastor or of the Ordinary respectively.[38]

The proper funeral church for the person who has more than one proper parish is his nearest parochial church, if the body of this person who has died outside the limits of all of his parishes can be brought easily to that church.[39] In this case the pastor to whose care the nearest proper parish church of the deceased is committed has the right and the duty to go in procession to the place of the person's death in order to escort the body even through other parishes to his own church and to conduct the exequies there. Again, the minister, before he enters the other

---

[37] Cf. *supra*, p. 91.

[38] C. 1232, § 1: "Sacerdos qui cadaver comitetur ad ecclesiam funeris . . . , libere transire poterit, cum stola quoque et cruce elevata, per territorium alius paroeciae vel dioecesis, etiam sine parochi vel Ordinarii licentia."

[39] Cf. *supra*, p. 92.

parish to receive the body, should inform the pastor of the place in which the minister's parishioner died that he (the minister) is entering his (the local pastor's) parish.

The proper funeral church for the person who dies so far away from his proper parish or parishes that the transfer of his body for the funeral to any one of the proper parish churches is inconvenient has also been determined.[40] If the persons who have an interest wish to have the body brought to any of the deceased's proper parishes, the church for the funeral is that which they select.[41] The proper pastor of the church selected is then the minister at all the ceremonies connected with the ecclesiastical burial of the deceased traveller.

In this instance, however, that is, when death occurs outside the proper parish, and when the transfer of the body to the proper parochial church is inconvenient but the relatives nevertheless undertake to bring the body to the proper parish church, it is difficult to determine which pastor has the right to receive the body in liturgical procession. The Code has no solution for the problem, since it directly gives to the proper pastor the right to receive the body only if the body can be brought easily to his church.

Coronata[42] and Beste[43] maintain that the pastor of the place of the death of the parishioner has the right to receive the body and to conduct it to the limits of the proper parish. Both of these authors base their contention on an analogy which they find in the comparison of canon 1230, § 2, with canon 1232, § 2. Canon 1232, § 2, states that the pastor of the funeral church cannot assert a right to accompany the body in procession to a place of burial outside the limits of the city when the body is to be buried in a cemetery to which it cannot easily be brought. Hence, it would seem, too, that the proper pastor cannot claim the right to go in procession to receive the body for the funeral when it cannot easily be brought to his parish church, but that this right belongs to the pastor of the place in which the parishioner died.

Their opinion appears reasonable only in the case in which the

---

40 Cf. *supra*, pp. 99–100.

41 Cf. *supra*, p. 100.

42 *De Locis et Temporibus Sacris*, n. 207, nota 1.

43 *Introductio in Codicem*, Commentary on can. 1230, § 2.

proper parish and the parish in which the death occurred are rather close to each other. In the event that the body must be brought or shipped a considerable distance, it seems that the reception of the body by the proper pastor as it arrives in his parish will fully satisfy the will of the legislator that all liturgical acts should be performed.

If the relatives or the friends of the deceased do not care to have the body brought to the church of any of his proper parishes, the funeral church is the church of the parish in which the person died. This is also the proper funeral church for the wanderer (*vagus*) and for the person who has only a diocesan domicile or quasi-domicile.[44] Obviously the pastor of the parish in which the person died exercises the rights and has the obligation to receive the body of any one of these persons, to escort it to his own church, and to conduct the exequies over it.

ARTICLE II. THE MINISTER IN CASES OF SELECTION OF THE FUNERAL CHURCH

All persons, except professed religious, when they have attained the age of puberty may freely select their funeral church and the cemetery for their burial.[45] The selection by any person of the funeral church implies the selection of its cemetery as the place for his burial, unless the deceased has chosen a particular cemetery or possesses a family plot.[46] On the other hand, the choice of a particular cemetery for his burial does not at the same time connote the selection of the particular funeral church. If only the cemetery is chosen, the funeral church must be determined according to the rules of canons 1216–1222. Since the interment will be the subject of a later chapter, the present discussion will be restricted to a consideration of the proper minister at the funeral of a person who has selected a particular church for his exequies.

Canon 1225 rules that the only churches which can be validly selected are parish churches, churches of the regular clergy, and

---

[44] Cf. *supra*, p. 86.
[45] Cf. *supra*, pp. 105–106.
[46] Cf. *supra*, p. 119.

other churches endowed with the right to conduct funerals. It permits the selection of the oratory of a convent of nuns, but only by those women who live continually within the cloister of the monastery.[47] In addition, a church of advowson may be selected as his funeral church by the avdowee or patron.

It is obvious that, if a person selects for his funeral his own parish church, the proper pastor has the right to receive the body, to escort it to his church, and to perform the exequies there. In this article, therefore, the selection of a parish church refers always to a parish church different from the proper parochial church.

The churches endowed with the right to conduct funerals are either exempt from the jurisdiction of the pastor, e.g., a church of the regular clergy, or subject to his jurisdiction, e.g., a church of a confraternity. The Code first presents the law to be observed when the funeral is held in an exempt church, and secondly, the rule governing the conduct of funerals in churches subject to the jurisdiction of the pastor.

A. Funerals at Churches Exempt from the Jurisdiction of the Pastor

Canon 1230, § 3: **Si ecclesia funeris sit ecclesia regularis aliave exempta a iurisdictione parochi, parochus, sub cruce ecclesiae funerantis, cadaver levat ac deducit ad ecclesiam; sed exsequias rector ecclesiae celebrat.**

The Constitution "*Dum intra*" of Pope Leo X (1513–1521) ruled that the regular clergy did not have by common law the right to remove the remains of those persons who had chosen to be buried in their churches; that the right of bestowing burial when granted to the regular clergy did not include the right to enter processionally into the parishes for this purpose, but that the regulars needed first to consult the pastor; that they could come in procession to receive the body in two instances, namely, if the pastor refused to conduct the body to their church, or if there was a custom which favored their right to remove the body from

[47] Cf. *supra*, p. 109.

the home of the deceased to their own church for the obsequies.

During the subsequent centuries the Sacred Roman Congregations were asked to settle many disputes which arose in practice as the result of misunderstandings of the provisions of the Constitution. The constant jurisprudence of the Roman Curia made it very clear that, in the event a parishioner chose for his burial either a church of the regular clergy or any other church exempt from the jurisdiction of the pastor, certain very definite regulations were to be observed by the clergy both of the proper parish church and of the church selected by the person for his burial.

The regular clergy and the chapters of collegiate churches[48] were not to enter processionally with a cross the proper parish of the deceased in order to receive the body,[49] but they were to invite the pastor to receive the body and to conduct it to their churches. If the pastor refused to bring the body,[50] or if the clergy of the funeral church had waited a reasonable length of time beyond the hour set for the funeral and the pastor had not brought the body,[51] they could go in procession to receive the corpse and escort it to their church for the funeral.

The proper pastor alone had the right to receive the body of

---

[48] S. R. C., *Thelesina,* 18 aug. 1629—*Fontes,* n. 5322; *Montis Regalis,* 12 iul. 1664, ad 5, 6—*Fontes,* n. 5546.

[49] S. C. Ep. et Reg., decr. gen., 12 ian. 1604—*Fontes,* n. 1627; *Nepesina,* 11 dec. 1615, ad 4—*Fontes,* n. 1669; *Vulturarien.,* 13 mart. 1744, ad 3, 4—*Fontes,* n. 1860; S. C. C., *Tusculana,* 22 nov. 1732, 5 iun., 24 iul. 1734, ad 1, 2—*Fontes,* nn. 3398, 3430; S. R. C., *Tornacen.,* 25 sept. 1649, ad 8—*Fontes,* n. 5459; *Baren.,* 1 dec. 1657, ad 2—*Fontes,* n. 5495; *Aquen.,* 2 sept. 1741, ad 8—*Fontes,* n. 5780; *Bestana,* 3 mart. 1674—*Fontes,* n. 5596; *Senogallien.,* 22 iun. 1675, ad 3-4—*Fontes,* n. 5605; *Novarien.,* 20 nov. 1677, ad 1—*Fontes,* n. 5622; *Messanen.,* 24 febr. 1680, ad 11—*Fontes,* n. 5634.

[50] S. C. Ep. et Reg., decr. gen., 12 ian. 1604—*Fontes,* n. 1627; *Vulturarien.,* 13 mart. 1744, ad 3, 4—*Fontes,* n. 1860; S. C. C., *Nullius Messanen.,* 19 dec. 1857, ad II, III—*Fontes,* n. 4159; *Novarien.,* 1 et 15 mart. 1704, ad 2—*Fontes,* n. 3015; S. R. C., *Montis Regalis,* 12 iul. 1664, ad 5, 6—*Fontes,* n. 5546; *Vestana,* 3 mart. 1674—*Fontes,* n. 5596; *Senogallien.,* 22 iun. 1675, ad 3-5—*Fontes,* n. 5605.

[51] S. C. Ep. et Reg., *Montis Pelusii,* 23 sept. 1735 ad 2, 4 et 28 febr. 1749—*Fontes,* nn. 1853, 1865; S. C. C., *Tusculana,* 22 nov. 1732, 5 iun., 24 iul. 1734, ad 1, 2—*Fontes,* n. 3398; *Nullius Messanen.,* 19 dec. 1857, ad II, III—*Fontes,* n. 4159.

his parishioners.[52] He alone therefore had the right to wear the stole, to sprinkle the corpse with holy water and to intone the antiphon "*Exsultabunt Domino*" as the corpse was carried from the house.[53] It was also his duty to receive the body, even if the clergy of the funeral church did not appear to assist him.[54] The regular clergy were not obliged to accompany the pastor as he went to the house for the reception of the body, but they could await his arrival with the corpse at their own church.[55] In the procession to the funeral church the proper pastor had the right of precedence unless the canons and clerics of the cathedral chapter attended in a body.[56]

The only cross to be used in the procession from the house to the funeral church was the cross of the funeral church.[57] A sole exception to this rule was admitted in the event that the cathedral chapter in a body participated in the procession. In that in-

---

[52] S. C. Ep. et Reg., *Bisinianen.*, 25 febr. 1592—*Fontes*, n. 1450; *Castellaneten.*, 3 febr. 1593—*Fontes*, n. 1473; *Castellaneten.*, 10 ian. 1594—*Fontes*, n. 1501; decr. gen. 12 ian. 1604—*Fontes*, n. 1627; S. C. C., *Spoletana*, 19 apr. 1692, ad 4—*Fontes*, n. 2928; *Insularum Canariae*, 31 iul. 1694—*Fontes*, n. 2943; *Ebredunen.*, 25 iun. 1695, ad 9—*Fontes*, n. 2948; S. R. C., *Discalceatorum Sancti Augustini in Galliis*, 6 iul. 1641—*Fontes*, n. 5406; *Tornacen.*, 25 sept. 1649, ad 8—*Fontes*, n. 5459; *Baren.*, 1 dec. 1657, ad 2—*Fontes*, n. 5495; *Messanen.*, 24 febr. 1680, ad 11—*Fontes*, n. 5634; *Aquen.*, 2 sept. 1741, ad 8—*Fontes*, n. 5780; *Sabinen.*, 12 nov. 1831, ad 1—*Fontes*, n. 5959.

[53] S. R. C., *Sabinen.*, 12 nov. 1831, ad 1—*Fontes*, n. 5859.

[54] S. R. C., *Discalceatorum Sancti Augustini in Galliis*, 6 iul. 1641—*Fontes*, n. 5406; *Senogallien.*, 22 iun. 1675, ad 3-5—*Fontes*, n. 5605; *Ordinis Carmelitarum Discalceatorum Congregationis Italiae*, 27 ian. 1680—*Fontes*, n. 5633; *Firmana*, 7 maii 1763, ad 1—*Fontes*, n. 5805.

[55] S. C. Ep. et Reg., *Alben.*, 30 apr. 1717, ad 3 et 2 sept. 1718—*Fontes*, n. 1833; S. C. C., *Eugubina*, 22 maii 1762, ad 3—*Fontes*, n. 3718.

[56] S. R. C., *Meliten.*, 18 nov. 1606—*Fontes*, n. 5227; *Aquaependen.*, 10 dec. 1667—*Fontes*, n. 5227; *Alexanen.*, 21 mart. 1739, ad 2—*Fontes*, n. 5775.

[57] S. C. Ep. et Reg., *Castellaneten.*, 10 ian. 1594—*Fontes*, n. 1501; *Baren.*, 15 mart. 1595—*Fontes*, n. 1536; *Vulturarien.*, 13 mart. 1744, ad 3, 4—*Fontes*, n. 1860; S. C. C., *Ebredunen.*, 25 iun. 1695, ad 5—*Fontes*, n. 2948; S. R. C., *Sulmonen.*, 18 aug. 1629—*Fontes*, n. 5319; *Sutrina*, 6 apr. 1680—*Fontes*, n. 5638; *Lucen.*, 15 maii 1694, ad 1—*Fontes*, n. 5692; *Urbis seu Romana*, 9 aug. 1681, 18 aug. 1714—*Fontes*, n. 5642; *Meliten.*, 27 febr. 1723, ad 5—*Fontes*, n. 5763; *Sabinen.*, 12 nov. 1831, ad 1—*Fontes*, n. 5859.

stance the cross of the cathedral chapter supplanted the cross of the funeral church.[58]

The proper pastor did not have the right to escort the body to his own church first in order to have some kind of ceremony there before he accompanied it to the proper funeral church, but the body was to be brought directly by the pastor from the home to the funeral church.[59] Moreover the request of the relatives that the body be brought first to the parish church was to be disregarded.[60]

The proper pastor possessed the right to escort the body simply to the door of the funeral church.[61] While the body remained at the door of the church, he was allowed to give the "*ultimum*

---

[58] S. C. Ep. et Reg., *Castellaneten.*, 3 febr. 1593—*Fontes*, n. 1473; S. C. C., *Ruben.*, 8 et 28 iul. 1713, ad 2—*Fontes*, n. 3124; S. R. C., *Sutrina*, 6 apr. 1680—*Fontes*, n. 5638; *Urbis seu Romana*, 9 aug. 1681, 18 aug. 1714—*Fontes*, n. 5642; *Andrien.*, 19 iul. 1710, ad 6, 7—*Fontes*, n. 5744.

[59] S. C. Ep. et Reg., *Castellaneten.*, 10 ian. 1594—*Fontes*, n. 1501; *Baren.*, 15 mart. 1595—*Fontes*, n. 1536; *Nepesina*, 11 dec. 1615, ad 4—*Fontes*, n. 1669; *Pientina*, 5 aug. 1729, ad 1—*Fontes*, n. 1845; S. C. C., *Troiana*, 7 et 21 maii 1701, ad 3 et 17 iun. 1702—*Fontes*, n. 2984; *Massanen.*, 17 apr. 1706, ad 1—*Fontes*, n. 3040; *Lucana*, 17 ian., 7 et 28 febr., 14 mart. 1722, ad 1—*Fontes*, n. 3238; *Sabinen.*, 18 dec. 1734, 19 ian. 1735, ad II—*Fontes*, nn. 3436, 3439; *Ariminen.*, 16 iun. 1827, ad 3-5—*Fontes*, n. 4010; *Forolivien.*, 26 ian. 1833, ad I—*Fontes*, n. 4043; S. R. C., *Umbriaticen.*, 25 febr. 1606—*Fontes*, n. 5218; *Cassanen.*, 4 maii 1647—*Fontes*, n. 5452; *Ordinis Minorum Observantium S. Francisci*, 19 dec. 1671—*Fontes*, n. 5583; *Savonen.*, 19 dec. 1671, ad 4—*Fontes*, n. 5584; *Senogallien.*, 22 iun. 1675, ad 3—*Fontes*, n. 5605; *Monopolitana*, 16 dec. 1679—*Fontes*, n. 5631; *Ordinis Carmelitarum Discalceatorum Congregationis Italiae*, 27 ian. 1680—*Fontes*, n. 5633; *Avenionen.*, 3 dec. 1701—*Fontes*, n. 5720.

[60] S. R. C., *Ordinis Minorum Observantium S. Francisci*, 19 dec. 1671—*Fontes*, n. 5583.

[61] Clemens X, const. "*Nuper pro parte*," 18 ian. 1672—*Fontes*, n. 247; S. C. Ep. et Reg., *Castellaneten.*, 10 ian. 1594—*Fontes*, n. 1501; *Placentina*, 16 dec. 1661, ad 3—*Fontes*, n. 1795; *Montis Politiani*, mense mart. 1711, ad 4—*Fontes*, n. 1828; *Alben.*, 30 apr. 1717, ad 1, 2 et 2 sept. 1718—*Fontes*, n. 1833; S. C. C., *Insularum Canariae*, 31 iul. 1694—*Fontes*, n. 2943; *Ebredunen.*, 25 iun. 1695, ad 10—*Fontes*, n. 2948; *Lauden.*, 2 maii, ad 1—*Fontes*, n. 3101; *Volaterrana*, 30 ian. 1723, 23 febr., 16 mart. 1726, ad 5—*Fontes*, nn. 3257, 3313; *Bononien.*, 18 sept. 1751—*Fontes*, n. 3619; S. R. C., *Firmana*, 7 maii 1763, ad 1—*Fontes*, n. 5805.

vale," which consisted of a simple blessing of the body.[62] He was not permitted to enter the church with any outward indication that he was the minister at the exequies, e.g., by wearing a stole, or that he possessed jurisdiction in the funeral church, e.g., by having a cross borne before him.[63] However, he was permitted to be present at the exequies if he removed his stole and made no effort to take part in the function.[64]

Within the funeral church exempt from the jurisdiction of the pastor, whether it was a church of the regular clergy, a collegiate church, or a confraternity church which was endowed with the same funeral rights as the churches of the regular clergy,[65] only the rector had the right to conduct the exequies.[66] Even if the canons of a cathedral church were in attendance at the funeral in

[62] Clemens V, const. *"Nuper pro parte,"* 18 ian. 1672—*Fontes,* n. 247; S. C. Ep. et Reg., *Minorum Observantium Reformatorum,* 5 sept. 1710—*Fontes,* n. 1827; *Montis Politiani,* mense mart. 1711, ad 1—*Fontes,* n. 1828; *Alben.,* 30 apr. 1717, ad 1, 2 et sept. 1718—*Fontes,* n. 1833; S. C. C., *Insularum Canariae,* 31 iul. 1694—*Fontes,* n. 2943; *Lauden.,* 12 maii 1711, ad 1—*Fontes,* n. 3101; S. R. C., *Novarien.,* 20 nov. 1677, ad 2—*Fontes,* n. 5622; *Aquen.,* 2 sept. 1741, ad 8—*Fontes,* n. 5780.

[63] S. C. C., *Insularum Canariae,* 31 iul. 1694—*Fontes,* n. 2943; *Ebredunen.,* 25 iun. 1695, ad 10—*Fontes,* n. 2948; *Lauden.,* 12 maii 1711, ad 1—*Fontes,* n. 3101; *Volaterrana,* 30 ian. 1723, 23 febr., 16 mart. 1726, ad 5—*Fontes,* nn. 3257, 3313; *Bononien.,* 18 sept. 1751—*Fontes,* n. 3619.

[64] S. R. C., *Novarien.,* 20 nov. 1677, ad 2—*Fontes,* n. 5622; *Avenionen.,* 3 dec. 1701—*Fontes,* n. 5720.

[65] S. C. C., *Senogallien.,* 1 febr. 1908—*Fontes,* n. 4345.

[66] S. C. Ep. et Reg., *Bisinianen.,* 25 febr. 1592—*Fontes,* n. 1450; *Castellaneten.,* 10 ian. 1594—*Fontes,* n. 1501; 31 aug. 1657—*Fontes,* n. 1792; *Veliternen.,* 22 aug. 1670—*Fontes,* n. 1802; *Minorum Observantium,* 27 nov. 1671—*Fontes,* n. 1808; *Conventualium,* 20 mart. 1739, ad 2—*Fontes,* n. 1855; S. C. C., *Troiana,* 7 et 21 maii 1701, ad 3 et 17 iun. 1702—*Fontes,* n. 2995; *Ruben.,* 8 et 28 iul. 1713, ad 2—*Fontes,* n. 3124; S. R. C., *Meliten.,* 18 nov. 1606—*Fontes,* n. 5227; *Theatina Terrae Buccanici,* 11 dec. 1627, ad 1—*Fontes,* n. 5299; *Sulmonen.,* 18 aug. 1629—*Fontes,* n. 5319; *Firmana,* 26 ian. 1641—*Fontes,* n. 5392; *Oritana,* 11 maii 1641—*Fontes,* n. 5403; *Montis Regalis,* 12 iul. 1664, ad 6—*Fontes,* n. 5546; *Aquaependen.,* 10 dec. 1667—*Fontes,* n. 5567; *Lucerina,* 4 aug. 1674, ad 3—*Fontes,* n. 5601; *Urbis seu Romana,* 9 aug. 1681, 18 aug. 1714—*Fontes,* n. 5642; *Mexicana in Indiis Occidentalibus,* 3 sept. 1746—*Fontes,* n. 5787; *Neritonen.,* 12 sept. 1884, ad 1—*Fontes,* n. 6159.

a body, they were not permitted to usurp the right of the rector of the funeral church to conduct the exequies.[67]

In 1895 the Sacred Congregation of Rites presented in its decree on the exequies a summary of the rules to be observed in the conduct of funerals.[68] The decree provided that in all funeral processions only one cross was to be used; that this cross was the cross of the church to which the body was brought for the funeral, unless the chapter of the cathedral church was present, in which case the cross of the cathedral chapter alone was to be used. It stated further that, from the place of death to the entrance to the church where the funeral was to occur, the proper pastor, even if the chapter of the cathedral church was present, always had the right and the duty to wear the stole and to conduct over the deceased all the religious offices. It ruled also that the body was to be carried directly from the home to the funeral church; that to reach the funeral church the procession could pass freely through other parishes. In addition it prescribed that, if a deceased person was to be buried in another parish church, the rector of this parish church, likewise wearing a stole, had both the right and the duty to perform the exequies in the church over the body of the deceased; that the rector had the right of precedence over all other persons, not excepting the proper pastor who, after he had brought the body to the threshold of the funeral church, was to withdraw from further official ministrations. Finally it was ordered that these rules were to be observed by all churches, whether collegiate or non-collegiate, whether belonging to the secular or to the regular clergy.

The Code in canon 1230, § 3, contains the chief legal points of the decree. It rules that, if the funeral church is a church of the regular clergy, or some other church exempt from the jurisdiction of the proper pastor, e.g., a collegiate church or another parish church, the proper pastor in a liturgical procession led by the cross of the funeral church receives the body at the home and

---

[67] S. C. Ep. et Reg., *Veliternen.*, 22 aug. 1670—*Fontes*, n. 1802; S. C. C., *Ruben.*, 8 et 28 iul. 1713, ad 2—*Fontes*, n. 3124; S. R. C., *Aquaependen.*, 10 dec. 1667—*Fontes*, n. 5567; *Lucerina*, 4 aug. 1674, ad 3—*Fontes*, n. 5601.

[68] S. R. C., decr. super exsequiis, 23 apr. 1895, n. I, II, IV, V—*Fontes*, n. 6243.

escorts it to the funeral church; that the rector of the exempt church conducts the exequies in the church.

In the event that a person selects an exempt church for his funeral church the rules mentioned above are to be followed. The proper pastor, therefore, must go in procession to the home to receive the body. There he has the right to sprinkle the corpse with holy water, to say the antiphon "*Si iniquitates,*" to recite the psalm "*De profundis,*" and to repeat the antiphon. He also has the right to intone the antiphon "*Exsultabunt Domino*" as the body is being carried from the house. Finally, from his position in front of the casket he has the right to escort the body to the door of the funeral church.

The cross with which the bearer leads the procession from the home to the funeral church must be the cross of the funeral church.

At the threshold of the church, the rights of the proper pastor cease. As the procession moves into the church, the chanters sing the antiphon "*Exsultabunt.*" [69] From this moment until the last prayer of the Absolution over the body is said [70] the rector of the church is the minister of all the rites and ceremonies performed in the church. Since the priest who conducts the exequies has the right to accompany the body to the place of burial,[71] it can be said that he is in complete charge of the funeral and the burial of the person who has elected his church as a funeral church and its cemetery as the place of his burial.

B. Funerals at Churches Subject to the Jurisdiction of the Pastor

At the Council of Trent a number of cases involving the selection for burial of a church which was not exempt from the jurisdiction of the pastor were presented for decision to the Sacred Roman Congregations. Their conclusions varied somewhat from those reached in cases involving the selection for burial of churches that were exempt from the jurisdiction of the pastor.

It was decided that, in non-exempt churches of confraternities,[72]

---

[69] Rituale Rom., tit. VI, c. 3, *Exsequiarum ordo,* n. 3.

[70] Rituale Rom., tit. VI, c. 3, *Exsequiarum ordo,* nn. 3–10.

[71] C. 1231, § 2.

[72] S. C. C., *Bononien.,* 12 febr., 10 iun., 8 et 28 iul. 1724, ad 9—*Fontes,* nn.

or in churches subject to the right of patronage,[73] the pastor of the parish in which the church was situated had the right to conduct the exequies, provided that the deceased had been a subject of the pastor;[74] that the rector or chaplain of the non-exempt church did not have the right to conduct the exequies, unless the pastor refused to come to conduct the funeral,[75] or unless the person to be buried was not a subject of the pastor.[76] However, particular privileges given to certain churches according to which the chaplains could conduct the exequies of all who selected these churches for burial were recognized.[77]

The Sacred Congregation of Bishops and Regulars and the Sacred Congregation of the Council in two separate cases expressly decreed that the pastor of the parish in which the non-exempt church was located had the right to conduct the exequies of both parishioners and non-parishioners whose funerals were to be conducted at the non-exempt church, but it was necessary for them to reply in this vein for the reason that there were very special circumstances involved in each case.[78]

Canon 1230, § 4, is therefore a succinct expression of the constant jurisprudence of the Roman Curia. It states that in a funeral church which is not exempt from the jurisdiction of the pastor the celebration of the exequies, except for a special privilege to the contrary, pertains not to the rector of the church, but to the pastor in whose territory the church is situated, provided that the deceased was his subject.

3275, 3279; *Viterbien.*, 26 aug., 16 sept. 1826, ad 5—*Fontes*, n. 4006; S. R. C., *Urbis et Orbis*, 12 ian. 1704, ad 20—*Fontes*, n. 5733.

[73] S. R. C., *Capuana*, 22 dec. 1629—*Fontes*, n. 5323.

[74] S. C. C., *Viterbien.*, 26 aug., 16 sept. 1826—*Fontes*, n. 4006; S. R. C., *Urbis et Orbis*, 12 ian. 1704, ad 20—*Fontes*, n. 5733; *Venusina*, 27 aug. 1836—*Fontes*, n. 5885; *Casertana*, 7 iul. 1877—*Fontes*, n. 6099.

[75] S. C. C., *Bononien.*, 12 febr., 10 iun., 8 et 28 iul. 1724, ad 9—*Fontes*, nn. 3275, 3279; *Viterbien.*, 26 aug., 16 sept. 1826—*Fontes*, n. 4006; S. R. C., *Capuana*, 22 dec. 1629—*Fontes*, n. 5323.

[76] S. R. C., *Perusina*, 9 iul. 1718, ad 4—*Fontes*, n. 5757; *Perusina*, 13 maii 1719, ad 7—*Fontes*, n. 5759.

[77] S. C. C., *Tiburtina*, 27 ian., 17 mart. 1827, ad 2—*Fontes*, n. 4009.

[78] S. C. Ep. et Reg., *Lauden.*, 20 aug. 1601—*Fontes*, n. 1607; S. C. C., *Faventina*, 17 iul. 1773, ad 5 et 14 mart. 1778, ad 5—*Fontes*, nn. 3785, 3803.

The role of the proper pastor of the deceased is clear. If the deceased who had selected as his funeral church a non-exempt church located within the parish was the parishioner of the local proper pastor, the latter has the right to receive the body, to escort it to the non-exempt church, to conduct the exequies therein, and to accompany the body to the place of burial.[79]

If the deceased chose a church which likewise is not exempt from the jurisdiction of the pastor, but which is located outside the territory of his proper parish, the proper pastor of the deceased has the right to receive the body and to conduct it to the non-exempt church. The rector of this church then has the right to conduct the exequies over the body in the church. As the canon clearly states, the pastor of the parish in which the non-exempt church is located has the right to celebrate the exequies in that church only if two conditions are fulfilled simultaneously, namely, if the non-exempt church is within the limits of his parish and if the deceased was his parishioner.

It is clear that the exequies in the church selected for the funeral are celebrated by the rector of the church or by the pastor of the local parish. It is clear also that the proper pastor of the deceased should receive the body and conduct it to the selected church. Therefore if the body of a parishioner who has died within the parish can be brought conveniently in liturgical procession to the church selected, the pastor should receive the body and escort it there.

The Code does not contain any explicit provisions regarding the reception of the body by the proper pastor in the event that the body is to be transported a considerable distance from the proper parish to a church selected for the funeral. If the body of a parishioner who has died within the parish cannot easily be brought in procession, but must be transported a considerable distance by automobile or by railroad to the church selected for the funeral, it seems to the writer that the rector of the selected church should receive the body on its arrival within his district. Coronata [80] thinks that the proper pastor should receive the body and

---

[79] C. 1231, § 2.

[80] *De Locis et Temporibus Sacris*, n. 217.

conduct it to the point from which the shipment is made, e.g., the railroad station. The final answer to the problem, it appears, must be sought in the particular law or the local custom, either of which may determine exactly the part played by the proper pastor when from a place far removed from the proper parish the body is to be transported to a church selected for the funeral.

In the Code there are likewise no provisions regarding the reception of the body by the proper pastor in the event that the parishioner died outside his proper parish. It seems reasonable to assert that the proper pastor should receive the body of a parishioner who has died outside the parish and should conduct it to the church selected for the funeral if the body can be brought easily on foot in liturgical procession to that church. Rossi believes that, if the person who has selected a church for his funeral dies so far from his proper parish that it is inconvenient for the proper pastor to convey the body to the funeral church, but near enough to the selected church that the rector can easily bring the body to the funeral church for the exequies, the rector of the selected funeral church should receive the body after he has informed the pastor of the place in which the person died that he is coming for the body in liturgical procession. He also asserts that, if the person has died far from both the parish church and the church selected for the funeral, the rector of the church selected should receive the body upon its arrival in his district.[81] The solutions of these two cases offered by the learned author appear to be logical and, moreover, commendable.

It has been noted above [82] that the oratory of a convent of nuns may be selected by certain women, namely by students, servants, boarders or sick persons, who dwell constantly within the precincts of the monastery. The oratory of a convent of nuns who are subject to regular superiors is exempt from the jurisdiction of the pastor.[83] The oratory of nuns who are subject to the juris-

[81] *Sepultura Ecclesiastica,* p. 218.

[82] Cf. *supra,* p. 109.

[83] C. 615: "Regulares, novitiis non exclusis, sive viri sive mulieres, cum eorum domibus et ecclesiis, exceptis monialibus quae Superioribus regularibus non subsunt, ab Ordinarii loci iurisdictione exempti sunt, praeterquam in casibus a iure expressis."

diction of the local Ordinary seems to be exempt from the jurisdiction of the local pastor in regard to funerals as soon as the care of the monastery is confided to a chaplain. If the chaplain has not been appointed, the oratory of the convent is subject to the juridiction of the local pastor.

The lay women who under certain conditions have the right to select the oratory of the convent as their funeral church are obligated by the common law in regard to ecclesiastical burial as long as they do not exercise this right. If they have not selected the oratory as their funeral church, their proper pastor has the right to receive the body and to escort it to his church for the exequies, whether they died in or outside the monastery.

If after having selected the oratory for their funeral church they died outside the monastery, their proper pastor receives the body and escorts it to the monastery church. If the oratory is exempt from his jurisdiction, the chaplain of the monastery conducts the exequies.[84] If it is subject to the jurisdiction of the local pastor, the latter conducts the exequies.[85]

If these persons, after having selected the oratory as their funeral church, died within the monastery, the chaplain may receive the body, escort it to the oratory, and conduct the exequies. If a chaplain has not been appointed, the pastor of the parish in which the monastery is situated may perform each of these acts.

The patron may select the church of patronage as his funeral church.[86] His proper pastor has the right to receive the body of the deceased patron and to conduct it to this church. If the church of patronage is subject to the jurisdiction of a pastor and if the deceased patron is a subject of the same pastor, he conducts the exequies.[87] If the church of patronage is withdrawn from the jurisdiction of the local pastor, or if the deceased patron was not his subject, the rector of the church of patronage conducts the exequies in the church.[88]

---

[84] C. 1230, § 3.
[85] C. 1230, § 4.
[86] C. 1225.
[87] C. 1230, § 4.
[88] C. 1230, §§ 3, 4.

ARTICLE III. THE MINISTER OF THE FUNERALS OF SPECIAL CLASSES OF PERSONS

A. The Roman Pontiff

After the body of the deceased pope has been brought by the Chapter of the Vatican Basilica from the Vatican Palace to the Basilica of St. Peter, it lies in state in the Chapel of the Blessed Sacrament until its interment. At the altar of the Chair in the apse of the Basilica, the Cathedral Chapter conducts the solemn exequies on each of the first six days appointed by the cardinals in their first general congregation. Assisted by his colleagues one of the members of the Chapter sings the Requiem Mass and gives the Absolution at the large catafalque (*castrum doloris*).[89]

As ministers of the ceremonies which are conducted with greater solemnity on each of the last three days of the *Novendialia,* three cardinals are appointed to sing the Requiem Mass; four other cardinals are named to assist each of these cardinals with the Absolution at the catafalque.[90]

A day, which need not coincide with the last day fixed for the exequies, is appointed for the interment of the deceased pontiff. The Chapter of the Basilica escorts the body from the Chapel of the Blessed Sacrament to a position before the altar of the Chair. Here the members of the Chapter, some members of the Curia and the cardinals perform the last ceremonies associated with the burial of a pope. In the procession to the place of interment in the crypt of the Basilica, the cardinals led by the cardinal archpriest of the Basilica of St. Peter follow the casket.[91]

B. Cardinals

Canon 1230, § 6: **Defuncto S. R. E. Cardinali aut Episcopo extra Urbem in civitate episcopali, servetur praescriptum can. 397, n. 3.**

Canon 1230, § 6, rules that the prescription of canon 397, 3°, is to be observed in the event that a cardinal or a bishop dies out-

---

[89] "*Ssmi. Domini Nostri Pii Papae XI Extrema Aegrotatio, Obitus, Funebria*"—*AAS,* XXXI (1939), 40-41.

[90] *Ibid.,* pp. 48-50.

[91] *Ibid.,* p. 42.

side the city of Rome in an episcopal see. According to canon 397, 3°, the dignitaries and canons of the cathedral chapter in the order of precedence have the right and duty, unless it is stated otherwise in the statutes of the chapter, to perform all the ceremonies associated with the funeral of the deceased bishop.[92] Hence they have the right to receive the body of the deceased cardinal or bishop, to escort it to the cathedral church, and to conduct the exequies there.

If a cardinal dies within the city of Rome, his proper pastor receives the body and accompanies it in procession to the funeral church designated by the Roman Pontiff.[93] Unless the Holy Father has named a particular prelate, the right to conduct the exequies pertains to the dean of the Sacred College of Cardinals.[94] According to Wernz-Vidal[95] and Rossi[96] a prelate of the Roman Curia is ordinarily designated to celebrate the Mass of Requiem, and the dean of the Sacred College of Cardinals gives the Absolution in the name of the Holy Father.

If a cardinal dies outside an episcopal see, his body is to be brought for the funeral to the most prominent church of the city in which he died, unless those persons who have an interest in the case transfer the body to its proper funeral church. In the event that the transfer does not occur, the rector of the more important church of the city conducts all the funeral ceremonies.[97]

C. Bishops

It was noted above that the body of a deceased residential bishop, and of an abbot *nullius* or prelate *nullius*, should be brought for

---

92 " Nisi aliud in statutis capitularibus caveatur, dignitatibus et canonicis secundum ordinem praecedentiae ius et officium est: 3°. Eidem (Episcopo) decumbenti ministrare Sacramenta; defuncto iusta funebria persolvere."

93 Rossi, *Sepultura Ecclesiastica,* n. 86; Cocchi, *Commentarium,* V, n. 62.

94 Cocchi, *Commentarium,* V, n. 62; Coronata, *De Locis et Temporibus Sacris,* n. 209; Beste, *Introductio in Codicem,* Commentary on canon 1230, § 6.

95 *Ius Canonicum,* IV, Pars I, n. 580.

96 *Sepultura Ecclesiastica,* n. 86.

97 " Secus a Clero ecclesiae loci dignioris, nisi Episcopus aliud statuerit, v. gr., si ipse cum canonicis suae Ecclesiae velit funus peragere."—Wernz-Vidal, *Ius Canonicum,* IV, Pars I, n. 580, nota (22).

the funeral to the cathedral church, abbatial church or prelatic church respectively, if the transfer can readily be made; that, if the body cannot easily be brought to the proper funeral church, it should be carried to the most prominent church of the city in which the death occurred; that the church selected for their funeral by these persons is to be preferred to any of the churches designated expressly in the law.

Canon 1230, § 6, is applicable also to bishops who die outside the city of Rome. The whole control of the ceremonies associated with the funerals of residential bishops who die in their episcopal sees is reserved to the dignitaries and canons of the cathedral church according to their rank.

Moreover, canon 1230, § 6, in its use of the phrase "*in civitate episcopali,*" seems to indicate that, if a bishop dies in any episcopal city, even though this city is not the site of his own see, the local cathedral chapter has the right to conduct all the funeral ceremonies in the cathedral church. Such a conclusion is in harmony with the rule of canon 1219, § 2, which prescribes that the body of a deceased residential bishop should be brought to the most prominent church of the place in which he died, if his body cannot easily be brought to his own cathedral church. It must be recalled, of course, that the use of this right by the cathedral chapter is contingent on the fact that the body of the deceased prelate was allowed to remain there for the funeral, either inasmuch as he had not selected a particular funeral church, or inasmuch as those who had an interest did not care to bring the body to the deceased's proper cathedral church for the funeral.

If the residential bishop dies outside an episcopal city, whether this be his own or that of another diocese, and his body is not brought to the episcopal see, the minister at all the functions is the rector of the most prominent church of the place in which the bishop died.

Canon 397, 3°, fully concedes to the dignitaries and canons of the cathedral chapter the right to conduct all the funeral ceremonies of the deceased bishop. It does not restrict the chapter to an exercise of this right exclusively in the cathedral church. Hence it appears that, if the residential bishop has selected a church in an episcopal city which is not his cathedral church, and his body can be brought to that church for the funeral, the dignitaries and canons of the cathedral chapter, instead of the rector of the funeral church, have the right to perform all the ceremonies connected with the deceased bishop's funeral and burial.

The funerals of abbots *nullius* and of prelates *nullius* are to be conducted by the clergy of the abbatial and prelatic church respectively. However, if the abbot *nullius* dies in an episcopal city outside the city of Rome, the local cathedral chapter performs all the funeral ceremonies, provided that his body is not brought to his abbatial church, or that he has not selected a particular church as the church at which the funeral rites are to be held.

If he dies outside an episcopal city, the rector of the most prominent local church performs all the funeral ceremonies. The same principles are applicable also to the case of a deceased prelate *nullius*.

The funeral church of a deceased titular bishop is his proper parish church. Cocchi [98] believes that the determination of the minister at the funeral of a deceased titular bishop is established also by canons 1230, § 6, and 397, 3°. Rossi [99] holds that, if the titular bishop has died outside his proper parish but in an episcopal city, the local cathedral chapter are to perform all the funeral ceremonies. Coronata [100] asserts that the minister of the funeral of a titular bishop is the rector of his parish church or the rector of the church selected for his funeral by the titular bishop. He maintains that the minister must be determined in this case according to the ordinary law, and that canon 397, 3°, since it refers only to residential bishops, cannot be applied at any time to the funerals of titular bishops.

Canon 1230, § 6, uses simply the word "*Episcopo,*" and prescribes that, in the event a bishop dies outside the city of Rome in an episcopal city, canon 397, 3°, must be observed. Hence it seems that, if the titular bishop dies in the city of an episcopal see, the cathedral chapter has the right to perform all the cere-

---

[98] *Commentarium,* V, n. 62.

[99] *Sepultura Ecclesiastica,* n. 86.

[100] *De Locis et Temporibus Sacris,* n. 210.

monies associated with his funeral. It seems very probable that the opinion of Rossi, then, can be maintained.[101]

In the United States the board of diocesan consultors takes the place of the cathedral chapter as the council of the bishop. The Code states in canon 427 that whatever part in the government of the diocese the law of the Code gives to the cathedral chapter during the reign of the bishop, during the time that the exercise of his jurisdiction is impeded, or during the vacancy of the bishopric, is also assigned to the body of consultors.[102]

Canon 397, 3°, declares that the dignitaries and canons of the cathedral chapter in their order of precedence have the right and duty to conduct the ceremonies associated with the funeral and burial of the deceased residential bishop. The subject matter of this regulation does not seem to be included in matters that pertain to the government of the diocese. Moreover, the law seems to belong to that kind of legislation which immediately regulates the rights and the duties of the cathedral chapter considered as such, and not when considered as forming the council of the bishop. According to the strict interpretation of canon 427 the common law does not appear to attribute to the consultors according to their order of precedence the right and duty to officiate at the services on the occasion of the funeral and burial of the deceased bishop.

However, it may be noted that according to canon 397, 3°, the minister who is actually granted the right to conduct the funeral ceremonies of the deceased residential bishop is the ecclesiastical person who enjoys the first right of precedence in the council of the bishop. By analogy, it seems that, in the event there is not a cathedral chapter in the diocese, the ecclesiastical person who has the first right of precedence in the council of the bishop has

---

[101] "Episcopi mere titulares hac in re reguntur communi iure fidelium; quodsi decesserit extra suum domicilium in civitate aliqua episcopali, ecclesiae cathedrali funus tribuendum videtur."—Wernz-Vidal, *Ius Canonicum,* IV, Pars I, n. 580, nota (23).

[102] "Coetus consultorum dioecesanorum vices Capituli cathedralis, qua Episcopi senatus, supplet; quare quae canones ad gubernationem dioecesis, sive sede plena sive ea impedita aut vacante, Capitulo cathedrali tribuunt, ea de coetu quoque consultorum dioecesanorum intelligenda sunt."

the right and the duty to conduct the funeral ceremonies of the deceased residential bishop. In those dioceses therefore in which the board of diocesan consultors acts as a council of the bishop the senior consultor who enjoys the right of precedence over other members of the council should be acknowledged as the possessor of this right.[103] Incidentally it may be remarked that it has become a common practice in this country to invite neighboring bishops and friends of the deceased prelate among the bishops to participate in the performance of the ceremonies on the occasion of his funeral and burial.

D. Residential Beneficiaries: Pastors; Priests

Before the promulgation of the Code the funerals of the canons of the cathedral and collegiate churches were to be held at their proper parish church, and were to be conducted by their proper pastor, unless they had chosen a particular church for their funeral, or unless the chapter possessed a distinct place for the burial of their deceased members in their church.[104] However, in many cities there was a strongly entrenched custom to the effect that the cathedral and collegiate chapters conducted the exequies of their own deceased members in their own churches.[105]

A priest who had a residential benefice in a certain church but lived in a parish distinct from the parish of his benefice was to be buried not in the parish of his benefice but in the parish of his

---

[103] Jaeger, *The Administration of Vacant and Quasi-Vacant Episcopal Sees in the United States,* The Catholic University of America Canon Law Studies, n. 81 (Washington, D. C.: The Catholic University of America, 1932), p. 111.

[104] Many, *De Locis Sacris,* nn. 177, 178; Wernz-Vidal, *Ius Canonicum,* IV, Pars I, n. 580.

[105] " Disputationes auctorum et resolutiones etiam S. Sedis aliquando inter se contradictoriae ante Codicem datae circa ministrum funerum in hoc casu, iure mere particulari plurimum innitebantur, et aliquando contrariam iuri communi consuetudinem demonstrant, . . ."—Coronata, *De Locis et Temporibus Sacris,* n. 211; "*Canonicorum* exequiae, quamvis de iure praecedenti competerent *parocho,* in cuius parochia canonicus suum habuit domicilium, tamen ex legitima consuetudine multarum dioecesium, v.g. in Gallia et Belgio fieri potuit, ut a Capitulo in ecclesia cathedrali sint celebrandae."—Wernz-Vidal, *Ius Canonicum,* IV, Pars I, n. 580.

domicile. If the church of the benefice had a particular place for the burial of the beneficiaries, the funeral was to be held in the church of the benefice.[106] The common law did not contain any regulations regarding the persons who conducted the funerals of pastors. Their funerals were sometimes reserved by particular law to the vicars forane. The funerals of the vicars forane were occasionally reserved to the neighboring vicar forane or to another priest delegated by the bishop.[107]

It was noted above that the Code now indicates that the funeral church of all residential beneficiaries is the church of their benefice; that the funeral church of deceased canons of chapters of cathedral and of collegiate churches is the proper cathedral or collegiate church respectively. Consequently, the rector of the cathedral or of the collegiate church has the right to conduct the exequies over the body of a deceased member of the chapter. However, the proper pastor of the deceased retains the right to receive the body and to conduct it to the funeral church.[108] The rector of the church of the benefice conducts the exequies of other residential beneficiaries.

Although the Code does not expressly refer to the minister who performs the exequies at the funeral of a pastor it does name his own parish church as the funeral church for the deceased pastor. Moreover, in canon 472, 2°, it seems at least to point to the priest who is to conduct his exequies. It rules that before the administrator of a vacant parish is appointed, the assistant of the former pastor shall assume charge of the parish, unless other provision has been made; that, if there are several assistants in the parish, the first assistant is to take charge; that, if there are no assistants, the nearest pastor takes charge; that, moreover, the ordinary in the diocesan synod, or outside the synod, shall determine beforehand which parish is to be considered nearest. Whichever priest has charge of the vacant parish according to this law appears also to have the right to conduct all the funerals that take place in the parish, the funeral of the deceased pastor included.[109]

---

[106] Many, *De Locis Sacris,* n. 179.

[107] Wernz-Vidal, *Ius Canonicum,* IV, Pars I, n. 580.

[108] Wernz-Vidal, *loc. cit.;* Coronata, *De Locis et Temporibus Sacris,* n. 211.

[109] Rossi, *Sepultura Ecclesiastica,* n. 86; Cocchi, *Commentarium,* V, n. 62.

Vidal stated that the clergy of his parochial church conduct the deceased pastor's funeral. However, he likewise indicated that in instances in which the deceased pastor was the only priest in the parish, his funeral is sometimes reserved by particular law to the vicar forane.[110]

It seems to the writer that the minister at the funeral of the deceased pastor is very frequently determined according to the practice in vogue in each diocese. In the United States customs regarding the selection of the priests to conduct the funeral of their deceased colleague vary considerably. In some dioceses the vicars forane are chosen or at least empowered to select the priests who will conduct all the ceremonies at the funeral of a pastor. In other dioceses the friends of the deceased are selected. Occasionally the priests are named by the pastor before his death. Perhaps more often the ministers at the rites are appointed by the bishop. Not infrequently the bishop of the diocese either celebrates the Requiem Mass or at least performs the Absolution over the deceased pastor.

The funerals of priests who do not possess residential benefices are to be conducted according to the norms regulating the funerals of the faithful. If they do not select a funeral church, their proper pastor receives the body, escorts it to the parish church, and conducts the exequies. If they select for their funeral a church other than their proper parish church, their proper pastor receives the body and escorts it to the church selected. If the church selected is exempt from the jurisdiction of the pastor, the rector of the church celebrates the exequies. If the church selected is not exempt from the jurisdiction of a pastor, this pastor conducts the exequies.

E. Men Religious

The funeral church of deceased men religious is the oratory or the church of their religious house, or at least the oratory or the church of one of the houses of their institute. If the professed religious dies so far away from a house of his institute that in the judgment of the superior it would be too inconvenient to bring

[110] *Ius Canonicum,* IV, Pars I, n. 580.

the body to an oratory or a church of the institute, the funeral church is the church of the parish in which he died.[111]

Canon 1221, § 1, expressly concedes to the religious superior the right to receive the body and to escort it to the funeral church.[112] The religious superior, therefore, of the house to which the body is brought for the funeral is the minister, not only of the exequies which occur in the particular church of the institute selected for the exequies by the superior, but like the proper pastor in other cases, wearing a stole and with a cross borne before him, he may go in liturgical procession to the place where the body of the deceased religious rests, perform the rites prescribed for the reception of the body, and escort the body to the church of the institute. He may pass freely through the territory of any parishes or even of another diocese without the permission of the pastors or of the Ordinaries.[113]

If the deceased religious belonged to a lay congregation, the superior of the lay institute himself, if he is a priest,[114] or through the ministry of the chaplain, exercises the rights to receive the body and to escort it to the oratory or the church which has been selected by him for the funeral. However, if the religious house to which the body is to be brought is subject to the jurisdiction of a pastor, the superior exercises the same rights by means of the ministry of the pastor. Moreover, the pastor conducts the exequies in the oratory of the religious house if it is not exempt from his jurisdiction.[115]

Since the funeral church of the deceased religious, if he dies so far away from his religious house that in the judgment of the superior his body cannot be brought to an oratory or a church of his institute, is the parish church of the place in which the death

---

111 Cf. *supra*, pp. 128–131.

112 "... ius autem levandi cadaver et illud deducendi ad ecclesiam funerantem pertinet semper ad Superiorem religiosum."

113 C. 1232, § 2.

114 Larraona, "Commentarium Codicis," *CpR*, IX (1928), 209.

115 Beste, *Introductio in Codicem*, Commentary on canon 1221; Coronata, *De Locis et Temporibus Sacris*, n. 212; Cappello, *Summa*, II, n. 743.

occurred, the pastor of this parish exercises the same rights as he does in cases of death among his own parishioners.[116]

The funeral church of novices in institutes of men religious is the same as that of the professed religious, except in those cases in which the novices have selected a funeral church.[117] The religious superior has the right to receive the body of the deceased novice and to escort it to the funeral church. If the funeral is held in a church of the religious institute, the religious superior also conducts the exequies. If the novice has selected a particular funeral church, the religious superior as the proper pastor of the deceased conducts the body to the door of the church selected, but the rector of the church selected conducts the exequies.[118]

If the novice dies so far away from his religious house that in the judgment of the superior it is actually inconvenient to bring the body to an oratory of the institute, the local pastor has the right to receive the body, to escort it to his own church, and to conduct the exequies, provided that the novice has not selected a different church as his funeral church. In the event that a novice did select a particular funeral church, the common law regulating the transfer of the body to the funeral church and the conduct of the exequies is obligatory.[119]

F. Men Servants of Men Religious

The funeral church of men servants who die within a religious house is the church of the religious house,[120] unless they have selected a different particular funeral church. If without having selected such a funeral church they die within the religious house, the religious superior exercises all the functions of a pastor in regard to the funeral and burial of his subjects. If they have selected a different funeral church and die within the religious

---

[116] C. 1221, § 2; Larraona, "Commentarium Codicis,"—*CpR,* IX (1928), 209.

[117] C. 1221, §§ 1, 2.

[118] C. 1230, §§ 3, 4.

[119] Larraona, "Commentarium Codicis,"—*CpR,* IX (1928), 209.

[120] Cf. *supra,* pp. 133–134.

house, the religious superior receives the body and conducts it to the selected funeral church.

If they die outside the religious house, their complete funerals are conducted according to the common law. Hence, the proper pastor of the deceased or the pastor of the place in which he died, as determined by the regulations of canons 1216–1218, has the right to receive the body and to perform the exequies.

If the servant has legitimately selected the church of the religious house but dies while he is away from the monastery his proper pastor receives the body and escorts it to the selected church. If the church is exempt from the jurisdiction of the pastor, the religious superior conducts the exequies. If it is not exempt from the jurisdiction of the pastor, the pastor conducts the exequies.

G. Women Religious

It has been noted above that, if they die in the religious house, the funeral church for deceased nuns and sisters who were members of a community that has been withdrawn from the jurisdiction of the pastor is their own oratory or church.[121] In canon 1230, § 5, the Code expressly names the chaplain of the nuns and exempt sisters as the minister of the funeral.[122]

Before the promulgation of the Code the Sacred Roman Congregations in several particular cases designated the confessor of nuns as the minister at their exequies.[123] However, in one instance the Sacred Congregation of the Council named the chaplain of a monastery of nuns as the minister of the exequies.[124] In still another case the Sacred Congregation of Rites responded that the right to conduct the exequies over the bodies of deceased nuns did not belong to the canons of the cathedral church, but to the

---

[121] Cf. *supra*, p. 137–140.

[122] ". . . indeque, si de religiosis agatur iurisdictioni parochi non obnoxiis, ad propriam religiosae domus ecclesiam vel oratorium deducit et exsequias peragit cappellanus; . . ."

[123] S. C. Ep. et Reg., *Clodien.*, 12 iul. 1604—*Fontes*, n. 1631; *Tranen.*, 30 maii 1856, 17 sept. 1858—*Fontes*, nn. 1975, 1977; *Pinerolien.*, 19 apr. 1907—*Fontes*, n. 2055; S. R. C., *Camerinen.*, 16 mart. 1805—*Fontes*, n. 5824.

[124] *Syracusana*, 24 febr. 1872—*Fontes*, n. 4220.

confessor or the chaplain to whom the care of the monastery church was committed.[125]

In the present law, the chaplain, not the confessor, at the convent of nuns or of sisters who are exempt from the jurisdiction of the pastor enjoys the rights of a pastor regarding the conduct of their funerals. Incidentally, it may be noted that a distinction has been made in canon 1230 between the minister at the funerals of the nuns and the minister of Holy Viaticum and extreme unction in the case of their professed members and novices.[126]

Canon 1230, § 5, provides that the women religious of the particular convent should carry the bodies of their deceased sisters and novices who have died in the convent to the threshold of the enclosure; that thence, if the deceased belonged to a body of religious who are not subject to the jurisdiction of the pastor, the chaplain of the convent escorts the body to their own proper oratory or church of the religious house, and there conducts the exequies. The legislator obviously does not consider the reception of the body by the chaplain as a sufficient excuse for his entrance into the enclosure.[127] Hence only at the threshold of the enclosure does the chaplain have the right to perform the various rites associated with the reception of the body. Thence he escorts the body to the oratory or the church of the religious house for the obsequies, which he has the right to conduct. Since the priest who conducts the exequies also enjoys the right to accompany the body to the cemetery, the chaplain of a monastery of nuns or of a convent of sisters that has been withdrawn from the jurisdiction of the pastor exercises regarding those committed to his care all the funeral rights which the proper pastor is accustomed to exercise concerning his own parishioners.

The minister at the funerals of the novices in the monasteries of nuns or in the convents of sisters that have been withdrawn from the jurisdiction of the pastor is also the chaplain of the

---

[125] *Aesernien.*, 20 apr. 1641—*Fontes*, n. 5398.

[126] C. 514, § 2: "In monialium domo idem ius et officium habet ordinarius confessarius vel qui eius vices gerit."

[127] "Immo si alicubi consuetudo vigeat permittendi ingressum etiam in domum clausurae papalis, id tolerari poterit ab Ordinario."—Coronata, *Institutiones*, II, n. 805.

particular monastery or convent in which the novices die, unless they have chosen another church for their funeral. If they have chosen another church, it seems that the chaplain alone should have the right to receive the body and to conduct it to the church selected by the novices, for the chaplain alone has the funeral rights of a proper pastor regarding the novices who die in the convent. Moreover, it is difficult to understand how he would lose the right to receive the body and to conduct it to the church selected for the funeral simply because the funeral is to be conducted outside the monastery or the convent. It seems very improbable that the local pastor would obtain a right to receive and to escort the body of the deceased novice, since she was never his subject.

The funeral church for women religious and novices who are subject to the jurisdiction of the pastor is the local parish church. Canon 1230, § 5, declares that the provision of the first paragraph of the same canon is obligatory in the event that a member of a community subject to the pastor dies in the convent.[128] Hence the pastor of the parish in which the convent is situated has the right to receive the body at the entrance to the enclosure,[129] escort it to his parish church, and there conduct the obsequies.[130] Moreover, he accompanies the body to the cemetery.[131]

If the novice who belongs to a community of sisters subject to the jurisdiction of the pastor has chosen a funeral church other than the local parish church, the local pastor receives the body at the entrance to the enclosure and escorts it to the church selected. The rector of the church selected conducts the exequies, and then accompanies the body to the cemetery, unless the church is subject to the local pastor.

---

[128] ". . . si de aliis religiosis, valet praescriptum § 1; . . ."

[129] "Si agatur de religione clausurae episcopalis tanta severitas, nisi id praecipiatur ab Ordinario loci, qua ingressus sacerdotis ad levationem cadaveris prohibetur, non videtur de necessitate servanda."—Coronata, *Institutiones,* II, n. 805.

[130] C. 1230, § 1: "Proprius parochus defuncti non solum ius sed etiam officium habet, excepto gravi necessitatis casu, levandi per se vel per alium cadaver, illud comitandi ad suam ecclesiam paroecialem ibique exsequias persolvendi, . . ."

[131] C. 1231, § 2.

It was indicated above that the body of an exempt woman religious or novice who has died outside the convent ought to be brought for the funeral to the oratory or church of her convent, if the transfer can easily be made; that, if it is inconvenient to make the transfer, the funeral ought to take place in the church of the parish in which she died; that the persons who have an interest always have the right to bring the body to the proper funeral church, that is, to the oratory or church of the convent.[132]

It is obvious that, if the persons who have an interest in the case of an exempt woman religious or novice judge it to be too inconvenient to have the body brought to the oratory or church of the convent, the pastor of the parish in which she died has the right to receive the body, to escort it to his church, and to conduct the exequies. However, if the body can easily be brought to the oratory of the convent, or if the superior has the body brought to the convent, even though it may be inconvenient to do so, the chaplain of the convent has the right to receive the body and to conduct the other funeral ceremonies. In the event that a novice who dies outside her convent has chosen another funeral church, her funeral will be conducted by the rector of the selected church, unless that church be subject to the jurisdiction of the local pastor, in which case the right to conduct the funeral exequies belongs to the pastor.

The bodies of sisters who were subject to the jurisdiction of the pastor but who died outside the religious house are to be brought for the funeral to the church of the parish within whose limits they were stationed, if that can easily be done. The pastor of this parish church performs all the ceremonies connected with their funeral and burial. If the transfer to the parish church cannot be made conveniently, their funeral church is the parish church of the place in which they died. The local pastor then has the right to receive the body and to perform all the other ceremonies. If, however, the religious community of the deceased woman religious exercises its right to have the body brought to the parish church of the convent in which the sister was stationed

---

[132] Cf. *supra,* p. 142.

prior to her death, the pastor of the parish in which the convent is situated performs all the liturgical ceremonies.

The funerals of novices who pertain to a community subject to the jurisdiction of a pastor and who die outside the religious house are regulated in the same manner as those of the sisters of the community. However, if they have chosen their funeral church, the pastor in which the religious house is situated receives the body, if possible, and escorts it to the church selected. The exequies are conducted by the rector of the selected church, if it is exempt from the jurisdiction of the pastor. If the selected church is not exempt from the jurisdiction of the pastor, the pastor conducts the exequies.

H. Guests, Students, the Sick, in Religious Houses, Colleges and Hospitals

It was noted above that the common law of canons 1216–1218 must be followed in regard to the funerals of the guests, of the students and of the sick in any religious house, college, or hospital, unless the religious house, college, or hospital has a special privilege or is governed by a particular law which calls for a different procedure.[133] The funeral church of the guest, the student or the sick person who has died in a religious house, college, or hospital, is according to the common law his proper parish church, unless he has chosen another church for his funeral. The proper pastor of the deceased person has the right to receive the body, to escort it to his parish church, and to conduct the exequies.

It must be recalled that persons living in religious institutions may very easily acquire a quasi-domicile in the parish in which the religious institution is located. If the quasi-domicile has been actually established there, the pastor of the parish in which the institution is situated has the exclusive right to perform all the ceremonies connected with the funeral and the burial of the deceased.

If the deceased has chosen another church distinct from his proper parish church as his funeral church, his proper pastor nevertheless has the right to receive the body at the religious

[133] Cf. *supra*, p. 145.

house and to conduct it to the church selected by the deceased. The rector of the church selected conducts the exequies, if the church selected is exempt from the jurisdiction of the local pastor. If the church selected is subject to the jurisdiction of the local pastor, the latter conducts the exequies.

If the religious institution has a special privilege or is governed by a divergent particular law, the funeral church of the guest, of the student or of the sick person is the church or the oratory of the institution. The determination of the minister at the reception of the body, at its transferral to the church, and at the exequies, will be clear from the content of the privilege or the regulation of the particular law. Ordinarily, the minister is the chaplain of the institution or the priest to whom the care of the church in which the ceremonies occur is committed.

I. Persons Who Die in a Seminary

According to canon 1222 the rector of the seminary is empowered to conduct the funerals of the persons who as abiding residents died in the seminary.[134] He has therefore the right to receive their bodies, to escort them to the oratory of the institution, and to conduct the exequies.

If one of the inmates of the seminary has chosen another church as his funeral church, the rector, who according to canon 1368 has the office of a pastor in relation to the persons who live in a seminary, has the right to receive the body and to escort it to the church selected for the funeral by his deceased subject.

ARTICLE IV. THE MINISTER IN THE EXTRAORDINARY CASE

Canon 1230, § 7: **Si cadaver mittatur ad locum ubi nec defunctus propriam paroeciam habebat, nec ecclesia funeris legitime fuerat electa, ius levandi cadaver, peragendi exsequias, si peragendae sint, et cadaver ad sepulturam deducendi, pertinet ad ecclesiam cathedralem eiusdem loci; quae si desit, ad ecclesiam paroeciae in qua coemeterium situm sit, nisi aliud ferant loci consuetudo aut dioecesana statuta.**

---

[134] *supra*, pp. 149–150.

In the history of the Church there have been many and serious disputes among clerics regarding the determination of the minister who has the right to conduct the funerals of the faithful. Evidently the legislator in promulgating so many laws regarding the determination of the minister at funerals has striven to eliminate as much as possible any causes for dispute and the resultant scandal to the laity. He has expressly designated the minister at the funerals which are conducted according to the ordinary law, and also at those in which the selection of the funeral church is involved. Moreover, he has named the proper minister at the funerals of certain classes of persons. Finally, in canon 1230, § 7, the legislator has promulgated a new law which should serve to remove the last possible reason for controversy among clerics regarding the rights to conduct funerals or to assist at the interment of the deceased.[135]

Paragraph seven of canon 1230 provides that, if a body is sent to a place in which the deceased did not have his proper parish and in which he has not chosen a church for his funeral, the right to receive the body, to hold the exequies, if they are to be held in that place, and to accompany the body to the burial place belongs to the cathedral church; that, if there is no cathedral church, the same rights pertain to the pastor of the church to which the cemetery of interment belongs, unless local custom or the diocesan statutes ordain otherwise.

This canon is concerned with a special case. Obviously, it does not determine the solution to be given in the case in which the traveller has died in a certain parish without having chosen a funeral church and the persons who have an interest do not care to bring the body to its proper funeral church. The Code solves this case in canon 1218 by ruling that the funeral of the traveller is to occur in the parish church of the place in which he died. Canon 1230, § 7, does not propose a solution for the case in which the wanderer (*vagus*) has died in a certain parish without having selected his funeral church, since the funeral church of the wanderer is the parish church of the place in which he died. Moreover, the canon does not give the solution to be applied in the case in

[135] S. C. C., *Dioecesis V . . .*, 4 iul. 1936—*AAS*, XXIX (1937), 474–476.

which a person has selected for his burial a cemetery which is not that of the funeral church, but to which the officiating minister can readily accompany the body for the interment in accord with the regulations of canons 1231, §§ 1, 2, and 1232, § 2.[136] Finally, it does not contain the solution to govern the case in which a person has a family plot in a cemetery to which the minister of the exequies can easily accompany the corpse for the interment.

The canon gives the solution applicable to the case in which the body is simply sent to a place in which the deceased did not have a proper parish and in which a church for the funeral has not been selected by the deceased. Very frequently, after the exequies have been conducted in the proper funeral church according to the norms established by the Code, the corpse is sent to a place in which the deceased had been a parishioner at one time, and in which the family plot or the grave selected by the deceased is located. This place is often at such a distance that the minister of exequies cannot possibly assert the right to accompany the body to the place of interment.[137] The Code provides that in such a case the right to conduct the body to the cemetery for the burial pertains to the cathedral church; that, if there is not a cathedral church in the place, the right to accompany the body to the cemetery pertains to the church of the parish in which the cemetery is located, unless local custom or the diocesan statutes decree otherwise.

It may happen also that the proper pastor for some serious reason is unable to conduct the exequies of his deceased parishioner who has a family plot or who has selected a particular place of burial in a distant city. The body is, thereupon, sent to the place in which the cemetery is located. In this event the Code provides that the right to receive the body, the right to perform the exequies, and the right to accompany the body to the cemetery pertain to the cathedral church; that, if there is not a cathedral church in the city, these same rights pertain to the parish church in whose territory the cemetery is located, unless local custom or the diocesan statutes ordain otherwise.

---

136 Cf. *infra*, p. 199.

137 C. 1232, § 2.

An error in the shipping of the body to the proper parish for the funeral may also occur. As a result the body may arrive at a totally unexpected destination. If it is impossible to rectify the error within a short space of time, and if the persons for whom the case has an interest are not willing to pay the added costs involved in the transportation of the corpse to the proper parish and in the delay in the performance of the funeral ceremonies at the proper funeral church, it seems that the provisions of canon 1230, § 7, should be considered as obligatory.

There are other reasons on account of which the body may be sent to a place in which the person did not have a domicile and in which there does not exist the church selected for the funeral of the deceased. Moreover, there are instances in which it is impossible to determine the proper minister at the funeral and burial, e.g., in the case of a body washed ashore in a foreign land, or in the case in which a person dies on a train as it speeds through a certain parish and the body is prepared for the funeral and burial at a parish many miles distant from the place of death. In fact, whenever the usual norms for determining the minister of the funeral or of the burial are inapplicable, the rule of canon 1230, § 7, is to be invoked. It is, of course, a supplementary norm. However, its presence in the Code demonstrates that the legislator is concerned to have the minister at the funeral and at the burial clearly established in every case.

There is no difficulty in determining who is the proper minister at the funeral and at the burial in those cases in which there is only one parish in a city or in which the city to which the body is shipped is the cathedral city. However, many difficulties arise in those instances in which there is a common cemetery located within the territory of several parishes, e.g., within the limits of a territorial parish and of several national parishes. In these instances the determination of the proper minister must be found in the diocesan statutes or in the local custom. If all the parishes are territorial and the common cemetery is located in one of them, the exercise of the various rights pertains to the parish in which the cemetery is situated, unless the diocesan statutes or local custom ordain otherwise.[138]

---

[138] S. C. C., *Dioecesis V . . .*, 4 iul. 1936—*AAS*, XXIX (1937), 474–476.

CHAPTER VIII

THE MINISTER AT THE INTERMENT AND THE ATTENDANTS AT THE FUNERAL

ARTICLE I. THE INTERMENT

Canon 1231, § 1: **Expletis in ecclesia exsequiis, cadaver tumulandum est ad normam librorum liturgicorum in coemeterio ecclesiae funeris, salvis praescriptis can. 1228, 1229.**

The Code declares that, after the exequies have been performed in the church, the corpse is to be interred in the cemetery of the same church with the ceremonies prescribed by the liturgical books, unless the body is to be taken to another cemetery either because the deceased has selected a particular cemetery for his burial, or for the reason that he has a family plot therein.

Ordinarily the interment is to occur in the cemetery of the funeral church. The cemetery may be reserved for the use of the funeral church, or it may be a common cemetery which the funeral church uses for the interment of the persons whose funerals are held in the church.

However, in canon 1228 the Code permits to all persons, except professed religious, once they have attained the age of puberty, the selection of a burial place in a cemetery distinct from that of the proper parish of the deceased. The parents or guardian can select the cemetery for the burial of children below the age of puberty even after the children have died.[1] Moreover, the Code states that the corpse should be buried in the cemetery selected, provided that there is no objection on the part of the persons who control the cemetery. If the cemetery selected belongs to a religious institute, the consent of the superior, who according to the constitutions of the institute is empowered to grant the permission, is required before the body can be interred.[2]

[1] C. 1224, 1°.

[2] C. 1228, § 2.

Canon 1229 prescribes that, if any person possesses a family plot in a certain cemetery, he is to be buried there, provided that the body can conveniently be brought to it, or the persons interested in the case undertake to pay the expenses of the transfer to the place of burial. Further, the wife should be buried in the same cemetery as her husband. If she had several husbands, she should be buried in the tomb of the last one.[3] The rule in regard to the burial of the wife does not apply after a legitimate separation, or when one of the parties is a non-Catholic.[4] Of course, the married woman remains free to select the place of her burial.[5] When there are several family plots or when the husband has several, the relatives or heirs of the deceased may select the one they prefer for the interment.[6]

The Code commands that the body is to be interred with the ceremonies prescribed by the liturgical books. Hence it is the express will of the legislator that the ceremonies and prayers associated with the procession to the place of burial and the final interment as found in the Roman Ritual and the *Caerimoniale Episcoporum* should be performed.

According to the Roman Ritual the hymn "*In paradisum*" is sung as the body is carried in procession to the cemetery.[7] In the cemetery the officiating priest blesses the particular grave if this has not yet been done.[8] He then intones the antiphon "*Ego sum*" before the singing of the canticle of Zachary. The entire antiphon having been repeated at the completion of the canticle, he intones the "*Kyrie eleison.*" After the choir has responded, the celebrant intones the "*Pater noster.*" He then sprinkles the casket with holy water. Several versicles and responses are chanted alternately by the minister and the choir prior to the singing of the oration beginning "*Fac, quaesumus, Domine.*" Finally, the celebrant makes the sign of the cross with his right hand over the casket,

---

[3] C. 1229, § 2.

[4] Ayrinhac, *Administrative Legislation in the New Code of Canon Law*, p. 78.

[5] C. 1223, § 2.

[6] C. 1229, § 3.

[7] Tit. VI, c. 3, *Exsequiarum ordo*, n. 11.

[8] *Ibid.*, nn. 12, 13.

and then sings the last three versicles to which the choir responds.[9]

ARTICLE II. THE MINISTER AT THE INTERMENT

Canon 1231, § 2: **Qui exsequias in ecclesia peregit, non solum ius, sed etiam officium habet, excepto gravi necessitatis casu, comitandi per se vel per alium sacerdotem cadaver ad locum sepulturae.**

The second paragraph of canon 1231 expressly designates the minister at the interment. It states that the priest who has conducted the exequies in the church has not only the right but also the duty, except in cases of grave necessity, to accompany, either in person or through another priest, the body to the place of the burial.

Since there is obviously an intimate connection between the funeral services and the interment, it has always been the common practice for the pastor of a parish to accompany to the place of burial the body of the person whose funeral services he conducted in the church. It has not always been so clear that the regular clergy could accompany to the cemetery the bodies of their deceased confrères or of persons who had selected their church as the funeral church. When burial in the churches and in cemeteries located next to the churches came to be forbidden in many places about the end of the eighteenth century,[10] some doubt was cast on the right of the regular clergy to accompany in procession to the common cemeteries the bodies of those persons whose exequies had been performed in their churches.

In the settlement of a number of controversies the Sacred Roman Congregations during the nineteenth century declared that the regular clergy without any interference on the part of the local pastor could accompany to the cemetery in procession the body of a deceased confrère, provided that the body was carried to the cemetery both directly and without any solemnity by the religious family of the monastery alone;[11] that the regular clergy

[9] *Ibid.*, n. 14.

[10] Many, *De Locis Sacris*, n. 206.

[11] S. C. C., *Ordinis Praedicatorum*, 24 ian. 1846, ad 2-4—*Fontes*, n. 4091; S. R. C., *Neritonen.*, 12 sept. 1884, ad II—*Fontes*, n. 6159.

had the same right to be exercised under the same conditions in regard to those persons whose exequies were celebrated in their churches and whose bodies were to be interred in the common cemetery of the city; [12] that a confessor of nuns without interference on the part of the pastor had the right to accompany the body of a deceased member of the community to a public cemetery, provided that the body was carried to the cemetery directly and without solemnity.[13] The Sacred Congregations, therefore, clearly upheld the right of the minister at the exequies to accompany the body to the cemetery.[14]

The priest, then, who conducts the exequies in the church has the right to accompany the body to the place of burial. The place of burial may be the cemetery of the funeral church or the cemetery of another church. Moreover, if there is a cemetery common to many parishes situated in one of the parishes, all the pastors of these parishes without any interference on the part of the local pastor have the right to bring the bodies there for interment.[15]

Occasionally in some common cemeteries, especially in those of great cities, chaplains are named to care for the interment of every corpse which is brought for burial. The appointment of a chaplain to such a cemetery does not appear to impair the right of the minister of the exequies to accompany the body to the cemetery and to perform the ceremonies at the interment, since the common law, as expressed in canon 1231, § 2, clearly establishes the right of the minister of the exequies to perform the various rites prescribed by canon 1231, § 1. Moreover, the law obligates the minister of the exequies to accompany the body to the place of burial. It may be recalled also that canon 462, 5°, reserves to the pastor the performance of all the ceremonies on the occasion of the funeral and burial of his parishioners.[16]

---

[12] S. C. Ep. et Reg., *Caven et Sarnen.*, 17 sept. 1880, ad 1, 3—*Fontes*, n. 2006.

[13] S. C. C., *Syracusana*, 24 febr. 1872—*Fontes*, n. 4220.

[14] Cf. *infra*, p. 198 concerning the conditions placed by the *Sacred Congregation* for the exercise of this right on the part of the regular clergy.

[15] Beste, *Introductio in Codicem*, Commentary on canon 1231; cf. also S. C. C., *Apuana*, 12 nov. 1927—*AAS*, XX (1928), 142.

[16] Cf. also S. C. C., *Asten.*, 26 ian. 1907—*Fontes*, n. 4332; " Circa la facoltà del Vescovo di dichiarare l'esenzione dalla giurisdizione parrochiale "—Sac-

The minister of the exequies is granted other rights in

Canon 1232, § 1: **Sacerdos qui cadaver comitetur ad ecclesiam funeris vel ad locum sepulturae, libere transire poterit, cum stola quoque et cruce elevata, per territorium alius paroeciae vel dioecesis, etiam sine parochi vel Ordinarii licentia.**

The priest who escorts the body to the funeral church or to the cemetery is entitled to pass freely with stole and raised cross through another parish or diocese without the permission of the pastor or of the ordinary. This right of the pastor to escort the body to the funeral church in this manner, and of the minister of the exequies to conduct the body to the cemetery in the same fashion, is a logical consequence of the possession by the priest of the "*ius levandi et ius deducendi in ecclesiam*" and of the "*ius comitandi* [*cadaver*] *in locum sepulturae.*"

Since the stole is an indication of the priest's office as the minister during the ceremonies, it is to be worn by the minister as he officiates at each part of the ceremonies.[17] It may be recalled that according to many decrees of the Roman Congregations the stole had to be removed at the door of the church by the priest who escorted the body from the home to the church selected by the deceased for his funeral; that this was commanded in order to indicate that he was no longer the minister; that the rector of the church selected then wore the stole as the minister of the exequies.[18]

The phrase, "*cruce elevata,*" is used by the legislator to eliminate the presumption that on passing through the territory of another parish or diocese the cross had to be lowered in order to acknowledge the jurisdiction of the local pastor.[19]

The priest can pass freely in procession either to the funeral church or to the cemetery. He is not obligated to obtain the permission of the pastor of the parish through which the procession

---

coni, *Il Monitore Ecclesiastico* (Romae, 1876–), 4. Series, X (1928), 212–215.

[17] Rituale Rom., tit VI, c. 3, *Exsequiarum ordo*, n. 1.

[18] Cf. *Supra*, pp. 167–168.

[19] S. C. Ep. et Reg., *Placentina*, 24 nov. 1713, ad 1—*Fontes*, n. 1829.

passes. *A fortiori,* he need not cede his position as the minister to the local pastor during the procession. It was noted above that the proper pastor, before he goes in procession to receive the body of a parishioner who has died outside his proper parish, is to advise the local pastor that he is coming into his parish to receive the body.[20]

The Code maintains in great part the law which was in force before the promulgation of the Code. Prior to 1918 the right of the pastors to conduct freely with stole and cross the bodies of their parishioners to the funeral church was impugned very rarely.[21]

It has been noted above that the Sacred Roman Congregations during the nineteenth century declared that the regular clergy without any interference on the part of the pastor could accompany to the cemetery in procession the bodies of their deceased confrères and of other persons who had selected their church as a funeral church, provided that the procession followed a direct route to the cemetery and was conducted without solemnity. In the same decrees it was stated that the regular clergy had the right to wear the stole in the procession and to carry the conventual cross. Moreover, the cross was not to be lowered as the procession passed through the parishes on the way to the place of the interment.[22]

Before the promulgation of the Code, if the procession from the church of the regular clergy was to be conducted with great solemnity, e.g., if the family wished confraternities and the secular clergy to attend, or if the procession was to pass to the cemetery by an indirect route, it was necessary for the regular clergy to ask the local pastor to accompany the body as the minister.[23] It seems that this restriction on the freedom of the regular clergy has been removed by the present law, especially in view of the fact that there is no allusion in the Code to the clause which

---

[20] C. 1230, § 2.

[21] S. C. Ep. et Reg., *Placentina,* 24 nov. 1713, ad 1—*Fontes,* n. 1829; S. C. C., *Papien.,* 28 nov. 1671, ad 2—*Fontes,* n. 2824; S. R. C., *Lucerina in Apulia,* 17 nov. 1674—*Fontes,* n. 5602.

[22] Cf. *supra,* p. 195–196.

[23] Many, *De Locis Sacris,* n. 197; Ferraris, *Prompta Bibliotheca,* v. *Sepultura,* n. 36.

occurs so frequently in the decrees, namely, "*dummodo cadaver deferatur absque solemni pompa, recto tramite ad coemeterium.*" [24]

The obligation to accompany the body to the cemetery, which obligation the canon imposes on the minister of the exequies, is one of serious import since he is excused from the fulfillment of this duty only in the case of grave necessity. The sudden illness of the minister and his continuous physical infirmity would certainly constitute cases of grave necessity. The advanced age of the minister may be another excusing cause if other reasons are present, e.g., inclement weather. A more important demand for his services, e.g., to attend a dying parishioner, must also be considered a reason sufficient to exempt him from his duty.[25] The Code releases the minister from the obligation under the circumstances contemplated in canon 1232, § 2, where it states that, if the body is to be buried in a cemetery to which it cannot easily be brought, the pastor or the rector of the funeral church cannot assert the right to accompany it outside the limits of the city or the district.

> **Si cadaver tumulandum sit in coemeterio ad quod commode asportari nequeat, parochus vel rector ecclesiae funeris nequit sibi vindicare ius illud comitandi extra fines civitatis vel loci.**

The minister of the exequies is obliged, therefore, to accompany in procession to the cemetery the body of the person whose exequies have been celebrated in the church. It is of no moment whether the body is to be interred in the cemetery of the funeral church, or in the cemetery of another parish selected by the deceased, or in a cemetery in which the deceased has a family plot, provided only that the body can be readily carried to any of these cemeteries. If the body cannot be easily carried in procession, the right and the obligation of the minister of the exequies to accompany it in procession outside the limits of the city or the district cease. However, in this instance, although the minister does not have the right to accompany the body in procession, there

---

[24] Coronata, *De Locis et Temporibus Sacris,* n. 239.

[25] Rossi, *Ecclesiastica Sepultura,* n. 43.

is nothing to prevent him from continuing on to the place of burial in a private capacity.

It was noted above that the Code makes it the business of the local Ordinary to determine for his territory the distance and the other circumstances which render inconvenient the transfer of the body to the funeral church. In the same canon he is instructed to determine the distance and the other circumstances which render inconvenient the transfer of the body to the place of burial.[26] The various circumstances which should be weighed by the Ordinary have been discussed above.[27]

It is clear that, if the body can easily be carried in procession to the place of burial, the minister of the exequies is obligated to accompany it there. Very frequently, however, the body is brought a great distance to a cemetery selected by the deceased, or to one in which there is a family plot. If the body is sent or carried to a place in which there is only one parish and one cemetery, the local pastor obviously has the right to accompany the body on its arrival in his territory to the place of interment and to perform the ceremonies associated with the burial. If the body is sent to a place in which the deceased did not have a proper parish, the pastor of the cathedral parish has this right; if there is not a cathedral in the city, the right to accompany the body to the place of burial pertains to the pastor of the parish in which the cemetery is located, unless local custom or the diocesan statutes ordain otherwise.[28] Moreover, in view of the mind of the legislator as manifested by the laws of the Code, it is only in an exceptional case in which the priest who has the absolute right to assist at the interment is not available that it is permissible to perform the rites and prayers of interment immediately after the prayers of the Absolution.[29]

The legislator obviously presumes that the corpse will be carried from the church to the cemetery in a procession modeled after that in which the body was brought from the home to the church.

---

[26] C. 1218, § 2.

[27] Cf. *supra*, pp. 97–99.

[28] C. 1230, § 7.

[29] Beste, *Introductio in Codicem*, Commentary on canon 1232.

In this country, ordinarily, the priest does not accompany the casket on foot. After the services in the church the pallbearers followed by the mourners carry the coffin to the hearse. The pallbearers and the mourners enter the waiting automobiles which are then formed in a line behind the hearse. The priest and his assistants ride to the cemetery in the first automobile of the procession, that is, immediately in front of the hearse.

In a number of places it has been the practice of the priest not to accompany the body to the cemetery, but in every case to complete the rites of the interment in the church. The distance to the parochial or common cemetery, the necessity of teaching classes in the school, and the lack of priests necessary to fulfill all the tasks involved in the care of the living are among the reasons adduced for the establishment of the practice. The writer agrees with Woywod [30] when the latter states: "it is rather a cold and unchristian conclusion to the beautiful and consoling funeral rites of the Church, when the interment is left to the undertaker, and there is no priest at the grave to say the final prayer as the body is laid to rest."

Moreover, it appears to the writer that the reasons alleged are specious. Certainly it is most rare that automobiles are not employed by the undertaker and the family, even in those cases in which the poor are to be buried. The distance to the cemetery and the lack of time, therefore, are baseless foundations for the justification of the practice. Further, it must be admitted that the priest will in fact be taking the best of spiritual care of the living members of the flock committed to his charge if he is present at the interment, for it is precisely at this time that he may exert the greatest spiritual influence on the mourners, the friends, and the relatives of the deceased. To say the least, the practice seems to be opposed to the mind of the Church, it cannot but wound deeply the feelings of the laity, and it betrays an unsympathic ministry.[31]

---

[30] *A Practical Commentary on the Code of Canon Law,* II, p. 42.

[31] Beste, *Introductio in Codicem,* Commentary on canon 1232. Cf. S. C. C., *Asten.,* 26 ian. 1907—*Fontes,* n. 4332.

ARTICLE III. THE ATTENDANTS AT THE FUNERAL

Canon 1233, § 1, **Nequit parochus, sine iusta et gravi causa ab Ordinario probata, excludere clericos saeculares, religiosos ac pia sodalitia quae familia vel heredes advocare velint ad deducendum cadaver ad ecclesiam funeris et ad sepulturam, et assistendum funeri; clerici tamen ipsi ecclesiae addicti a familia vel heredibus prae aliis omnibus invitari debent.**

After the Council of Trent (1545–1563) the Sacred Roman Congregations were frequently called upon to defend the right of the relatives or heirs to invite whom they wished to be present at the ceremonies performed on the occasion of the funeral and burial of the deceased. Even before the promulgation of the Code, therefore, some of the salient points now stressed in canon 1233, § 1, were already well established by the practice of the Roman Curia.

The heirs were to have complete liberty to invite, besides the pastor, as many members of the clergy, whether secular or religious, as they wished.[32] They could not be forced by the secular clergy to invite as many of their number as they did of the regular clergy.[33] Moreover, notwithstanding a synodal decree to the contrary,[34] the right to determine the number of religious as well as the various kinds of religious institutes which would be invited to participate belonged exclusively to the heirs, not to the pastor.[35] The invitation to the regular clergy to participate in the funeral could be extended by the heirs without the knowledge of the pastor, who did not then for that reason have the right to prevent the persons invited from attending.[36]

[32] S. C. Ep. et Reg., *S. Severini,* 25 nov. 1639—*Fontes,* n. 1757.

[33] S. C. Ep. et Reg., *Ferrarien.,* 11 mart. 1579—*Fontes,* n. 1355; *Placentina,* 24 nov. 1713, ad 4—*Fontes,* n. 1829; S. C. C., *Papien.,* 12 dec. 1665—*Fontes,* n. 2797; *Novarien.,* 1 et 15 mart. 1704, ad 9—*Fontes,* n. 3015; *Eugubina,* 22 maii 1762, ad 4—*Fontes,* n. 3718.

[34] S. R. C., *Senarum,* 7 dec. 1641—*Fontes,* n. 5412.

[35] S. R. C., *Ordinis Minorum Observantium,* 14 ian. 1640—*Fontes,* n. 5383; *Canarien.,* 22 nov. 1643—*Fontes,* n. 5433.

[36] S. C. Ep. et Reg., *Ordinis Carmelitarum,* 16 dec. 1729, ad 1, 2—*Fontes,* n. 1846.

The pastor could invite other clerics to be present, provided that the heirs had not made other arrangements.[37] It was not permitted to the pastor, contrary to the will of the family, to prevent the regular clergy from being present at all the functions.[38] Further, if the regular clergy had been called by the family to accompany the body to a funeral which was to take place in the cathedral church, they were to be permitted to enter the church to assist at the funeral.[39] The bishop and the pastor were not allowed to prevent the attendance of confraternities, if they had been invited to attend the ceremonies.[40] Even if the cathedral chapter should not have been invited, the members of a confraternity could be invited and be present during the procession and at the funeral.[41]

The liberty of the family or of the heirs of the deceased to invite whomever they wish to be present at all the services associated with the processions and the funeral is maintained by the Code. Canon 1233, § 1, declares that, without a just and grave cause approved by the Ordinary, the pastor cannot prevent clerics, religious and pious societies, when these have been invited by the family or by the heirs, from accompanying the body in the procession to the church and to the place of burial, and from assisting at the funeral services in the church; that, however, the clergy of the church where the funeral services are held ought to be invited by the family or the heirs in preference to all others.

Members of the secular clergy, religious and confraternities may be invited by the family to participate in the processions from the home of the deceased to the church, and from the church to the cemetery, and to be present at the funeral. The Code also states that secular tertiaries may in a corporate attendance take part in

[37] S. C. C., *Ebredunen.*, 25 iun. 1695, ad 2—*Fontes*, n. 2948; S. R. C., *Ferrarien.*, 7 sept. 1613—*Fontes*, n. 5266.

[38] S. R. C., *Sulmonen.*, 17 aug. 1629—*Fontes*, n. 5319; *Ordinum Mendicantium,* 22 apr. 1633, ad 1—*Fontes*, n. 5352. Cf. also Urbanus VIII, const. "*Nuper pro parte*", 25 iun. 1633, §§ 1, 2—*Fontes*, n. 212.

[39] S. C. Ep. et Reg., *Monopolitana*, 18 febr. 1723, ad 3—*Fontes*, n. 1839.

[40] S. C. C., *Bononien.*, 12 febr., 10 iun., 8 et 28 iul. 1724, ad 10—*Fontes*, nn. 3275, 3279; S. R. C., *Sulmonen. et Vallacen.*, 18 aug. 1629—*Fontes*, n. 5320; *Gallipolitana*, 8 iun. 1630—*Fontes*, n. 5327; *Monopolitana*, 17 iun. 1673—*Fontes*, n. 5593; *Meliten.*, 9 febr. 1854—*Fontes*, n. 5968.

[41] S. R. C., *Gallipolitana*, 8 iun. 1630—*Fontes*, n. 5327.

funerals; that, if they are present, they must march under their own cross and wear the insignia of their order.[42]

The right to assist at the funeral in the church which the secular and the religious possess is not to be extended to include the right to be the minister of the exequies or even the assistants of the minister, e.g., the deacon in the solemn Mass of Requiem. It seems to the writer to signify that clerics have the right not only to be present at the exequies, but especially the right to take an active part in the ceremony of the Absolution which is described in the Roman Ritual. The Ritual states that after the subdeacon, bearing the cross and accompanied by the two acolytes, has taken up his position at the head of the deceased, all the other members of the clergy with lighted candles come in proper order according to their rank and stand in a circle about the casket.[43]

Canon 1233, § 1, expressly declares that the clergy assigned to the funeral church should be invited by the family or the heirs in preference to all others. The words, " to all others," are not to be restricted to include only secular clerics, but they obviously refer to all those whom the family according to this canon have the right to invite. Hence the family, in preference to other secular clerics, religious and pious societies, should invite the clerics assigned to the funeral church.[44]

It is of no importance whether the funeral church is a parochial church or another church endowed with the right of conducting funerals. In any case the clergy assigned to the funeral church should be preferred to other persons by the family. It may be of interest to note that the Pontifical Commission for the Authentic Interpretation of the Code, when it was asked whether the words of canon 1233, § 1, " clerics . . . assigned to the church itself,"

---

[42] C. 706.

[43] " Finita Missa, . . . Tum Subdiaconus accipit Crucem, et praecedentibus duobus acolythis, uno cum thuribulo et navicula incensi, alio cum vase aquae benedictae et aspersorio, accedit ad feretrum et se sistit ad caput defuncti cum Cruce, medius inter duos acolythos seu ceroferarios cum candelabris et candelis accensis. Post eum omnes alii de Clero veniunt ordinatim in gradu suo cum candelis accensis, et stant in circuitu feretri: "—Tit. VI, c. 3, *Exsequiarum ordo,* n. 7.

[44] Cocchi, V, *Commentarium,* n. 66; Cappello, *Summa,* II, n. 749.

included also the capitulars of a cathedral or collegiate church, responded in the negative.[45]

According to Augustine,[46] the apparent precept to invite the clergy of the funeral church in preference to all other persons is merely a timely admonition to the family and the heirs to show respect to their own clergy. Coronata [47] maintains that the opinion of Augustine must be held as the only true interpretation, since there is no reason to believe that the legislator wished to change the legislation which was in existence before the promulgation of the Code. Regatillo [48] remarks that this preference which is to be shown for the clergy of the funeral church is for them not a strict right but simply a claim in equity.

In the judgment of the writer their opinion seems to be well founded. Moreover, it is difficult to understand how the family would be obligated even in equity to invite the clergy assigned to the funeral church, if the funeral church is not the parish church of the deceased, but rather a church selected by the deceased for his funeral.

The pastor cannot exclude the persons invited by the family of the deceased without a just and grave cause to be approved by the Ordinary.[49] It seems that the cause for the exclusion must be one of exceptional gravity, e.g., a grave scandal or a clear case of injustice to the pastor. It does not seem that, if the family did not invite the clergy assigned to the funeral church in preference to others, a just and grave cause to exclude those who were invited would be present.[50]

Whatever reason the pastor may judge to be a just and grave cause must be approved by the Ordinary before the persons mentioned in this canon can be excluded from the processions and

---

[45] *AAS,* XXXIII (1941), 173; reported in Bouscaren, *The Canon Law Digest,* II, 354.

[46] *A Commentary on Canon Law,* VI, 143.

[47] *Institutiones,* II, n. 808.

[48] *Institutiones Iuris Canonici* (2 vols., Santander: Sal Terrae, 1942), II, n. 71.

[49] ". . . ut si multi sacerdotes invitarentur ad funus infimae classis."—Regatillo, *Institutiones Iuris Canonici,* II, n. 71.

[50] Coronata, *Institutiones,* II, n. 808.

from the church. If there is not sufficient time to present the cause to the Ordinary for his consideration, the pastor would certainly have the right to exclude the persons mentioned in canon 1233, § 1, e.g., in view of the danger of public scandal which would arise from their admission to the procession and to the funeral. It seems to be beyond the pastor's competence, however, to exclude anyone from the funeral when the cause alleged for this exclusion is the injustice to himself which would arise as the result of their admission.

On the other hand, societies clearly hostile to the Catholic religion should never be permitted to participate in the ceremonies. Insignia, also, which are hostile to our faith must not be allowed to be exhibited or worn in the processions or in the church at the exequies. These prohibitions are contained in canon 1233, § 2:

> **Nunquam admittantur societates vel insignia religioni catholicae manifeste hostilia.**

Among the societies evidently hostile to the Catholic religion must be included those organizations which persons are forbidden to join under the threat of an excommunication,[51] e.g., the Freemasons, the Fenians,[52] the Carbonari, the nihilistic, anarchistic and perhaps some socialistic societies.[53] There are other associations clearly hostile to the Catholic religion, which associations the Church declares unlawful under penalty of grave sin without censure, e.g., non-Catholic Bible societies, cremation and theosophical societies.[54] In this latter group must be numbered those societies which demand of their members an oath of secrecy and

[51] C. 2335: "Nomen dantes sectae massonicae aliisve eiusdem generis associationibus quae contra Ecclesiam vel legitimas civiles potestates machinantur, contrahunt ipso facto excommunicationem Sedi Apostolicae simpliciter reservatam."

[52] S. C. C. Off., decr. 12 ian. 1870—*Fontes*, n. 1012.

[53] Beste, *Introductio in Codicem*, Commentary on canon 2335; Woywod, *A Practical Commentary on the Code of Canon Law*, II, 484; Ayrinhac-Lydon, *Penal Legislation in the New Code of Canon Law* (2. ed., New York, N. Y.: Benziger Bros., 1936), n. 256; Quigley, *Condemned Societies*, The Catholic University of America Canon Law Studies, n. 46 (Washington, D. C.: The Catholic University of America, 1927), p. 7.

[54] *Quigley, op. cit.*, pp. 26–28, 35–36; Beste, *loc. cit.;* Woywod, *loc. cit.*

of blind obedience to their leaders. Several of these have been expressly condemned, e.g., the Odd Fellows, the Sons of Temperance, the Knights of Pythias [55] and the Independent Order of Good Templars.[56]

Enrollment in the associations of women affiliated with these secret societies, e.g., the Rebekahs, the Pythian Sisters, is forbidden under the same penalty. In the United States there are so many of these fraternal organizations that it is often difficult for the outsider to determine to which category of forbidden societies they belong. Some of them are directly connected with the Freemasons, e.g., the Eastern Star and the Order of De Molay, while others resemble more closely the condemned American secret societies, e.g., the Independent Order of Redmen, the Modern Woodman.

The pastor should not allow any of these societies to enter the church or to assist at ecclesiastical functions. Moreover, he must not allow in the church or during the funeral processions any display of their standards, banners, badges, emblems, or insignia of any kind that would be unbecoming to the sacredness of the place or the character of the ceremony.[57]

In the nineteenth century the Supreme Congregation of the Holy Office repeatedly forbade the use of the masonic emblems in funeral processions or in the church. In the response to the question whether it was lawful to celebrate the funeral services and to grant ecclesiastical burial to those persons who had received the sacraments before death, but who had been members of the Freemasons, and on whose caskets the emblems of this sect were placed, the Sacred Congregation stated that it was lawful, provided that the masonic emblems were removed and the placing of the emblems on the casket had not been requested by the deceased person after he had received the sacraments. In addition, the Supreme Congregation of the Holy Office declared that the emblems should be removed as soon as it was known that they

---

[55] S. C. S. Off., instr. 20 aug. 1894—*Fontes*, n. 1171.

[56] S. C. S. Off., 9 aug. 1895—*Fontes*, n. 1167.

[57] Ayrinhac, *Administrative Legislation in the New Code of Canon Law*, n. 73.

had been placed on the casket, and that they must certainly be removed before the procession starts from the house.[58]

Moreover, the Sacred Penitentiary stressed another practical norm to be followed by the priests in those cases in which the masonic emblems were in evidence in the processions or in the church. It stated that, if the banners with symbols which are obviously godless or perverse were displayed in the funeral procession, the clergy was to withdraw from it; that, if such standards were brought by force into the church and the Mass had not yet begun, the priest was to withdraw; that, if the Mass had been started before the banners were brought into the church, the ecclesiastical authority, after the Mass had been completed, should solemnly protest against the profanation of the church and of the sacred functions.[59]

The Sacred Penitentiary tolerated the use of the national flag in funeral processions provided that it did not display any emblem which was in itself forbidden and that it was carried after the casket. Yet the Sacred Tribunal did not tolerate its use in the churches except in those cases in which on account of the prohibition disturbances among the people or other dangers were feared.[60] In 1911 the Holy Office in a letter sent by Cardinal Rampolla (1843–1913) to the Apostolic Delegate declared that, since there was wholly absent any contempt for the Church or the Sacred Liturgy, nothing hindered the use of the national flag of the United States in the church or on the occasion of funerals.[61]

In 1887 the Supreme Congregation of the Holy Office permitted in the church only the banners of confraternities and the blessed banners of Catholic societies whose statutes were approved by the Church and which in some manner depended on the Church; that

[58] S. C. S. Off., 2 dec. 1840—*Fontes,* n. 884. Cf. also, S. C. S. Off. (Portus Aloisii), 1 aug. 1855—*Fontes,* n. 932; instr. (ad Ordinarios imperii Brasil.), 2 iul. 1878—*Fontes,* n. 1056.

[59] S. C. S. Off., 31 aug. 1887—*Collectanea S. Congregationis de Propaganda Fide* (2 vols., Romae: ex Typographia Polyglotta Vaticana, 1907), n. 1681, nota 2; hereafter cited as *Coll. S. C. P. F.*

[60] *Loc. cit.*

[61] "Attentis expositis a R. P. D. Delegato Apostolico, quatenus absit omnino quilibet Ecclesiae vel Sacrae Liturgiae contemptus, nihil obstare."—*AER,* XLIV (1911), 590.

the banners themselves were not to contain any disapproved symbol, but had to show some indication of the Catholic religion.[62] However, in response to the petition of some local Ordinaries for a rule or instruction in regard to the admission of banners into the church and the blessing of banners, the Sacred Congregation of Rites, after hearing also the opinion of the Pontifical Commission for the Authentic Interpretation of the Code, replied as follows: " When the insignia or banners do not belong to societies which are clearly contrary to the Catholic religion, when the statutes of these societies have not been disapproved, and when the insignia or the banners themselves do not display any symbol which is in itself forbidden or disapproved, they may be admitted into the churches. When, in fact, the blessing of the above-mentioned insignia or of the banners is peacefully requested as a gesture of goodwill and as a mark of respect to the Catholic religion, this blessing according to the formula of the Roman Ritual may be granted." [63]

The insignia or banners of all societies of Catholics may certainly be admitted into the churches and carried in funeral processions. According to the explicit words of the Code and of the Instruction of the Sacred Congregation of Rites, it is very clear that the insignia and banners of many organizations which are not specifically Catholic, e.g., the American Legion, the Boy Scouts, may be permitted also.

The Code and the Instruction of the Sacred Congregation are very explicit in providing a norm of action. However, in practice, it may be very difficult for the pastor to apply it. Thus, Beste warns that there is need of great prudence on the part of the pastor in dealing with certain types of organizations, whose prin-

---

[62] S. C. S. Off., 31 aug. 1887—*Coll. S. C. P. F.*, n. 1681.

[63] " Mens est: Quando insignia seu vexilla non pertineant ad Societates religioni catholicae manifeste contrarias, nec reprobata sint harum statuta, neque ipsa insignia seu vexilla aliquod emblema de se vetitum ac reprobatum praeseferant, in ecclesiis admitti possunt. Quum vero in favorem et obsequium eiusdem religionis catholicae pacifice postuletur supradictorum insignium seu vexillorum benedictio, haec concedi potest, adhibita formula Ritualis Romani."—S. R. C., *Plurium Dioecesium,* De vexillis in ecclesia admittendis vel benedicendis, 15 dec. 1922, 26 mart. 1924—*AAS,* XVI (1924), 171.

ciples are not directly and clearly opposed to the Catholic religion, but whose leaders and members in their activities, works and speeches reveal a mentality that is certainly not religious.[64] Such organizations are to be found in ever increasing number in the fields of politics and labor.

Beste and Cocchi[65] maintain that in and of themselves they are to be excluded from the church and from ecclesiastical functions, inasmuch as they are imbued with a spirit and zeal that are totally irreligious; that, if strife or disturbances among the people or other grave inconveniences are prudently to be feared on account of their exclusion from attendance at these ceremonies, it is permitted to the pastor, in order to avoid greater evils, to tolerate their presence instead of actively opposing them.

It seems to the writer that Vermeersch-Creusen[66] present a rather practical norm according to which the pastor may judge whether such organizations are to be admitted to or barred from the churches. They feel that the customs of each country must be considered. Hence, they state, that, even if the society is not clearly condemned, its emblems and insignia are to be excluded as long as the society is looked upon by most of the people of a nation as hostile to the Church, e.g., the Socialist parties in Belgium.

Certain kinds of societies, then, are permitted to take part in funeral processions. It has also been noted above that the pastor is not to exclude from the church or from participation in the processions the secular clergy, the religious and the pious societies invited by the family of the deceased. However, the pastor is constituted the regulator of the procession by the third paragraph of canon 1233.

> **Associantes cadaver tenentur morem gerere parocho circa ductum funeris, salvis uniuscuiusque praecedentiae iuribus.**

This canon states that the persons who accompany the body in the

---

[64] *Introductio in Codicem,* Commentary on canon 1233.

[65] *Commentarium,* V, n. 66.

[66] *Epitome Iuris Canonici,* II, n. 539.

procession are held to comply with the wishes of the pastor regarding the funeral arrangements, with due regard, of course, to the rights of precedence.

Before the promulgation of the Code the Sacred Roman Congregations determined that the pastor could set the hour for the reception of the body at the home,[67] and had the right to decide in which direction or through which streets the funeral procession should march.[68] Regarding the regular clergy and the confraternities, it has often been decided that they should not join the procession at the house of the deceased or wait for its approach in the street, but that, if they are to participate in the procession,[69] they must go to the parish church and proceed with the pastor to the home of the deceased;[70] that, if the cathedral chapter has been invited to participate in the procession, all participants in the procession must meet at the cathedral church before the procession to the home.[71]

Canon 1233, § 3, grants to the pastor the right to make all the arrangements for the funeral procession, and commands the participants to follow his orders. Since it is the pastor who has the right and the duty to receive the body and to escort it to the church, it is only logical that he should arrange the order of the procession.

It seems to the writer that the term "pastor" must be understood as applicable to all the priests who have the right to receive the body and to escort it to the funeral church. In the previous chapter it was determined which priest has this right in particular cases.

Although the pastor has the right to arrange the order of the funeral procession, he must not act arbitrarily, but must take into consideration the rights of precedence enjoyed by the societies and the persons participating in it. In funeral processions precedence

---

[67] S. R. C., *Nullius Messanen.*, 18 dec. 1857, ad IV—*Fontes*, n. 4159.

[68] S. C. C., *Ebredunen.*, 25 iun. 1695, ad 6—*Fontes*, n. 2948; S. R. C., *Savonen.*, 19 dec. 1671, ad 3, 5—*Fontes*, n. 5584.

[69] Cf. *supra*, p. 165.

[70] S. R. C., *Tornacen.*, 25 sept. 1649, ad 8—*Fontes*, n. 5459; *Nicien.*, 9 aug. 1670, ad 1—*Fontes*, n. 5577; *Senogallien.*, 12 aug. 1673, ad 3—*Fontes*, n. 5594; *Firmana*, 4 aug. 1674—*Fontes*, n. 5600; *Marsicen.*, 21 mart. 1699—*Fontes*, n. 5700.

[71] S. R. C., *Savonen.*, 19 dec. 1671, ad 3—*Fontes*, n. 5584.

is reckoned in relation to the casket. The position in the procession of the person who enjoys the right of precedence over all other persons is immediately before the casket.

It has been frequently decided by the Roman Congregations that the pastor precedes all other persons in funeral processions unless the canons of the cathedral chapter attend in a body.[72] The decree of the Sacred Congregation of Rites concerning the exequies stated that the pastor enjoyed the right of precedence over all other clerics except the chapter of the cathedral church, which, if present, was to walk in procession immediately behind the pastor. It provided further that, if there was a custom in any place to the effect that the chapter of a collegiate church enjoyed precedence over the pastor, it was to be observed. It declared that in these instances the greatest dignity of the chapter should wear the stole and cope, the pastor only the stole.[73]

The cathedral chapter, of course, precedes all other chapters [74] and all religious everywhere in the respective diocese.[75] The secular clergy precedes all lay persons and also the religious outside the churches of the religious. Moreover, the secular clergy precedes the members of lay religious institutes even in the churches of these institutes.[76]

Among the secular clergy the vicar general has precedence over all priests, even the dignitaries and the canons of the cathedral chapter. If however there is present a cleric with the episcopal character, he precedes the vicar general unless the vicar general is himself a bishop.[77] The vicar forane precedes all pastors and

---

[72] Cf. *supra,* p. 165.

[73] S. R. C., decr. super exequiis, 23 apr. 1895, ad III: "Eumdem Parochum primas habere super omnem Clerum; excepto (si interfuerit) Capitulo Cathedralis Ecclesiae, quod in associatione incedet post ipsum Parochum: excepto etiam Capitulo Ecclesiae Collegiatae, si ita consuetudo ferat. Hoc tamen in casu dignior Capituli Cathedralis incedat cum Stola et etiam cum pluviali, quod tamen non ferat Parochus: et id ipsum servabitur, si Capitulum Ecclesiae Collegiatae post Parochum incedat."—*Fontes,* n. 6243.

[74] C. 408. Cf. this canon also for the rights of precedence within the same chapter.

[75] C. 491, § 2.

[76] C. 491, § 2.

[77] C. 370, § 1.

other priests of his deanery.[78] The pastor of the cathedral church or the parochial vicar of the cathedral chapter precedes all other pastors or vicars.[79] Vicars substitute and adjutant vicars precede while in office the assistant priests; the assistant priests precede other priests assigned to the parochial church.[80] To determine the rights of precedence of other priests and secular clerics, the general norms established by canon 106 are to be observed.

The religious also precede lay persons. Among the religious the order of precedence is as follows: clerical institutes precede lay institutes; canons regular precede monks; monks precede other regulars; regulars precede religious congregations; congregations of papal approval precede congregations of diocesan approval.[81] Among moral persons of the same kind and rank, that moral person precedes who is in peaceful quasi-possession of precedence. If it is not clear which moral person or, in other words, which religious group is in quasi-possession of precedence, that person precedes which was first established in the place where the question of precedence arises.[82]

Among the pious societies of lay people, the order of precedence is as follows:

1. Third orders
2. Archconfraternities
3. Confraternities
4. Primary unions
5. Other pious unions [83]

These societies have their right of precedence in the funeral procession only when the members take part in it as a body under their own banner and wearing their own peculiar dress or the insignia of their society.[84] If there is a question of precedence

[78] C. 450, § 2.

[79] C. 478, § 1.

[80] C. 478, § 2.

[81] C. 491, § 1.

[82] C. 106, 5o.

[83] C. 701, § 1.

[84] C. 701, § 3. These societies, except the Tertiaries, do not appear to have the right to carry their own cross in the funeral procession. Cf. Coronata, *De Locis et Temporibus Sacris,* n. 232.

among societies of the same kind and rank, it is to be settled according to the norm mentioned in the preceding paragraph.[85]

In the funeral procession, then, from the home of the deceased to the funeral church, the following order will be observed, with due regard for the rights of precedence among the various groups as described above:

1. Pious societies
2. The cross-bearer [86]
3. The regular clergy
4. The secular clergy
5. The pastor
6. The cathedral chapter, if it is present
7. The pallbearers with the casket
8. The mourners and friends of the deceased

The last point mentioned by the Code in regard to the funeral procession is found in the fourth paragraph of canon 1233.

> **Laici cadaver, generis aut dignitatis cuiusvis ille fuerit, clerici ne deferant.**

The canon repeats almost word for word the instruction of the Roman Ritual which was edited during the reign of Pius X (1903–1914).[87] It states that clerics should not act as pallbearers for a deceased member of the laity, no matter what his rank or dignity may have been. The reason for this prohibition is evi-

[85] C. 701, § 1.

[86] "The procession now goes to the church. Confraternities of laymen go first; the cross is borne before the clergy, that is, all who wear cassock and surplice."—Fortescue-O'Connell, *The Ceremonies of the Roman Rite Described* (5. ed., London: Burns, Oates and Washbourne, Ltd., 1934), 446. "Mox ordinatur processio, praecedentibus laicorum confraternitatibus, si adsint; tum sequitur Clerus regularis et saecularis per ordinem; binique procedunt, praelata cruce, devote Psalmos, ut infra, decantantes, Parocho praecedente feretrum cum luminibus; inde sequuntur alii funus comitantes, et pro defuncto Deum rite deprecantes sub silentio."—Rituale Rom., tit. VI, c. 3, *Exsequiarum ordo,* n. 1.

[87] "Laici cadaver, quolibet generis, aut dignitatis titulo praeditus ille fuerit, Clerici ne deferant, sed laici."—*Rituale Romanum Pauli V Pontificis Maximi iussu editum a Benedicto XIV et a Pio X castigatum et auctum* (2. ed., Taurini: Marietti, 1922), tit. VI, c. 1, *De Exsequiis,* n. 16.

dently to be found in the distinction between the clergy and the laity, and in the fact that the clergy are of a superior dignity than laymen of any rank.[88]

Rossi [89] notes that laymen can act as pallbearers for clerics. However, he and Cocchi [90] agree that it would be a praiseworthy usage if clerics of the same or of a lesser order would act as the pallbearers for deceased clerics.

---

[88] Augustine, *A Commentary on Canon Law,* VI, 144.

[89] *Ecclesiastica Sepultura,* n. 41.

[90] *Commentatrium,* V, n. 66.

CONCLUSIONS

1. By the time of Pope Leo III (795–816) the right of the parochial church to bury its parishioners was recognized as a parochial right, modified only by the right of the faithful to select the place of their burial and by the right to seek burial in the family tomb.

2. Those persons who were below the age of puberty were never allowed to select for themselves a place of burial.

3. The opinion of Oldradus and Panormitanus relative to the right of the regular clergy to enter the parishes processionally with a cross in order to remove the bodies of the faithful who had selected their churches as a place of burial was abandoned after the publication of the Constitution "*Dum intra*" of Pope Leo X (1513–1521) in the V General Council of the Lateran (1512–1517).

4. After the Council of Trent (1545–1563) the decisions of the Sacred Roman Congregations constantly favored burial in the parish church for all those who had lived within the parish limits, unless they had clearly gained and established the right to be buried elsewhere.

5. The third and fourth paragraphs of canon 1230 are succinct expressions of the mind of the Roman Curia as manifested in numerous decisions before the promulgation of the Code of Canon Law.

6. There was never an official definition of the clause: "*Dummodo absque periculo ad ipsam* (*ecclesiam*) *valeat deportari.*"

7. The meaning of the terms "*exsequiae,*" "*ordo exsequiarum*" and "*funus*" in the Code of Canon Law differs from the meaning of the term "*Exsequiarum ordo*" in the Roman Ritual.

8. The funeral church is the church in which the Requiem Mass is offered and the Absolution over the corpse is given.

9. The better interpretation of the words of canon 1218, § 1, namely, "*ecclesiam paroeciae propriae quae vicinior sit,*" is the

"nearer parochial church" rather than "the church of the nearer proper parish."

10. Canon 1221 contains the law regarding the funerals of men religious. The provisions of this canon are not applicable to women religious.

11. The bodies of sisters who are subject to the jurisdiction of the pastor, in the event that death occurs outside the convent, are to be brought for the funeral to the church of the parish within whose limits the sisters were stationed, if the transfer of the body to this church can be made easily.

12. The term "*parochus*" of canon 1233, § 3, includes all priests who have the right to receive the body at the place where it rests and to escort it to the funeral church.

BIBLIOGRAPHY

SOURCES

Acta Apostolicae Sedis, Commentarium Officiale, Romae, 1909–

Acta Sanctae Sedis, 41 vols., Romae, 1865–1908.

Bouscaren, T. Lincoln, *The Canon Law Digest,* 2 vols., Milwaukee: Bruce, 1934–1943.

Bullarum Diplomatum et Privilegiorum Romanorum Pontificum Taurinensis Editio, 25 vols., Augustae Taurinorum, 1857–1872.

Canones et Decreta Sacrosancti et Oecumenici Concilii Tridentini, Parisiis, 1754.

Codex Iuris Canonici Pii X Pontificis Maximi iussu digestus, Benedicti Papae XV auctoritate promulgatus, Romae: Typis Polyglottis Vaticanis, 1917. Reimpressio, 1933.

Codicis Iuris Canonici Fontes cura Emi Petri Card. Gasparri editi, 9 vols., Romae: Typis Polyglottis Vaticanis, 1923–1939. (Vols. VII–IX ed. cura et studio Emi Iustiniani Card. Serédi.)

Collectanea S. Congregationis de Propaganda Fide, 2 vols., Romae: ex Typographia Polyglotta Vaticana, 1907.

Corpus Iuris Canonici, ed. Lipsiensis 2. post Aemilii Ludovici Richteri curas . . . instruxit Aemilius Friedberg, Lipsiae: Ex Officina Bernhardi Tauchnitz, 1879–1881. Editio anastatice repetita, Lipsiae: Tauchnitz, 1928.

Decretales D. Gregorii IX una cum Glossis Restitutae, Romae, 1582.

Decretum Gratiani Emendatum et Notationibus illustratum una cum Glossis, Gregorii XIII, Pont. Max. iussu editum, 2 vols., Romae, 1582.

Jaffé, Philippus, *Regesta Pontificum Romanorum ab condita Ecclesia ad annum post Christum natum MCXCVIII,* ed. 2, correctam et auctam auspiciis Gulielmi Wattenbach, curaverunt F. Kaltenbrunner, P. Ewald, S. Loewenfeld, 2 vols. in 1, Lipsiae, 1885–1888.

Liber Sextus Decretalium D. Bonifacii Papae VIII suae integritati una cum Clementinis et Extravagantibus earumque Glossis restitutis, Romae, 1582.

Mansi, Joannes Dominicus, *Sacrorum Conciliorum Nova et Amplissima Collectio,* 53 vols. in 60, Paris-Arnhem-Leipzig, 1901–1927.

Monumenta Germaniae Historica, Epistolarum Tomi I et II, Gregorii Papae Registrum Epistolarum, P. Ewald and L. M. Hartmann, Berolini, 1887–1899.

Potthast, Augustus, *Regesta Pontificum Romanorum inde ab anno post Christum natum MCXCVIII ad annum MCCCIV,* 2 vols., Berolini, 1874–1875.

Rituale Romanum Pauli Pontificis Maximi iussu editum, a Benedicto XIV et a Pio X castigatum et auctum. Editio secunda Taurinensis juxta typicam, Taurini: Marietti, 1917.

Rituale Romanum Pauli V Pontificis Maximi iussu editum aliorumque Pontificum cura recognitum atque auctoritate Sanctissimi D. N. Pii Papae XI ad normam Codicis Iuris Canonici accommodatum, Editio iuxta typicam Vaticanam, Novi Eboraci: Benziger Brothers, 1944.

Sacrae Romanae Rotae Decisiones seu Sententiae, 24 vols., Romae: Typis Polyglottis Vaticanis, 1912–

Schroeder, Henry J., *Disciplinary Decrees of the General Councils,* St. Louis: B. Herder Book Co., 1937.

REFERENCE WORKS

Augustine, Charles, *A Commentary on the New Code of Canon Law,* 8 Vols., St. Louis: Herder, 1931–1938. Vol. VI, 3. ed., *Administrative Law,* 1936.

———, *Canonical and Civil Status of Catholic Parishes,* St. Louis: B. Herder Book Co., 1924.

———, *The Pastor According to the New Code of Canon Law,* 2. ed., St. Louis: B. Herder Book Co., 1924.

Ayrinhac, H. A., *Administrative Legislation in the New Code of Canon Law,* London: Longmans, Green and Co., 1930.

———, –Lydon, P. J., *Penal Legislation in the New Code of Canon Law,* 2. ed., New York, N. Y.: Benziger Bros, 1936.

Barbosa, Augustinus, *De Officio et Potestate Parochi,* Romae, 1774.

———, *Tractatus Varii, De appellativa verborum utriusque Iuris significatione,* Lugduni: 1660.

Bernardus Papiensis, *Summa Decretalium,* ed. E. A. T. Laspeyres, Ratisbonae, 1860.

Beste, Udalricus, *Introductio in Codicem,* ed. altera, Collegeville, Minn.: St. John's Abbey Press, 1944.

Blat, Albertus, *Commentarium Textus Codicis Iuris Canonici,* 6 vols., Romae: Collegio "Angelico," 1921–1927; Liber III, Pars II–VI, *De Rebus,* Romae: Collegio Angelico, 1923.

Bonal, A., *Institutiones Canonicae,* 2 vols., Parisiis, 1898.

Bouix, D., *Tractatus de Parocho,* 3. ed., Parisiis, 1880.

Cappello, Felix M., *Summa Iuris Canonici,* 3 vols., Romae: Universitas Gregoriana, Vol. I, 3. ed., 1938; Vol. II, 3. ed., 1939; Vol. III, 1936.

Chelodi, J., *Ius de Personis iuxta Codicem Iuris Canonici,* 2. ed., Tridenti, 1927.

Cocchi, Guidus, *Commentarium in Codicem Iuris Canonici ad Usum Scholarum,* 8 vols. in 5, Taurinorum Augustae, 1922–1930. Vol. V, *De Rebus,* 3. ed., Taurinorum Augustae: Marietti, 1932.

Coronata, Matthaeus Conte a, *Institutiones Iuris Canonici,* 5 vols., Taurini: Marietti, 1928–1936. Vol. II, *De Rebus,* 1931.

——, *De Locis et Temporibus Sacris,* Augustae Taurinorum: Marietti, 1922.

Costello, J., *Domicile and Quasi-Domicile,* The Catholic University of America Canon Law Studies, n. 60, Washington, D. C.: The Catholic University of America, 1930.

Creusen, J.–Garesché, E.–Ellis, A., *Religious Men and Women in the Code,* 4. English ed., Milwaukee: Bruce, 1942.

DeHerdt, J. B., *Praxis Sacrae Liturgiae iuxta Ritum Romanum,* 8. ed., 4 vols., Lovanii: Universitas Catholica, 1889.

DeMeester, Alphonsus, *Iuris Canonici et Iuris Canonico-Civilis Compendium,* Nova editio, 3 vols. in 4, Brugis, 1921–1928.

Devoti, Joannes, *Institutionum Canonicarum Libri IV,* Romae, 1830.

Drumm, William, *Hospital Chaplains,* The Catholic University of America Canon Law Studies, n. 178, Washington, D. C.: The Catholic University of America Press, 1943.

Duchesne, Louis, *Le Liber Pontificalis, texte, introduction, et commentaire,* 2 vols., Paris, 1886–1892.

Fanfani, L., *De Iure Parochorum ad normam Codicis Iuris Canonici,* Taurini-Romae: Marietti, 1924.

——, *De Iure Religiosorum ad normam Codicis Iuris Canonici,* 2. ed., Taurini-Romae: Marietti, 1925.

Ferraris, Lucius, *Prompta Bibliotheca Canonica Juridica Moralis Theologica necnon Ascetica Polemica Rubricistica Historica,* 9 vols., Romae, 1885–1899.

Fortescue, Adrian–O'Connell, J. B., *The Ceremonies of the Roman Rite Described,* 5. ed., London: Burns, Oates & Washbourne, 1934.

Genicot, E., et Salsmans, I., *Institutiones Theologiae Moralis,* 10. ed., 2 vols., Bruxellis, 1922.

Geser, Fintan, *The Canon Law Governing Communities of Sisters,* St. Louis, Mo.: B. Herder Book Co., 1939.

Gonzalez-Tellez, Emmanuel, *Commentaria Perpetua in Singulos Textus Quinque Librorum Decretalium Gregorii IX,* 5 vols. in 4, Venetiis, 1699.

Hefele, Carolus–Leclercq, Henricus, *Histoire des Conciles,* 10 vols. in 19, Paris: Letouzey et Ané, 1907–1938.

Hostiensis, Cardinalis (Henricus de Segusia), *Commentaria in Quinque Decretalium Libros,* 5 vols. in 3, Venetiis, 1581.

——, *Summa Aurea,* Venetiis, 1570.

Jaeger, Leo, *The Administration of Vacant and Quasi-Vacant Episcopal Sees in the United States,* The Catholic University of America Canon Law Studies, n. 81, Washington, D. C.: The Catholic University of America, 1932.

Kerin, Charles, *The Privation of Christian Burial,* The Catholic University of America Canon Law Studies, n. 136, Washington, D. C.: The Catholic University of America Press, 1941.

Kühner, R.–Stegmann, C., *Ausführliche Grammatik der lateinischen Sprache,* 2. ed., 2 vols., Hannover, 1912–1914.

Leurenius, Petrus, *Forum Ecclesiasticum in quo ius canonicum universum librorum ac titulorum ordine explanatur,* 5 vols. in 4, Venetiis, 1729.

Many, S., *De Locis Sacris,* Parisiis, 1904.

Maroto, P., *Institutiones Iuris Canonici ad normam Novi Codicis,* 2 vols., Vol. I, 3. ed., 1921; Vol. II, 1919, Romae.

McBride, J., *Incardination and Excardination of Seculars,* The Catholic University of America Canon Law Studies, n. 145, Washington, D. C.: The Catholic University of America Press, 1941.

Ojetti, B., *Commentarium in Codicem Iuris Canonici,* 4 vols., Romae: Universitas Gregoriana, 1927–1931.

Panormitanus, Abbas (Nicolaus de Tudeschis), *Commentaria in Quinque Libros Decretalium,* 5 vols. in 7, Venetiis, 1588.

Pirhing, Ernricus, *Jus Canonicum Nova Methodo Explicatum,* 5 vols. in 4, Dilingae, 1674–1678.

Quigley, Joseph, *Condemned Societies,* The Catholic University of America Canon Law Studies, n. 46, Washington, D. C.: The Catholic University of America, 1927.

Raymundus de Pennafort, *Summa,* Veronae, 1744.

Regatillo, E. F., *Institutiones Iuris Canonici,* 2 vols., Santander: Sal Terrae, 1941–1942.

Reiffenstuel, Anacletus, *Ius Canonicum Universum,* 5 vols. in 7, Parisiis, 1864–1870.

Rossi, Giuseppe, *La Sepultura Ecclesiastica e l' "Ius Funerum," nel Diritto Canonico,* Bergamo: Arnoldi, 1920.

Rufinus, *Summa Decretorum,* ed. H. Singer, Paderborn, 1902.

Santi, Franciscus, *Praelectiones Iuris Canonici,* 4 vols. in 2, Ratisbonae, Neo Eboraci et Cincinnati, 1886.

Schaefer, T., *De Religiosis ad Normam Codicis Iuris Canonici,* 3. ed., Romae: S. A. L. E. R., 1940.

Schmalzgrueber, Franciscus, *Jus Ecclesiasticum Universum,* 5 vols. in 12, Romae: 1843–1845.

Sipos, Stephanus, *Enchiridion Iuris Canonici,* Pécs: Ex Typographia "Haladás R. T.," 1926.

Van Espen, Zegerus, *Jus Ecclesiasticum Universum,* 4 vols., Lovanii, 1753.

Van Hove, A., *Commentarium Lovaniense in Codicem Iuris Canonici,* Vol. I, Tom. I, *Prolegomena ad Codicem Iuris Canonici,* Mechliniae et Romae: Dessain, 1928.

Vermeersch, A.–et Creusen, J., *Epitome Iuris Canonici,* 3 vols., Mechliniae–Romae: H. Dessain. Vol. I, 6. ed., 1937; Vol. II, 6. ed., 1940; Vol. III, 5. ed., 1936.

Waldron, J., *The Minister of Baptism.* The Catholic University of America Canon Law Studies, n. 170, Washington, D. C.: The Catholic University of America Press, 1942.

Wernz, Franciscus Xaverius, *Ius Decretalium,* 6 vols., Romae et Prati, 1898–1905.

Wernz, F.–Vidal, P., *Ius Canonicum,* 7 vols. in 8, Romae: Apud Aedes Universitatis Gregorianae, 1927–1938. Vol. II, *De Personis,* ed. Tertia, 1943. Vol. IV, *De Rebus,* Pars I, 1934.

Woywod, Stanislaus, *A Practical Commentary on the Code of Canon Law,* 2 vols., New York: Joseph F. Wagner. Vol. I, Sixth Printing, 1941. Vol. II, Seventh Printing, 1943.

PERIODICALS

Apollinaris, Romae, 1928–

Commentarium pro Religiosis, Romae, 1920– ; from 1935: *Commentarium pro Religiosis et Missionariis.*

Ecclesiastical Review, The, Philadelphia, 1889–

Irish Ecclesiastical Record, The, Dublin, 1864–

Monitore Ecclesiastico, Il, Romae, 1876–

Nouvelle Revue Théologique, Tournai, 1869–

Periodica de Religiosis et Missionariis, Brugis, 1905–1919; *Periodica de Re Canonica et Morali Utili praesertim Religiosis et Missionariis,* Brugis, 1920–1927; *Periodica de Re Morali, Canonica, Liturgica,* Brugis, 1927–1936; Romae, 1937–

ARTICLES

Cappello, F. M., "Annotationes,"—*Periodica de Re Canonica, Morali, Liturgica,* XXII (1933), 149–152.

Creusen, I., "Ubi tumulus ibi funus?",—*Nouvelle Revue Théologique,* LIV (1927), 782–784.

Kinane, J., "Funeral Offerings—Important Decision of the Congregation of the Council on the Celebrated Armagh Statute,"—*Irish Ecclesiastical Record,* 5 Series, XXVI (1925), 518–522.

Larraona, A., "Commentarium Codicis,"—*Commentarium pro Religiosis,* IX (1928), 204–211; 313–324.

Maroto, P., "Annotationes ad Responsum Quartum,"—*Commentarium pro Religiosis,* X (1929), 334–341.

———, "De Axiomate 'Ubi tumulus ibi funus.'"—*Apollinaris,* I (1928), 22–35; 125–139; 263–279.

Sacconi, Vincenzo, "Circa la facoltà del Vescovo di dichiarare l'esenzione dalla giurisdizione parrochiale,"—*Il Monitore Ecclesiastico,* 4. Series, X (1928), 212–215.

Schaaf, V., "Right to Choose Church of Funeral,"—*The Ecclesiastical Review,* XCIV (1936), 309–311.

Vermeersch, A., "'Ubi tumulus ibi funus': Axioma (?),"—*Periodica de Re Canonica, Morali, Liturgica,* XVI (1927), 57–66.

Anonymous, "National Pastors and Assistance at Marriage,"—*The Ecclesiastical Review,* LXXX (1929), 88–94.

ABBREVIATIONS

AAS—Acta Apostolicae Sedis.
ASS—Acta Sanctae Sedis.
AER—The American Ecclesiastical Review.
Fontes—Codicis Iuris Canonici Fontes cura . . . Gasparri editi.
Jaffé—Regesta Pontificum Romanorum.
Mansi—Sacrorum Conciliorum Nova et Amplissima Collectio.
Potthast—Regesta Pontificum Romanorum.
S.C.C.—Sacra Congregatio Concilii
S. C. Ep. et Reg.—Sacra Congregatio Episcoporum et Regularium
S.R.C.—Sacrorum Rituum Congregatio

INDEX

BIOGRAPHICAL NOTE

Joseph F. Hale was born on October 2, 1906, at Madelia, Minnesota. He attended Mater Dolorosa Grade and High School of that village, and St. Mary's Academy and College, Winona, Minnesota. In September, 1925, he was admitted to Basselin College, The Catholic University of America, where he obtained the degree of Master of Arts in 1928. In the fall of that year he was sent to the North American College, Rome, Italy, to pursue his Theological Studies. He received the degree S.T.L. from the University of Propaganda, in May of 1931. He was ordained to the Holy Priesthood on October 25, 1931. In the month of September, 1943, he enrolled in the School of Canon Law of the Catholic University of America, where he received the degree of J.C.B. in May, 1944, and the degree of J.C.L. in May, 1945.

Canon Law Studies *

1. Freriks, Rev. Celestine A., C.PP.S., J.C.D., Religious Congregations in Their External Relations, 121 pp., 1916.
2. Galliher, Rev. Daniel M., O.P., J.C.D., Canonical Elections, 117 pp., 1917.
3. Borkowski, Rev. Aurelius L., O.F.M., J.C.D., De Confraternitatibus Ecclesiasticis, 136 pp., 1918.
4. Castillo, Rev. Cayo, J.C.D., Disertacion Historico-Canonica sobre la Potestad del Cabildo en Sede Vacante o Impedida del Vicario Capitular, 99 pp., 1919 (1918).
5. Kubelbeck, Rev. William J., S.T.B., J.C.D., The Sacred Penitentiaria and Its Relation to Faculties of Ordinaries and Priests, 129 pp., 1918.
6. Petrovits, Rev. Joseph J. C., S.T.D., J.C.D., The New Church Law on Matrimony, X-461 pp., 1919.
7. Hickey, Rev. John J., S.T.B., J.C.D., Irregularities and Simple Impediments in the New Code of Canon Law, 100 pp., 1920.
8. Klekotka, Rev. Peter J., S.T.B., J.C.D., Diocesan Consultors, 179 pp., 1920.
9. Wanenmacher, Rev. Francis, J.C.D., The Evidence in Ecclesiastical Procedure Affecting the Marriage Bond, 1920 (Printed 1935).
10. Golden, Rev. Henry Francis, J.C.D., Parochial Benefices in the New Code, IV-119 pp., 1921 (Printed 1925).
11. Koudelka, Rev. Charles J., J.C.D., Pastors, Their Rights and Duties According to the New Code of Canon Law, 211 pp., 1921.
12. Melo, Rev. Antonius, O.F.M., J.C.D., De Exemptione Regularium, X-188 pp., 1921.
13. Schaaf, Rev. Valentine Theodore, O.F.M., S.T.B., J.C.D., The Cloister, X-180 pp., 1921.
14. Burke, Rev. Thomas Joseph, S.T.D., J.C.D., Competence in Ecclesiastical Tribunals, IV-117 pp., 1922.
15. Leech, Rev. George Leo, J.C.D., A Comparative Study of the Constitution "Apostolicae Sedis" and the "Codex Juris Canonici," 179 pp., 1922.
16. Motry, Rev. Hubert Louis, S.T.D., J.C.D., Diocesan Faculties According to the Code of Canon Law, II-167 pp., 1922.
17. Murphy, Rev. George Lawrence, J.C.D., Delinquencies and Penalties in the Administration and the Reception of the Sacraments, IV-121 pp., 1923.

* All published numbers are available from the Catholic University of America Press, 621 Michigan Ave., N.E., Washington 17, D. C., except the following numbers: 1-114 inclusive, and numbers 116, 118, 120, 122, 123, 162 and 198.

18. O'Reilly, Rev. John Anthony, S.T.B., J.C.D., Ecclesiastical Sepulture in the New Code of Canon Law, II-129 pp., 1923.
19. Michalicka, Rev. Wenceslas Cyrill, O.S.B., J.C.D., Judicial Procedure in Dismissal of Clerical Exempt Religious, 107 pp., 1923.
20. Dargin, Rev. Edward Vincent, S.T.B., J.C.D., Reserved Cases According to the Code of Canon Law, IV-103 pp., 1924.
21. Godfrey, Rev. John A., S.T.B., J.C.D., The Right of Patronage According to the Code of Canon Law, 153 pp., 1924.
22. Hagedorn, Rev. Francis Edward, J.C.D., General Legislation on Indulgences, II-154 pp., 1924.
23. King, Rev. James Ignatius, J.C.D., The Administration of the Sacraments to Dying Non-Catholics, V-141 pp., 1924.
24. Winslow, Rev. Francis Joseph, M.M., J.C.D., Vicars and Prefects Apostolic, IV-149 pp., 1924.
25. Correa, Rev. Jose Servelion, S.T.L., J.C.D., La Potestad Legislativa de la Iglesia Catolica, IV-127 pp., 1925.
26. Dugan, Rev. Henry Francis, A.M., J.C.D., The Judiciary Department of the Diocesan Curia, 87 pp., 1925.
27. Keller, Rev. Charles Frederick, S.T.B., J.C.D., Mass Stipends, 167 pp., 1925.
28. Paschang, Rev. John Linus, J.C.D., The Sacramentals According to the Code of Canon Law, 129 pp., 1925.
29. Piontek, Rev. Cyrillus, O.F.M., S.T.B., J.C.D., De Indulto Exclaustrationis necnon Saecularizationis, XIII-289 pp., 1925.
30. Kearney, Rev. Richard Joseph, S.T.B., J.C.D., Sponsors at Baptism According to the Code of Canon Law, IV-127 pp., 1925.
31. Bartlett, Rev. Chester Joseph, A.M., LL.B., J.C.D., The Tenure of Parochial Property in the United States of America, V-108 pp., 1926.
32. Kilker, Rev. Adrian Jerome, J.C.D., Extreme Unction, V-425 pp., 1926.
33. McCormick, Rev. Robert Emmett, J.C.D., Confessors of Religious, VIII-266 pp., 1926.
34. Miller, Rev. Newton Thomas, J.C.D., Founded Masses According to the Code of Canon Law, VII-93 pp., 1926.
35. Roelker, Rev. Edward G., S.T.D., J.C.D., Principles of Privilege According to the Code of Canon Law, XI-166 pp., 1926.
36. Bakalarczyk, Rev. Richardus, M.I.C., J.U.D., De Novitiatu, VIII-208 pp., 1927.
37. Pizzuti, Rev. Lawrence, O.F.M., J.U.L., De Parochis Religiosis, 1927. (Not Printed.)
38. Bliley, Rev. Nicholas Martin, O.S.B., J.C.D., Altars According to the Code of Canon Law, XIX-132 pp., 1927.
39. Brown, Mr. Brendan Francis, A.B., LL.M., J.U.D., The Canonical Juristic Personality with Special Reference to its Status in the United States of America, V-212 pp., 1927.

40. Cavanaugh, Rev. William Thomas, C.P., J.U.D., The Reservation of the Blessed Sacrament, VIII-101 pp., 1927.
41. Doheny, Rev. William J., C.S.C., A.B., J.U.D., Church Property: Modes of Acquisition, X-118 pp., 1927.
42. Feldhaus, Rev. Aloysius H., C.PP.S., J.C.D., Oratories, IX-141 pp., 1927.
43. Kelly, Rev. James Patrick, A.B., J.C.D., The Jurisdiction of the Simple Confessor, X-208 pp., 1927.
44. Neuberger, Rev. Nicholas J., J.C.D., Canon 6 or the Relation of the Codex Juris Canonici to the Preceding Legislation, V-95 pp., 1927.
45. O'Keefe, Rev. Gerald Michael, J.C.D., Matrimonial Dispensations, Powers of Bishops, Priests, and Confessors, VIII-232 pp., 1927.
46. Quigley, Rev. Joseph A. M., A.B., J.C.D., Condemned Societies, 139 pp., 1927.
47. Zaplotnik, Rev. Johannes Leo, J.C.D., De Vicariis Foraneis, X-142 pp., 1927.
48. Duskie, Rev. John Aloysius, A.B., J.C.D., The Canonical Status of the Orientals in the United States, VIII-196 pp., 1928.
49. Hyland, Rev. Francis Edward, J.C.D., Excommunication, Its Nature, Historical Development and Effects, VIII-181 pp., 1928.
50. Reinmann, Rev. Gerald Joseph, O.M.C., J.C.D., The Third Order Secular of Saint Francis, 201 pp., 1928.
51. Schenk, Rev. Francis J., J.C.D., The Matrimonial Impediments of Mixed Religion and Disparity of Cult, XVI-318 pp., 1929.
52. Coady, Rev. John Joseph, S.T.D., J.U.D., A.M., The Appointment of Pastors, VIII-150 pp., 1929.
53. Kay, Rev. Thomas Henry, J.C.D., Competence in Matrimonial Procedure, VIII-164 pp., 1929.
54. Turner, Rev. Sidney Joseph, C.P., J.U.D., The Vow of Poverty, XLIX-217 pp., 1929.
55. Kearney, Rev. Raymond A., A.B., S.T.D., J.C.D., The Principles of Delegation, VII-149 pp., 1929.
56. Conran, Rev. Edward James, A.B., J.C.D., The Interdict, V-163 pp., 1930.
57. O'Neill, Rev. William H., J.C.D., Papal Rescripts of Favor, VII-218 pp., 1930.
58. Bastnagel, Rev. Clement Vincent, J.U.D., The Appointment of Parochial Adjutants and Assistants, XV-257 pp., 1930.
59. Ferry, Rev. William A., A.B., J.C.D., Stole Fees, V-136 pp., 1930.
60. Costello, Rev. John Michael, A.B., J.C.D., Domicile and Quasi-Domicile, VII-201 pp., 1930.
61. Kremer, Rev. Michael Nicholas, A.B., S.T.B., J.C.D., Church Support in the United States, VI-136 pp., 1930.
62. Angulo, Rev. Luis, C.M., J.C.D., Legislation de la Iglesia sobre la intencion en la application de la Santa Misa, VII-104 pp., 1931.

63. FREY, REV. WOLFGANG NORBERT, O.S.B., A.B., J.C.D., The Act of Religious Profession, VIII-174 pp., 1931.
64. ROBERTS, REV. JAMES BRENDAN, A.B., J.C.D., The Banns of Marriage, XIV-140 pp., 1931.
65. RYDER, REV. RAYMOND ALOYSIUS, A.B., J.C.D., Simony, IX-151 pp., 1931.
66. CAMPAGNA, REV. ANGELO, PH.D., J.U.D., Il Vicario Generale del Vescovo, VII-205 pp., 1931.
67. COX, REV. JOSEPH GODFREY, A.B., J.C.D., The Administration of Seminaries, VI-124 pp., 1931.
68. GREGORY, REV. DONALD J., J.U.D., The Pauline Privilege, XV-165 pp., 1931.
69. DONOHUE, REV. JOHN F., J.C.D., The Impediment of Crime, VII-110 pp., 1931.
70. DOOLEY, REV. EUGENE A., O.M.I., J.C.D., Church Law on Sacred Relics, IX-143 pp., 1931.
71. ORTH, REV. CLEMENT RAYMOND, O.M.C., J.C.D., The Approbation of Religious Institutes, 171 pp., 1931.
72. PERNICONE, REV. JOSEPH M., A.B., J.C.D., The Ecclesiastical Prohibition of Books, XII-267 pp., 1932.
73. CLINTON, REV. CONNELL, A.B., J.C.D., The Paschal Precept, IX-108 pp., 1932.
74. DONNELLY, REV. FRANCIS B., A.M., S.T.L., J.C.D., The Diocesan Synod, VIII-125 pp., 1932.
75. TORRENTE, REV. CAMILO, C.M.F., J.C.D., Las Procesiones Sagradas, V-145 pp., 1932.
76. MURPHY, REV. EDWIN J., C.PP.S., J.C.D., Suspension Ex Informata Conscientia, XI-122 pp., 1932.
77. MACKENZIE, REV. ERIC F., A.M., S.T.L., J.C.D., The Delict of Heresy in its Commission, Penalization, Absolution, VII-124 pp., 1932.
78. LYONS, REV. AVITUS E., S.T.B., J.C.D., The Collegiate Tribunal of First Instance, XI-147 pp., 1932.
79. CONNOLLY, REV. THOMAS A., J.C.D., Appeals, XI-195 pp., 1932.
80. SANGMEISTER, REV. JOSEPH V., A.B., J.C.D., Force and Fear as Precluding Matrimonial Consent, V-211 pp., 1932.
81. JAEGER, REV. LEO A., A.B., J.C.D., The Administration of Vacant and Quasi-Vacant Episcopal Sees in the United States, IX-229 pp., 1932.
82. RIMLINGER, REV. HERBERT T., J.C.D., Error Invalidating Matrimonial Consent, VII-79 pp., 1932.
83. BARRETT, REV. JOHN D. M., S.S., J.C.D., A Comparative Study of the Third Plenary Council of Baltimore and the Code, IX-221 pp., 1932.
84. CARBERRY, REV. JOHN J., PH.D., S.T.D., J.C.D., The Juridical Form of Marriage, X-177 pp., 1934.
85. DOLAN, REV. JOHN L., A.B., J.C.D., The Defensor Vinculi, XII-157 pp., 1934.

86. HANNAN, REV. JEROME D., A.M., S.T.D., LL.B., J.C.D., The Canon Law of Wills, IX-517 pp., 1934.
87. LEMIEUX, REV. DELISE A., A.M., J.C.D., The Sentence in Ecclesiastical Procedure, IX-131 pp., 1934.
88. O'ROURKE, REV. JAMES J., A.B., J.C.D., Parish Registers, VII-109 pp., 1934.
89. TIMLIN, REV. BARTHOLOMEW, O.F.M., A.M., J.C.D., Conditional Matrimonial Consent, X-381 pp., 1934.
90. WAHL, REV. FRANCIS X., A.B., J.C.D., The Matrimonial Impediments of Consanguinity and Affinity, VI-125 pp., 1934.
91. WHITE, REV. ROBERT J., A.B., LL.B., S.T.B., J.C.D., Canonical Ante-Nuptial Promises and the Civil Law, VI-152 pp., 1934.
92. HERRERA, REV. ANTONIO PARRA, O.C.D., J.C.D., Legislacion Ecclesiastica sobra el Ayuno y la Abstinencia, XI-191 pp., 1935.
93. KENNEDY, REV. EDWIN J., J.C.D., The Special Matrimonial Process in Cases of Evident Nullity, X-165 pp., 1935.
94. MANNING, REV. JOHN J., A.B., J.C.D., Presumption of Law in Matrimonial Procedure, XI-111 pp., 1935.
95. MOEDER, REV. JOHN M., J.C.D., The Proper Bishop for Ordination and Dimissorial Letters, VII-135 pp., 1935.
96. O'MARA, REV. WILLIAM A., A.B., J.C.D., Canonical Causes for Matrimonial Dispensations, IX-155 pp., 1935.
97. REILLY, REV. PETER, J.C.D., Residence of Pastors, IX-81 pp., 1935.
98. SMITH, REV. MARINER T., O.P., S.T.Lr., J.C.D., The Penal Law for Religious, VII-169 pp., 1935.
99. WHALEN, REV. DONALD W., A.M., J.C.D., The Value of Testimonial Evidence in Matrimonial Procedure, XIII-297 pp., 1935.
100. CLEARY, REV. JOSEPH F., J.C.D., Canonical Limitations on the Alienation of Church Property, VIII-141 pp., 1936.
101. GLYNN, REV. JOHN C., J.C.D., The Promoter of Justice, XX-337 pp., 1936.
102. BRENNAN, REV. JAMES H., S.S., M.A., S.T.B., J.C.D., The Simple Convalidation of Marriage, VI-135 pp., 1937.
103. BRUNINI, REV. JOSEPH BERNARD, J.C.D., The Clerical Obligations of Canons 139 and 142, X-121 pp., 1937.
104. CONNOR, REV. MAURICE, A.B., J.C.D., The Administrative Removal of Pastors, VIII-159 pp., 1937.
105. GUILFOYLE, REV. MERLIN JOSEPH, J.C.D., Custom, XI-144 pp., 1937.
106. HUGHES, REV. JAMES AUSTIN, A.B., A.M., J.C.D., Witnesses in Criminal Trials of Clerics, IX-140 pp., 1937.
107. JANSEN, REV. RAYMOND J., A.B., S.T.L., J.C.D., Canonical Provisions for Catechetical Instruction, VII-153 pp., 1937.
108. KEALY, REV. JOHN JAMES, A.B., J.C.D., The Introductory Libellus in Church Court Procedure, XI-121 pp., 1937.

109. McManus, Rev. James Edward, C.SS.R., J.C.D., The Administration of Temporal Goods in Religious Institutes, XVI-196 pp., 1937.
110. Moriarty, Rev. Eugene James, J.C.D., Oaths in Ecclesiastical Courts, X-115 pp., 1937.
111. Rainer, Rev. Eligius George, C.SS.R., J.C.D., Suspension of Clerics, XVII-249 pp., 1937.
112. Reilly, Rev. Thomas F., C.SS.R., J.C.D., Visitation of Religious, VI-195 pp., 1938.
113. Moriarity, Rev. Francis E., C.SS.R., J.C.D., The Extraordinary Absolution from Censures, XV-334 pp., 1938.
114. Connolly, Rev. Nicholas P., J.C.D., The Canonical Erection of Parishes, X-132 pp., 1938.
115. Donovan, Rev. James Joseph, J.C.D., The Pastor's Obligation in Prenuptial Investigation, XII-322 pp., 1938.
116. Harrigan, Rev. Robert J., M.A., S.T.B., J.C.D., The Radical Sanation of Invalid Marriages, VIII-208 pp., 1938.
117. Boffa, Rev. Conrad Humbert, J.C.D., Canonical Provisions for Catholic Schools, VII-211 pp., 1939.
118. Parsons, Rev. Anscar John, O.M.Cap., J.C.D., Canonical Elections, XII-236 pp., 1939.
119. Reilly, Rev. Edward Michael, A.B., J.C.D., The General Norms of Dispensation, XII-156 pp., 1939.
120. Ryan, Rev. Gerald Aloysius, A.B., J.C.D., Principles of Episcopal Jurisdiction, XII-172 pp., 1939.
121. Burton, Rev. Francis James, C.S.C., A.B., J.C.D., A Commentary on Canon 1125, X-222 pp., 1940.
122. Miaskiewicz, Rev. Francis Sigismund, J.C.D., Supplied Jurisdiction According to Canon 209, XII-340 pp., 1940.
123. Rice, Rev. Patrick William, A.B., J.C.D., Proof of Death in Prenuptial Investigation, VIII-156 pp., 1940.
124. Anglin, Rev. Thomas Francis, M.S., J.C.D., The Eucharistic Fast, VIII-183 pp., 1941.
125. Coleman, Rev. John Jerome, J.C.D., The Minister of Confirmation, VI-153 pp., 1941.
126. Downs, Rev. John Emmanuel, A.B., J.C.D., The Concept of Clerical Immunity, XI-163 pp., 1941.
127. Esswein, Rev. Anthony Albert, J.C.D., Extrajudicial Penal Powers of Ecclesiastical Superiors, X-144 pp., 1941.
128. Farrell, Rev. Benjamin Francis, M.A., S.T.L., J.C.D., The Rights and Duties of the Local Ordinary Regarding Congregations of Women Religious of Pontifical Approval, V-195 pp., 1941.
129. Feeney, Rev. Thomas John, A.B., S.T.L., J.C.D., Restitutio in Integrum, VI-169 pp., 1941.
130. Findlay, Rev. Stephen William, O.S.B., A.B., J.C.D., Canonical

Norms Governing the Deposition and Degradation of Clerics, XVII-279 pp., 1941.

131. Goodwine, Rev. John, A.B., S.T.L., J.C.D., The Right of the Church to Acquire Property, VIII-119 pp., 1941.
132. Heston, Rev. Edward Louis, C.S.C., Ph.D., S.T.D., J.C.D., The Alienation of Church Property in the United States, XII-222 pp., 1941.
133. Hogan, Rev. James John, A.B., S.T.L., J.C.D., Judicial Advocates and Procurators, XIII-200 pp., 1941.
134. Kealy, Rev. Thomas M., A.B., Litt.B., J.C.D., Dowry of Women Religious, IX-152 pp., 1941.
135. Keene, Rev. Michael James, O.S.B., J.C.D., Religious Ordinaries and Canon 198, V-164 pp., 1942.
136. Kerin, Rev. Charles A., S.S., M.A., S.T.B., J.C.D., The Privation of Christian Burial, XVI-279 pp., 1941.
137. Louis, Rev. William Francis, M.A., J.C.D., Diocesan Archives, X-101 pp., 1941.
138. McDevitt, Rev. Gilbert Joseph, A.B., J.C.D., Legitimacy and Legitimation, X-247 pp., 1941.
139. McDonough, Rev. Thomas Joseph, A.B., J.C.D., Apostolic Administrators, X-217 pp., 1941.
140. **Meier, Rev. Carl Anthony, A.B., J.C.D., Penal Administrative Pro**cedure Against Negligent Pastors, XI-240 pp., 1941.
141. Schmidt, Rev. John Rogg, A.B., J.C.D., The Principles of Authentic Interpretation in Canon 17 of the Code of Canon Law, XII-331 pp., 1941.
142. Slafkosky, Rev. Andrew Leonard, A.B., J.C.D., The Canonical Episcopal Visitation of the Diocese, X-197 pp., 1941.
143. Swoboda, Rev. Innocent Robert, O.F.M., J.C.D., Ignorance in Relation to the Imputability of Delicts, IX-271 pp., 1941.
144. Dubé, Rev. Arthur Joseph, A.B., J.C.D., The General Principles for the Reckoning of Time in Canon Law, VIII-299 pp., 1941.
145. McBride, Rev. James T., A.B., J.C.D., Incardination and Excardination of Seculars, XX-585 pp., 1941.
146 Król, Rev. John T., J.C.D., The Defendant in Ecclesiastical Trials, XII-207 pp., 1942.
147. Comyns, Rev. Joseph J., C.SS.R., A.B., J.C.D., Papal and Episcopal Administration of Church Property, XIV-155 pp., 1942.
148. Barry, Rev. Garrett Francis, O.M.I., J.C.D., Violation of the Cloister, XII-260 pp., 1942.
149. Bolduc, Rev. Gatien, C.S.V., A.B., S.T.L., J.C.D., Les Études dans les Religions Cléricales, VIII-155 pp., 1942.
150. Boyle, Rev. David John, M.A., J.C.D., The Juridic Effects of Moral Certitude on Pre-Nuptial Guarantees, XII-188 pp., 1942.
151. **Canavan, Rev. Walter Joseph, M.A., Litt.D., J.C.D., The Profes**sion of Faith, XII-143 pp., 1942.

152. Desrochers, Rev. Bruno, A.B., Ph.L., S.T.B., J.C.D., Le Premier Concile Plénier de Quèbéc et le Code de Droit Canonique, XIV–186 pp., 1942.
153. Dillon, Rev. Robert Edward, A.B., J.C.D., Common Law Marriage, X-148 pp., 1942.
154. Dodwell, Rev. Edward John, Ph.D., S.T.B., J.C.D., The Time and Place for the Celebration of Marriage, X-156 pp., 1942.
155. Donnellan, Rev. Thomas Andrew, A.B., J.C.D., The Obligation of the Missa pro Populo, VII-131 pp., 1942.
156. Eltz, Rev. Louis Anthony, A.B., J.C.D., Cooperation in Crime, XII-208 pp., 1942.
157. Gass, Rev. Sylvester Francis, M.A., J.C.D., Ecclesiastical Pensions, XI-206 pp., 1942.
158. Guiniven, Rev. John Joseph, C.SS.R., J.C.D., The Precept of Hearing Mass, XIV-188 pp., 1942.
159. Gluczynski, Rev. John Theophilus, J.C.D., The Desecration and Violation of Churches, X-126 pp., 1942.
160. Hammill, Rev. John Leo, M.A., J.C.D., The Obligations of the Traveler According to Canon 14, VIII-204 pp., 1942.
161. Haydt, Rev. John Joseph, A.B., J.C.D., Reserved Benefices, XI-148 pp., 1942.
162. Huser, Rev. Roger John, O.F.M., A.B., J.C.D., The Crime of Abortion in Canon Law, XII-187 pp., 1942.
163. Kearney, Rev. Francis Patrick, A.B., S.T.L., J.C.D., The Principles of Canon 1127, X-162 pp., 1942.
164. Linahen, Rev. Leo James, S.T.L., J.C.D., De Absolutione Complicis In Peccato Turpi, 114 pp., 1942.
165. McCloskey, Rev. Joseph Aloysius, A.B., J.C.D., The Subject of Ecclesiastical Law According to Canon 12, XVII-246 pp., 1942.
166. O'Neill, Rev. Francis Joseph, C.SS.R., J.C.D., The Dismissal of Religious in Temporary Vows, XIII-220 pp., 1942.
167. Prince, Rev. John Edward, A.B., S.T.B., J.C.D., The Diocesan Chancellor, X-136 pp., 1942.
168. Riesner, Rev. Albert Joseph, C.SS.R., J.C.D., Apostates and Fugitives from Religious Institutes, IX-168 pp., 1942.
169. Stenger, Rev. Joseph Bernard, J.C.D., The Mortgaging of Church Property, 186 pp., 1942.
170. Waldron, Rev. Joseph Francis, A.B., J.C.D., The Minister of Baptism, XII-197 pp., 1942.
171. Willett, Rev. Robert Albert, J.C.D., The Probative Value of Documents in Ecclesiastical Trials, X-124 pp., 1942.
172. Woeber, Rev. Edward Martin, M.A., J.C.D., The Interpellations, XII-161 pp., 1942.
173. Benko, Rev. Matthew Aloysius, O.S.B., M.A., J.C.D., The Abbot *Nullius*, XVI-148 pp., 1943.

174. CHRIST, REV. JOSEPH JAMES, M.A., S.T.L., J.C.D., Dispensation from Vindicative Penalties, XIV-285 pp., 1943.
175. CLANCY, REV. PATRICK M. J., O.P., A.B., S.T.Lr., J.C.D., The Local Religious Superior, X-229 pp., 1943.
176. CLARKE, REV. THOMAS JAMES, J.C.D., Parish Societies, XII-147 pp., 1943.
177. CONNOLLY, REV. JOHN PATRICK, S.T.L., J.C.D., Synodal Examiners and Parish Priest Consultors, X-223 pp., 1943.
178. DRUMM, REV. WILLIAM MARTIN, A.B., J.C.D., Hospital Chaplains, XII-175 pp., 1943.
179. FLANAGAN, REV. BERNARD JOSEPH, A.B., S.T.L., J.C.D., The Canonical Erection of Religious Houses, X-147 pp., 1943.
180. KELLEHER, REV. STEPHEN JOSEPH, A.B., S.T.B., J.C.D., Discussions with Non-Catholics: Canonical Legislation, X-93 pp., 1943.
181. LEWIS, REV. GORDIAN, C.P., J.C.D., Chapters in Religious Institutes, XII-169 pp., 1943.
182. MARX, REV. ADOLPH, J.C.D., The Declaration of Nullity of Marriages Contracted Outside the Church, X-151 pp., 1943.
183. MATULENAS, REV. RAYMOND ANTHONY, O.S.B., A.B., J.C.D., Communication, a Source of Privileges, XII-225 pp., 1943.
184. O'LEARY, REV. CHARLES GERARD, C.SS.R., J.C.D., Religious Dismissed After Perpetual Profession, X-213 pp., 1943.
185. POWER, REV. CORNELIUS MICHAEL, J.C.D., The Blessing of Cemeteries, XII-231 pp., 1943.
186. SHUHLER, REV. RALPH VINCENT, O.S.A., J.C.D., Privileges of Regulars to Absolve and Dispense, XII-195 pp., 1943.
187. ZIOLKOWSKI, REV. THADDEUS STANISLAUS, A.B., J.C.D., The Consecration and Blessing of Churches, XII-151 pp., 1943.
188. HENEGHAN, REV. JOHN JOSEPH, S.T.D., J.C.D., The Marriages of Unworthy Catholics: Canons 1065 and 1066, XVI-213 pp., 1944.
189. CARROLL, REV. COLEMAN FRANCIS, M.A., S.T.L., J.C.L., Charitable Institutions.
190. CIESLUK, REV. JOSEPH EDWARD, Ph.B., S.T.L., J.C.D., National Parishes in the United States, VI-178 pp., 1944.
191. COBURN, REV. VINCENT PAUL, A.B., J.C.D., Marriages of Conscience, XII-172 pp., 1944.
192. CONNORS, REV. CHARLES PAUL, C.S.Sp., A.B., J.C.D., Extra-Judicial Procurators in the Code of Canon Law, X-94 pp., 1944.
193. COYLE, REV. PAUL RAYMOND, A.B., J.C.D., Judicial Exceptions, X-142 pp., 1944.
194. FAIR, REV. BARTHOLOMEW FRANCIS, A.B., S.T.L., J.C.D., The Impediment of Abduction, XII-122 pp., 1944.
195. GALLAGHER, REV. THOMAS RAPHAEL, O.P., A.B., S.T.Lr., J.C.D., The Examination of the Qualities of the Ordinand, X-166 pp., 1944.
196. GANNON, REV. JOHN MARK, S.T.L., J.C.D., The Interstices Required for the Promotion to Orders, XII-100 pp., 1944.

197. Goldsmith, Rev. J. William, B.C.S., S.T.L., J.C.D., The Competence of Church and State over Marriage—Disputed Points, X-128 pp., 1944.
198. Goodwine, Rev. Joseph Gerard, A.B., S.T.D., J.C.D., The Reception of Converts, XIV-326 pp., 1944.
199. Kowalski, Rev. Romuald Eugene, O.F.M., A.B., J.C.D., Sustenance of Religious Houses of Regulars, X-174 pp., 1944.
200. McCoy, Rev. Alan Edward, O.F.M., J.C.D., Force and Fear in Relation to Delictual Imputability and Penal Responsibility, XII-160 pp., 1944.
201. McDevitt, Rev. Vincent John, Ph.B., S.T.L., J.C.L., Perjury.
202. Martin, Rev. Thomas Owen, Ph.D., S.T.D., J.C.D., Adverse Possession, Prescription and Limitation of Actions: The Canonical "Praescriptio," XX-208 pp., 1944.
203. Miklosovic, Rev. Paul John, A.B., J.C.L., Attempted Marriages and Their Consequent Juridic Effects.
204. Mundy, Rev. Thomas Maurice, A.B., S.T.L., J.C.D., The Union of Parishes, X—164 pp., 1944.
205. O'Dea, Rev. John Coyle, A.B., J.C.D., The Matrimonial Impediment of Nonage, VIII-126 pp., 1944.
206. Olalia, Rev. Alexander Ayson, S.T.L., J.C.D., A Comparative Study of the Christian Constitution of States and the Constitution of the Philippine Commonwealth, XII—136 pp., 1944.
207. Poisson, Rev. Pierre-Marie, C.S.C., A.B., Ph.L., Th.L., J.C.L., Droits Patrimoniaux des Maisons et des Églises Religieuses.
208. Stadalnikas, Rev. Casimir Joseph, M.I.C., J.C.D., Reservation of Censures, X-141 pp., 1944.
209. Sullivan, Rev. Eugene Henry, S.T.L., J.C.D., Proof of the Reception of the Sacraments, X—165 pp., 1944.
210. Vaughan, Rev. William Edward, J.C.D., Constitutions for Diocesan Courts, X-210 pp., 1944.
211. Paro, Rev. Gino, S.T.D., J.C.L., The Right of Apostolic Legation.
212. Balzer, Rev. Ralph Francis, C.P., J.C.D., The Computation of Time in a Canonical Novitiate, X—227 pp., 1945.
213. Dougherty, Rev. John Whelan, A.B., S.T.L., J.C.D., De Inquisitione Speciali, XII—195 pp., 1945.
214. Dziob, Rev. Michael Walter, J.C.D., The Sacred Congregation for the Oriental Church, XII—181 pp., 1945.
215. Eidenschink, Rev. John Albert, O.S.B., B.A., J.C.D, The Election of Bishops in the Letters of Pope Gregory the Great, VII—200 pp., 1945.
216. Gill, Rev. Nicholas, C.P., J.C.D., The Spiritual Prefect in Clerical Religious Houses of Study, X—140 pp., 1945.
217. Hynes, Rev. Harry Gerard, S.T.L., J.C.D., The Privileges of Cardinals, XII-183 pp., 1945.
218. McDevitt, Rev. Gerald Vincent, S.T.L., J.C.D., The Renunciation of an Ecclesiastical Office, XIV—179 pp., 1945.

219. MANNING, REV. JOSEPH LEROY, J.C.D., The Free Conferral of Offices, VIII—116 pp., 1945.

220. **MEYER, REV. LOUIS G., O.S.B., A.B., S.T.B., J.C.D., Alms-Gathering** by Religious, XII—163 pp., 1945.

221. O'DONNELL, REV. CLETUS FRANCIS, M.A., J.C.D., The Marriage of Minors, XII—268 pp., 1945.

222. **PRUNSKIS, REV. JOSEPH, J.C.D., Comparative Law, Ecclesiastical and Civil, in Lithuanian Concordat, X—161 pp., 1945.**

223. **SWEENEY, REV. FRANCIS PATRICK, C.SS.R., J.C.D., The Reduction of Clerics to the Lay State, X—199 pp., 1945.**

224. VOGELPOHL, REV. HENRY JOHN, J.C.D., The Simple Impediments to Holy Orders, XVI—190 pp., 1945.

225. BROCKHAUS, REV. THOMAS AQUINAS, O.S.B., A.B., J.C.D., Religious who Are Known as *Conversi*, X—127 pp., 1945.

226. GRIESE, REV. N. ORVILLE, S.T.D., J.C.D., The Marriage Contract and the Procreation of Offspring, XVI-224 pp., 1946.

227. BOUDREAUX, REV. WARREN LOUIS, J.C.D., The "*ab acatholicis nati*" of Canon 1099, § 2, XII-110 pp., 1946.

228. BOWE, REV. THOMAS JOSEPH, A.B., J.C.D., Religious Superioresses, VIII-206 pp., 1946.

229. DIEDERICHS, REV. MICHAEL FERDINAND, S.C.J., J.C.D., The Jurisdiction of the Latin Ordinaries over their Oriental Subjects, XIV-153 pp., 1946.

230. DINGMAN, REV. MAURICE JOHN, A.B., S.T.L., J.C.L., The Plaintiff in Contentious Trials.

231. FRISON, REV. BASIL, C.M.F., M.MUS., J.C.D., The Retroactivity of Law, X-221 pp., 1946.

232. GALVIN, REV. WILLIAM ANTHONY, M.A., J.C.D., The Administrative Transfer of Pastors, XII-288 pp., 1946.

233. GORACY, REV. JOSEPH C., J.C.L., The Diriment Matrimonial Impediment of Major Orders.

234. HALE, REV. JOSEPH FRANCIS, M.A., S.T.L., J.C.L., The Pastor of Burial.

235. HENRY, REV. JOSEPH ARTHUR, A.B., J.C.D., The Mass and Holy Communion: Inter-Ritual Law, XII-138 pp., 1946.

236. LINENBERGER, REV. HERBERT, C.PP.S., J.C.L., The False Denunciation of an Innocent Confessor.

237. LOWRY, REV. JAMES MARTIN, A.B., J.C.D., Dispensation from Private Vows, XII-266 pp., 1946.

238. LYNCH, REV. GEORGE EDWARD, A.B., S.T.L., J.C.D., Coadjutors and Auxiliaries of Bishops, X-107 pp., 1947.

239. LYNCH, REV. TIMOTHY, M.S.SS.T., J.C.D., Contracts between Bishops and Religious Congregations, XIV-232 pp., 1946.

240. MCCLUNN, REV. JUSTIN DAVID, A.B., S.T.L., J.C.D., Administrative Recourse, VII-142 pp., 1946.

241. LOHMULLER, REV. MARTIN NICHOLAS, A.B., J.C.D., The Promulgation of Law, XII-140 pp., 1947.
242. MCGRATH, REV. JAMES, A.B., J.C.D., The Privilege of the Canon, XII-156 pp., 1946.
243. MARBACH, REV. JOSEPH FRANCIS, A.B., J.C.D., Marriage Legislation for the Catholics of the Oriental Rites in the United States and Canada, XIV-314 pp., 1946.
244. SHIMKUS, REV. BERNARD ALOYSIUS, A.B., J.C.L., The Determination and Transfer of Rite.
245. SMITH, REV. VINCENT MICHAEL, A.B., S.T.L., J.C.L., Ignorance Affecting Matrimonial Consent.
246. WACHTRLE, REV. PAUL ANTHONY, A.B., J.C.L., The Baptism of the Children of Non-Catholics.
247. CROTTY, REV. MATTHEW MICHAEL, J.C.D., The Recipient of First Holy Communion, X-142 pp., 1947.
248. EAGLETON, REV. GEORGE, J.C.L., The Quinquennial Faculties, Formula IV.
249. GIBBONS, REV. MARION LEO, C.M., J.C.D., Domicile of the Wife Unlawfully Separated from Her Husband, XIV-171 pp., 1947.
250. KELLY, REV. BERNARD MATTHEW, S.T.L., J.C.D., The Functions Reserved to Pastors, X-150 pp., 1947.
251. KILCULLEN, REV. THOMAS JOHN, LL.M., J.C.D., The Collegiate Moral Person as Party Litigant, X-150 pp., 1947.
252. LAFONTAINE, REV. GERMAIN JOSEPH, W.F., J.C.L., Relations Canoniques entre le Missionaire et Ses Superieurs.
253. LANE, REV. LORAS THOMAS, J.C.L., Matrimonial Procedure in Ordinary Court of Second Instance.
254. LOVER, REV. JAMES FRANCIS, C.Ss.R., J.C.D., The Master of Novices, X-168 pp., 1947.
255. MCNICHOLAS, REV. TIMOTHY JOSEPH, J.C.L., The *Septimae Manus* Witness.
256. MAROSITZ, REV. JOSEPH JOHN, M.S.C., J.C.D., Obligations and Privileges of Religious Promoted to the Episcopal or Cardinalitial Dignities, XII-180 pp. 1947.
257. MURPHY, REV. FRANCIS JOSEPH, J.C.D., Legislative Powers of the Provincial Council, XII-158 pp., 1947.
258. O'BRIEN, REV. ROMAEUS WILLIAM, O.Carm., J.C.D., The Provincial Superior in Religious Orders of Men, X-294 pp., 1947.
259. PFALLER, REV. BENEDICT ANTHONY, O.S.B., J.C.L., *The ipso facto* Effected Dismissal of Religious.
260. POPEK, REV. ALPHONSE SYLVESTER, J.C.D., The Rights and Obligations of Metropolitans, XVIII-460 pp., 1947.
261. RISTUCCIA, REV. BERNARD JOSEPH, C.M., J.C.L., Quasi-Religious.
262. SONNTAG, REV. NATHANIEL LOUIS, O.F.M.Cap., J.C.D., Censorship of Special Classes of Books, XII-147 pp., 1947.

263. Stadler, Rev. Joseph Nicholas, J.C.L., Frequent Holy Communion.
264. Szal, Rev. Ignatius Joseph, J.C.L., The Communication of Catholics with Schismatics, XII-217 pp., 1947.
265. Wagner, Rev. Urban Stanley, O.F.M.Conv., J.C.D., Parochial Substitute Vicars and Supplying Priests, IX-126 pp., 1947.
266. Quinn, Rev. Joseph, M.A., J.C.L., Documents Required for the Reception of Orders.
267. Bennington, Rev. James Clement, A.B., J.C.L., The Recipient of Confirmation.
268. Blaher, Rev. Damian Joseph, O.F.M., A.B., J.C.L., The Ordinary Processes in Causes of Beatification and Canonization.
269. Clune, Rev. Robert Bell, B.A., J.C.L., The Judicial Interrogation of the Parties.
270. Courtemanche, Rev. Basil F., B.A., J.C.L., The Total Simulation of Matrimonial Consent.
271. Dlouhy, Rev. Maur John, O.S.B., A.B., J.C.L., The Ordination of Exempt Religious.
272. Donovan, Rev. John Thomas, Ph.B., S.T.L., J.C.L., The Clerical Obligations of Canons 138 and 140.
273. Freking, Rev. Frederick W., A.B., S.T.B., J.C.L., The Canonical Installation of Pastors.
274. Fulton, Rev. Thomas B., J.C.L., Prenuptial Investigation.
275. Godley, Rev. James P., J.C.L., The Time and the Place for the Celebration of Mass.
276. Kane, Rev. Thomas A., A.B., B.S., J.C.L., Jurisdiction of Patriarchs until 1439.
277. Kennedy, Rev. Andrew A., J.C.L., The Annual Pastoral Report to the Local Ordinary.
278 Konrad, Rev. Joseph George, J.C.L., Transfer of Religious.
279. Kress, Rev. Alphonse, J.C.L., Contumacy in Ecclesiastical Trials.
280. McCartney, Rev. Marcellus Anthony, O.F.M., M.A., J.C.L., Faculties of Regular Confessors.
281. McCaslin, Rev. Edward Patrick, M.A., S.T.L., J.C.L., The Division of Parishes.
282. McElroy, Rev. Francis J., A.B., J.C.L., The Privileges of Bishops.
283. Quinn, Rev. Stephen, M.S.SS.T., J.C.L., Relation of the Local Ordinary to Religious of Diocesan Approval.
284. Schneider, Rev. Edelhard Louis, S.D.S., M.A., J.C.L., The Status of Secularized Ex-Religious Clerics.
285. Thompson, Rev. Chester J., A.B., J.C.L., The Simple Removal from Office.

www.ingramcontent.com/pod-product-compliance
Lightning Source LLC
LaVergne TN
LVHW050251080826
844660LV00012B/622

* 9 7 8 0 8 1 3 2 2 4 1 4 5 *